IMAGES
of America

PINE ISLAND

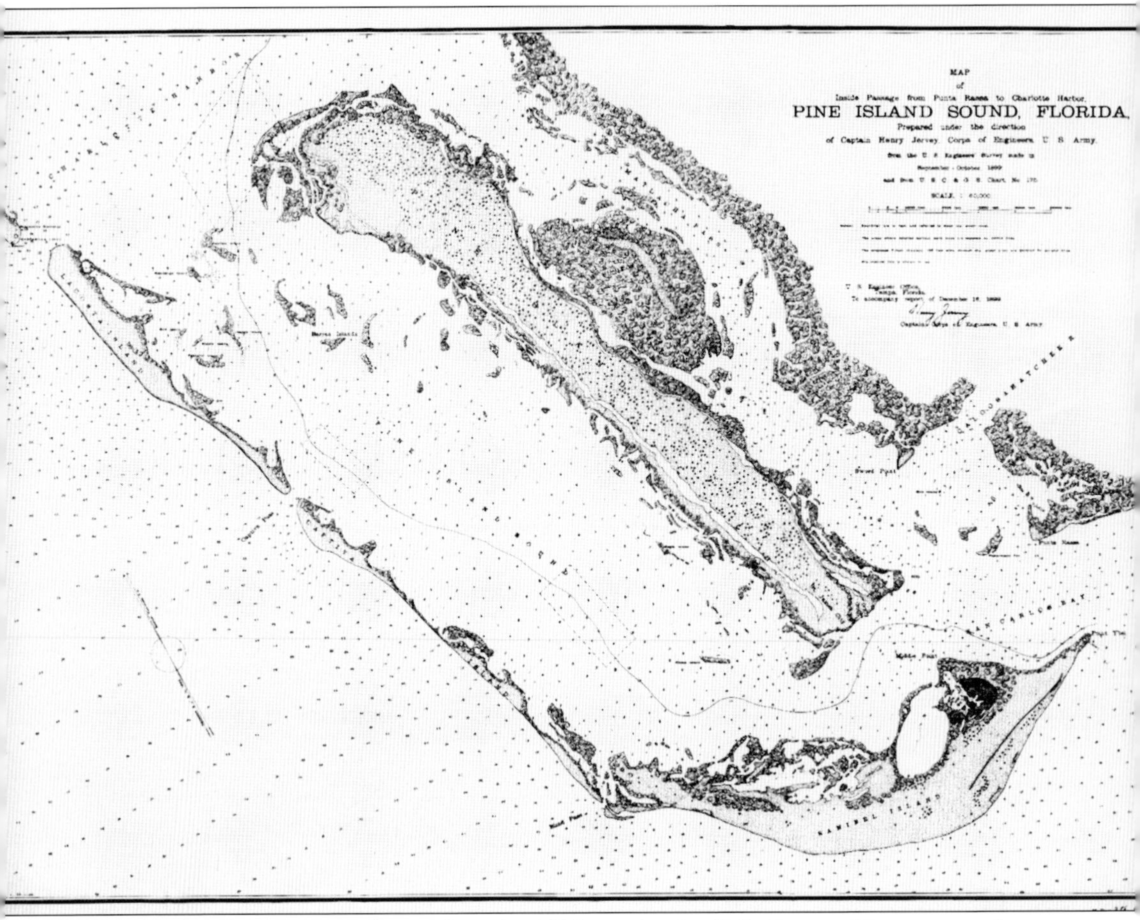

Pine Island Sound, as it is depicted on the 1899 map by the U.S. Corps of Engineers, is home to Pine Island, as well as some 75 smaller islands called keys. Shown here, the mainland is top right, Punta Rassa is to the center right at the mouth of the Caloosahatchee River, and the islands of Sanibel and Captive run from bottom right up to top left. The island between the mainland and Pine Island is Little Pine Island. (Florida State Archives.)

ON THE COVER: The Henry Martin family and friends enjoy a day of oystering in Charlotte Harbor off Pine Island. As Bokeelia's first settlers, the Martins are credited with building a boardinghouse, a sawmill, a sugarcane mill, and Bokeelia's landmark pier. (Museum of the Islands.)

IMAGES
of America

PINE ISLAND

Mary Kaye Stevens

ARCADIA
PUBLISHING

ISBN 978-0-7385-5448-8

Published by Arcadia Publishing
Charleston, South Carolina

Printed in the United States of America

Library of Congress Catalog Card Number: 2008925868

For all general information contact Arcadia Publishing at:
Telephone 843-853-2070
Fax 843-853-0044
E-mail sales@arcadiapublishing.com
For customer service and orders:
Toll-Free 1-888-313-2665

Visit us on the Internet at www.arcadiapublishing.com

To my husband, Dan, for his belief in my dreams and his patience in living with a wife-writer on a deadline.

Contents

ACKNOWLEDGMENTS

Many individuals and organizations made this production possible, but none so much as the individuals from Pine Island's past. Without their diligence in preserving the history of this island, projects like this would not be possible. During the research for this book, I had help from at least one member of almost every family mentioned. I am grateful to the following Pine Islanders for their time, courtesy, and help: Nancy Brooks, Dot Goodwin, Joey and Virginia Morton, Susie Robertson-Lupp, Frank and Kay DellaBitta, Sharon DellaBitta, Bill and Joan McNagny, Rob Wells, Randy Kersey, Arthur Thibeault, Mel Meo, Bobbi Shanks, Frank Padilla, Al Zeller, Judy Baxley, Rhonda and Mike Dooley, Susan Laffitte, John Honc, Pat Cordy, Paula and Robert Montgomery, Barb Peckenpaugh, Dottie Muske, Elaine Jordan, Alexa Groth, Maurie and Dorie Stevens, Ann McLemore, Genev Koonce, Karen Long, Ed Pritchard, Ole Odland, Rick Odland, Breese Glennon, David Overholt, Shirley and Johnny Nielson, Dave and Cece Lewis, and Mike and Patty Burman. Also, my gratitude to the late Corella Stahl, who did not survive to see the finished book.

When I needed professional assistance, images, and technical expertise, I found them from the following: Daisy Nijoku at the Smithsonian Museum of Anthropology, Victor Zarich with Fort Myers Museum of History, Dr. William Marquardt of the Florida Museum of Natural History, Jennifer Farr with the University of Florida Library, Adam Watson with the State Archives of Florida, and Mary McMurray with the Department of Environmental Protection. A special thank-you goes to Sharon Traylor and those who have preserved our island heritage through supporting the Museum of the Islands.

My assistant, Julie Talmadge, has saved my sanity too many times to enumerate. As always I am grateful for her good humor and hard work. My gratitude extends to Luke Cunningham, my editor, who has guided me through this rewarding project. I do not think I could have had a finer editor. And a special thank-you to my family for their unwavering belief that this book would reach publication. For their ceaseless encouragement I thank: Karisa, Scott, Ali, and Clayton Workman; Craig, Staci, and Skyla Stevens; Ruth Loeber; and Maurie and Dorie Stevens. My husband, Dan, deserves the ultimate thanks for his tireless support of me and my dreams.

The memories of over a hundred individuals interviewed for this book provide the captions for the majority of the images. I can promise that the conversations and events are recorded as truthfully as I can relay them. Where possible, I researched the facts. Please understand that despite my efforts toward accuracy, if some factual errors or faulty remembrances are in these pages, they are not intentional.

Thanks to the following sources for photograph and artwork usage throughout this book:
www.AntiqueFishingReels.com
Celander, Bill. Florida Museum of Natural History.
Clark, Merald. Florida Museum of Natural History.
National Anthropological Archives, Smithsonian Institution.
Cushing #02644400 and Demory's Key #09652000.

Introduction

Almost hidden from contemporary civilization, Pine Island lays between mainland Southwest Florida and the islands of Sanibel and Captiva. Although Pine Island is the size of New York's Manhattan Island, at 17 miles long and 2 miles wide, size is the only similarity between the islands. With a single drawbridge, first built in 1927, Pine Island seems remote in comparison. Leaving steel and glass high-rises, mega malls, and elbow-to-elbow humanity on the mainland, islanders enjoy a small-town environment, free of crowded beaches, glitzy tourist attractions, and even traffic lights. With only one four-way stop sign at the island center, Pine Island is entirely free of traffic lights!

Twenty years after Florida was granted statehood in 1845, Pine Island remained basically unexplored and uninhabited. A fatal injury during a skirmish with Calusa Indian warriors on Pine Island's northern shore, led to Spanish explorer Ponce de Leon's death. Plying the water surrounding Pine Island, legendary pirate Brewster Baker left his mark and perhaps a buried fortune in treasure on the island in the late 1700s. Leading a team of explorers along Southwest Florida's coastline in 1865, Smithsonian Institute's Frank Hamilton Cushing noted a lack of inhabitants and the remains of an advanced Calusa Indian culture on Pine Island. By the beginning of the 20th century, a few hardy fisherfolk settlers had formed communities in Pineland, Bokeelia, and Matlacha. With the first tarpon caught on a lure right off the southern tip of the island, entrepreneurs began building a fisherman's haven called St. James City in the 1870s. Two extravagant hotels, businesses, and a hemp-rope factory sprang up shortly thereafter, only to be abandoned within a few years.

Living on the bounties of nature found on the island and in her surrounding waters, early settlers were a fiercely self-sufficient and somewhat quirky lot. With the building of Matlacha Bridge in 1927, fill dirt was piled in both directions leading up to the bridge. As the dirt was leveled and hardened, squatters quickly set up housekeeping in shanties and beached houseboats. For years the area was referred to as simply the "fill." The movie, *Follow That Dream*, starring Elvis Presley, was based on this new shanty-lined causeway. From a captain with a sordid past enjoying Caruso's voice blaring across Bokeelia, to a recluse known as the Swamp Angel who befriended Matlacha's children, to a host who entertained guests with vulture/eagle fights in an ancient Calusa amphitheater, Pine Island has been home to those seeking independent living away from the confines of society.

The isolated lifestyles of the island's earlier dwellers set the stage for today's residents. Not surprising, Pine Islanders pride themselves in being just a little more eccentric than the mainlanders. The shanties of old are now vibrantly painted cottages, galleries, and shops, welcoming visitors and residents to the island. Sports fishermen still line the "Fishingest Bridge" connecting the island to the mainland. The enduring spirit of the Calusa nation is preserved for future generations at Pineland's Randall Research Center. The north-south island road is still lined with palms, however, replacing the scrub palms and slash pines of the past, are fields of cultivated cocos, washingtonia, and coconut palms. The put-put drum of the hot-head boat engines of the past is gone, but a few determined commercial fishermen still make their living on the water. Barefoot children of today still share the carefree life of past generations. As they cross the bridge connecting the mainland's stress-driven responsibilities with the island's sylvan refuge, islanders shrug off the cares of mainland society. It is this air of tropical quietude that permeates the island and invites us to make Pine Island home.

One

Calusa, Explorers, and Buried Treasure

The rich blue-green waters of southwest Florida's estuaries . . . provided the Calusa with such abundance that they thrived for many centuries.

—*The Calusa and Their Legacy*, Darcie A. MacMahon and William H. Marquardt

Scientists say that humans have inhabited Pine Island for some 12,000 years. Beginning about 5,000 years ago, the Calusa Indians set up an advanced culture based on the reliance of an abundant supply of fish and shellfish found in the rich estuaries surrounding Pine Island. In addition to shell mounds riddled with ancient remains of the Calusa civilization, island history includes the discovery of a Calusa gold medallion supposedly possessing supernatural powers by two young boys. After a series of mysterious misfortunes surrounding the boys, the medallion changed hands several times. The whereabouts of the medallion remain unknown today.

After living in relative isolation for 1,500 years, Ponce de Leon led the first documented Spanish landing party to visit the Pineland Calusa settlement in 1513. On de Leon's final voyage, the crew fought a fierce battle with the Calusa Indians on Pine Island. Beaten and injured, de Leon and his men sailed for Cuba, where Ponce de Leon died of his wounds. A Pine Island legend tells of a rock engraved with the words, "Ponce de Leon—1513," on top, discovered in the mid-1920s by fisherman Lee Willas on the sand flats along Pine Island's southwestern shore. Some islanders claim a storm buried the rock before it could be excavated and studied, while others say it was stolen away under cover of night.

By the late 1700s, Pine Island was home to the legendary pirate Brewster Baker. Now known as the charming community of Bokeelia, the sandy beaches and plentiful fish made this an ideal home for Baker and his crew until around 1820, when the U.S. government put a stop to his pirating lifestyle. In haste, the pirate and his crew evacuated their Pine Island camp and sailed at high tide. Island legend tells of abandoned loot, which the pirates intended to later retrieve. However, Baker and his men never had the opportunity to return. Ever hopeful that Baker indeed left behind buried loot, treasure hunters still expectantly search the island.

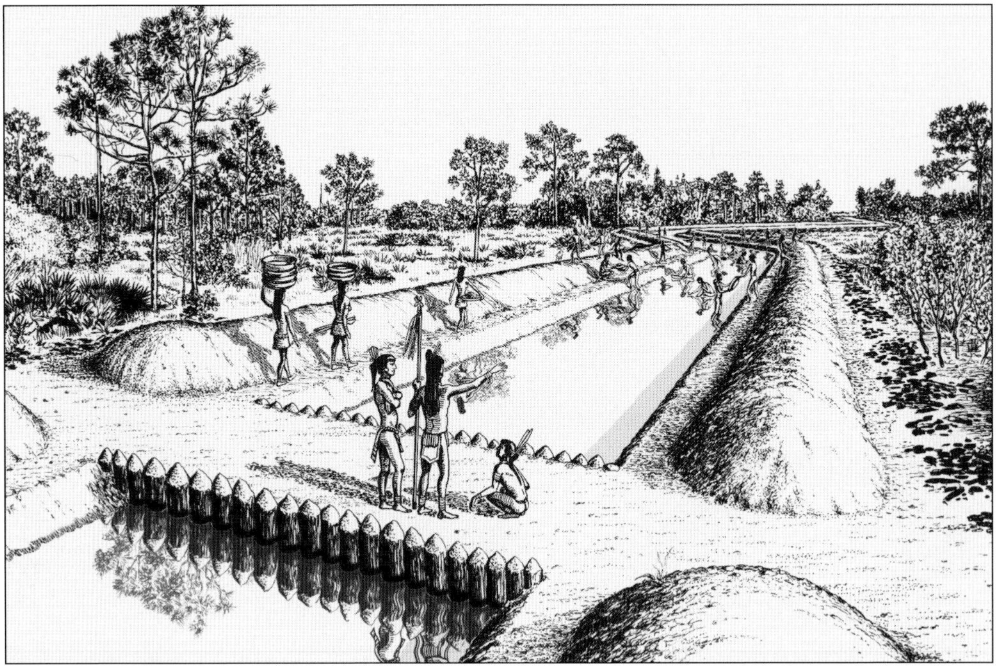

Following a visit to Pine Island in 1895, Smithsonian anthropologist Frank Hamilton Cushing described the remains of the Calusa Canals as remarkable. Dug by hand, these canoe highways measured 30 feet wide and 5–6 feet deep. Not only did the canal system serve as a mode of transportation, it also connected the communities by providing an avenue for communication and trade. (William Marquardt.)

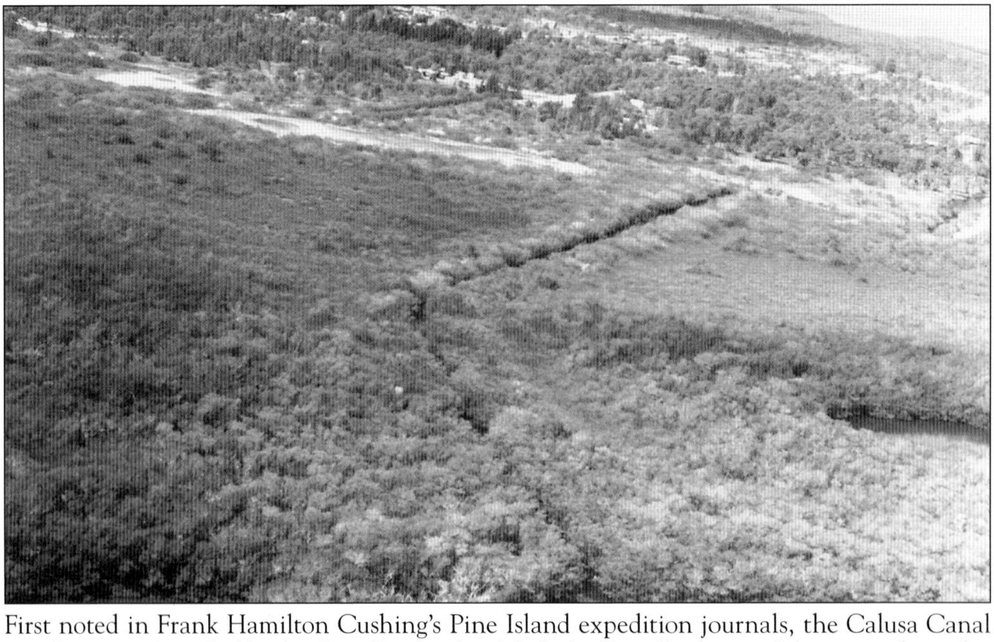

First noted in Frank Hamilton Cushing's Pine Island expedition journals, the Calusa Canal travels two and one half miles from Pineland to Matlacha Pass. Evidence of the original canal is still visible from the air. Preservation efforts have secured most of the original waterway, and it is now known as the Calusa Canal Preserve. (Judy Baxley.)

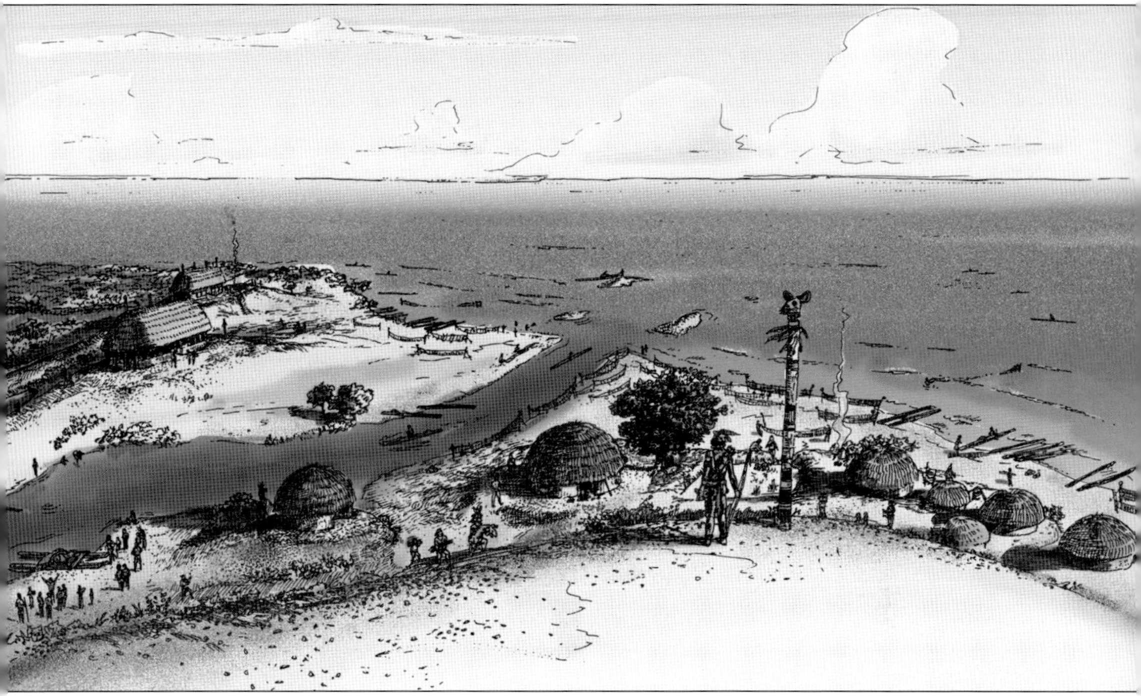

Beginning around 50 AD and spanning some 1,500 years, Pineland was an important Calusa town. With its prime location on the Charlotte Harbor/Pine Island Sound Estuary, Pineland may have been an early capital of the Calusa domain. Described in the writings of Frank Hamilton Cushing, the Pineland Complex was a place of "shell heaps, canals, central lagoon and all . . . was on a scale so vast that I could scarcely believe it to have been artificial, wholly the work of human hands." (William Marquardt.)

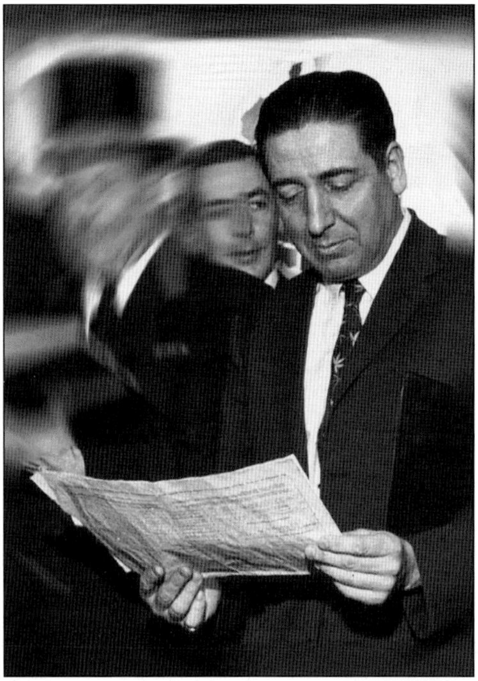

As a Princeton-trained economist, Col. Donald Randell provided sound financial strategies to his clients. During his retirement in Pineland, he and his wife, Patricia, made the generous donation of 56 acres of Calusa Indian mound land in August 1994. Today the Randell Research Center, named in honor of the initial benefactors, consists of 200 preserved acres, exhibits, trails, and active archeological digs. (Debra Randell.)

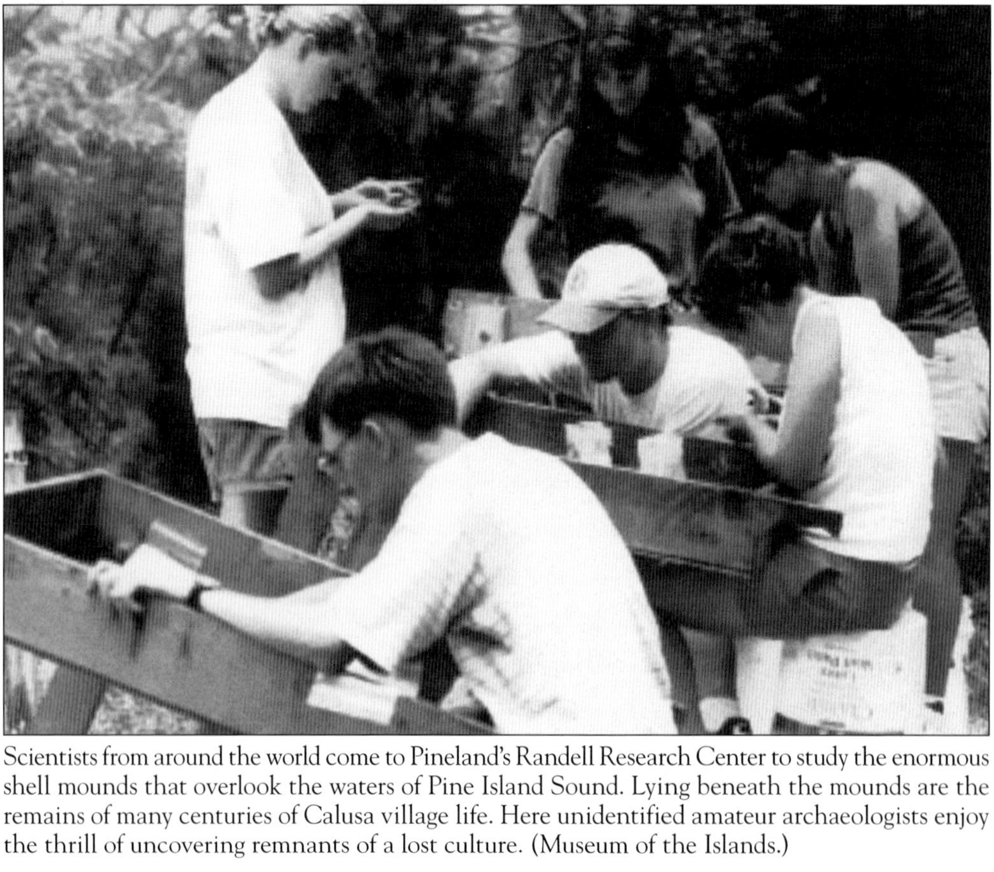

Scientists from around the world come to Pineland's Randell Research Center to study the enormous shell mounds that overlook the waters of Pine Island Sound. Lying beneath the mounds are the remains of many centuries of Calusa village life. Here unidentified amateur archaeologists enjoy the thrill of uncovering remnants of a lost culture. (Museum of the Islands.)

Juan Ponce de Leon, a Spanish conquistador, is credited with naming Florida in honor of his discovery of the land on April 2, 1513, during Easter Advent. From that date forward, the land became known as "La Florida," referring to the Easter season. (Florida State Archives.)

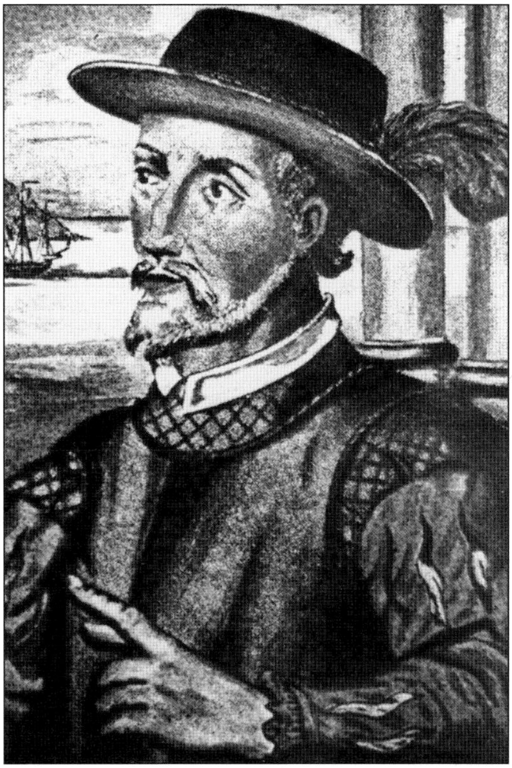

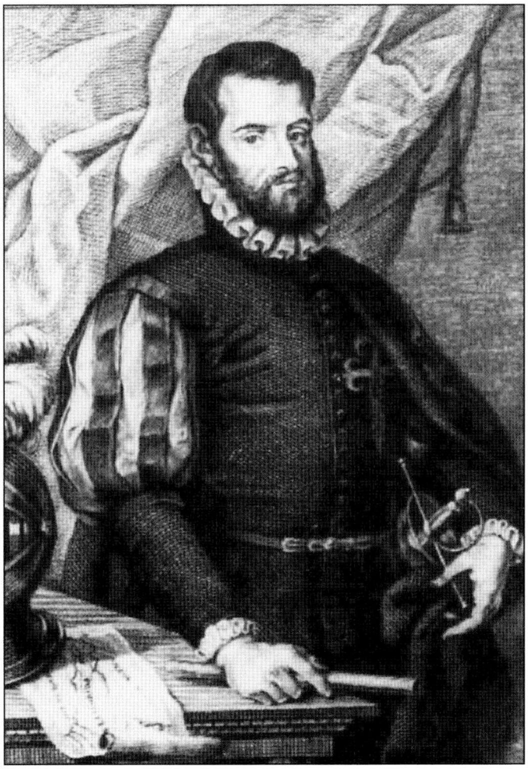

Florida founder Pedro Menendez De Aviles's goal was to bring the Calusa and Seminole native peoples of South Florida into his new colony. Beginning in 1566, Menendez began placing Spanish garrisons and Jesuit missionaries at forts in Southwest Florida. In Menendez's documents, he expressed frustration with the Calusas saying, "they have many times ruptured the peace." Giving up on dominating the Calusas, by June 1569, the last garrison in Calusa territory had been abandoned. (Florida State Archives.)

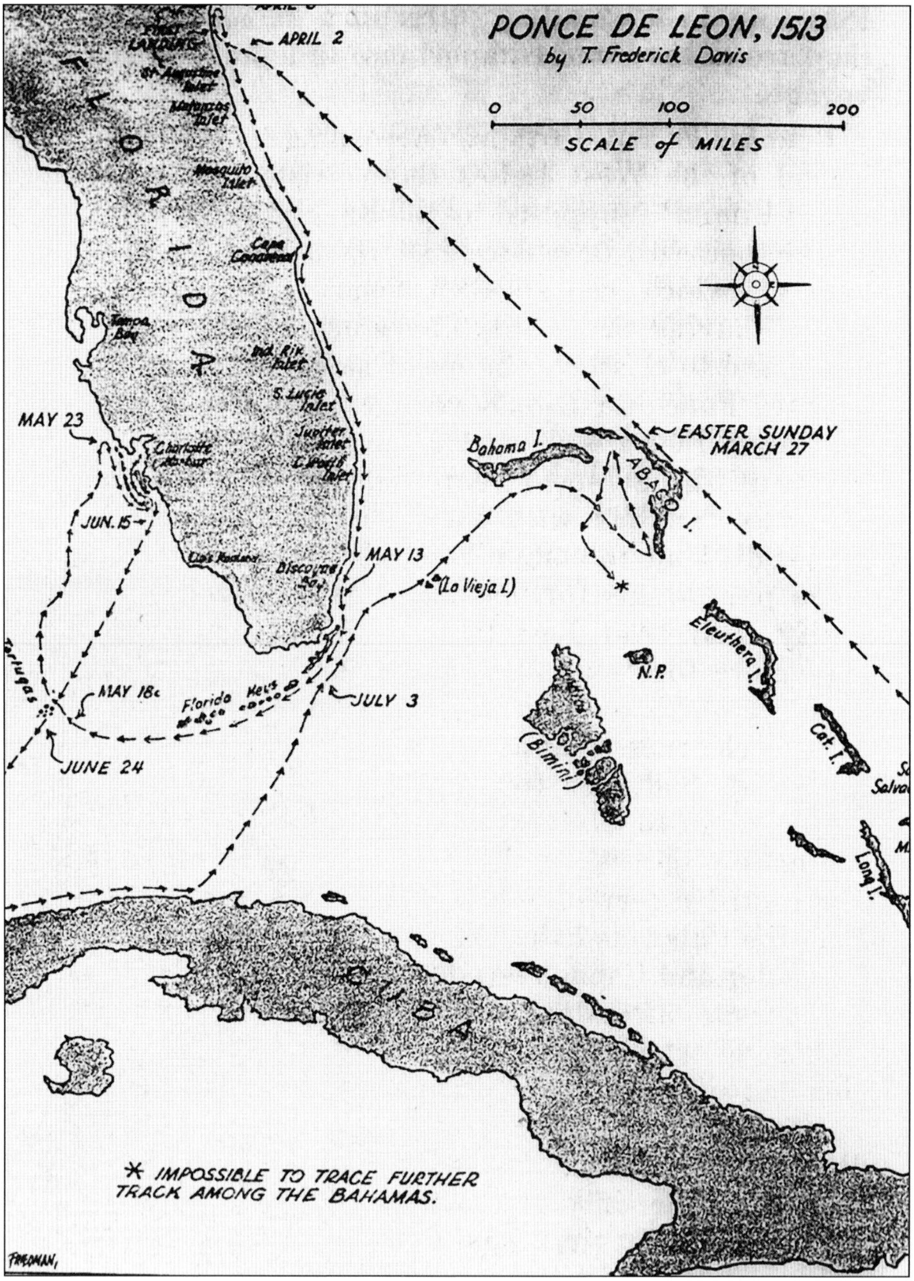

At his own expense, Spanish explorer Ponce de Leon equipped three ships for his first voyage to the New World in 1513. Making landfall along the eastern peninsula during Easter season in April 1513, he is credited with naming Florida after the Spanish term for "Flowery Passover." This map shows his later course around Pine Island. De Leon's second voyage was a return to Florida in search of the fountain of eternal youth. Having no success in locating the elusive waters, de Leon once again equipped ships with men and supplies needed for colonizing Southwest Florida, and set out on his third and final voyage in 1521. Landing on what historians believe to be Pine Island, the colonists were attacked by the Calusa Indians. Suffering a poisoned-arrow injury, de Leon was taken to Cuba, where he died from his wound. (Florida State Archives.)

In 1895, the Smithsonian Institution sent highly acclaimed archaeologist Frank Hamilton Cushing on a Southwest Florida anthropological expedition. One of his most impressive discoveries was evidence of the Calusa Indian culture, found on Demere Key, at the time spelled Demorey Key. (Smithsonian Archives.)

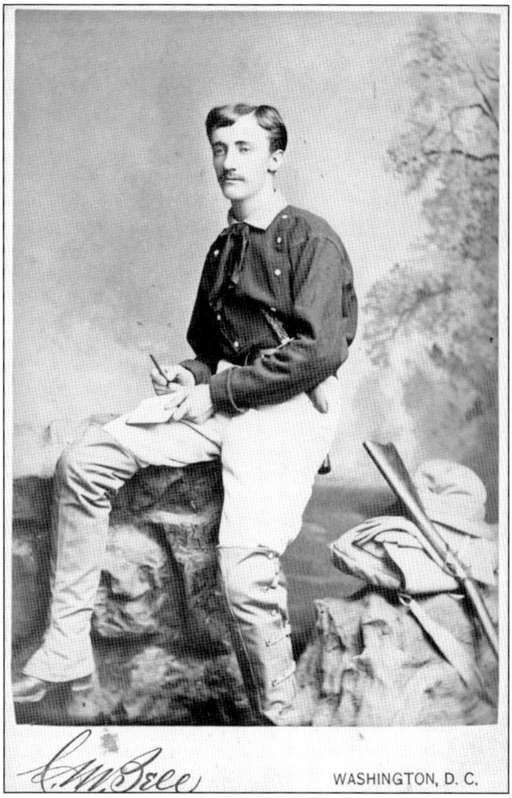

The remains of what archaeologist Frank Hamilton Cushing determined to be a temple mound structure, along with walls and altars, were all constructed of large whelk shells. This image (below), taken during Cushing's 1885 expedition, shows the intact shell wall. (Smithsonian Archives.)

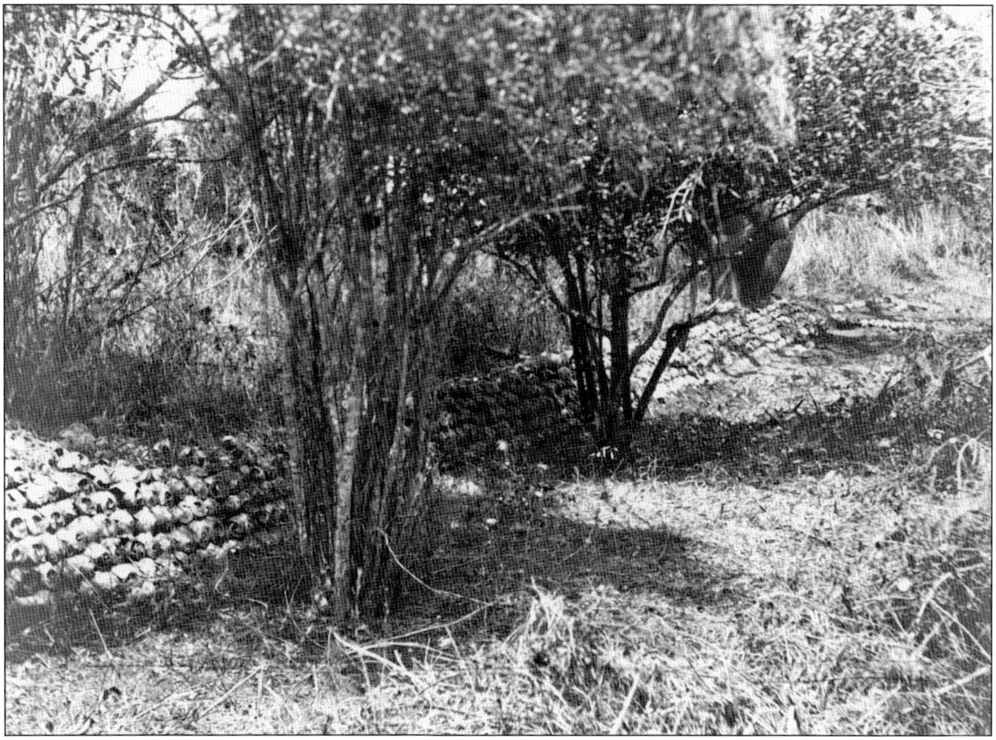

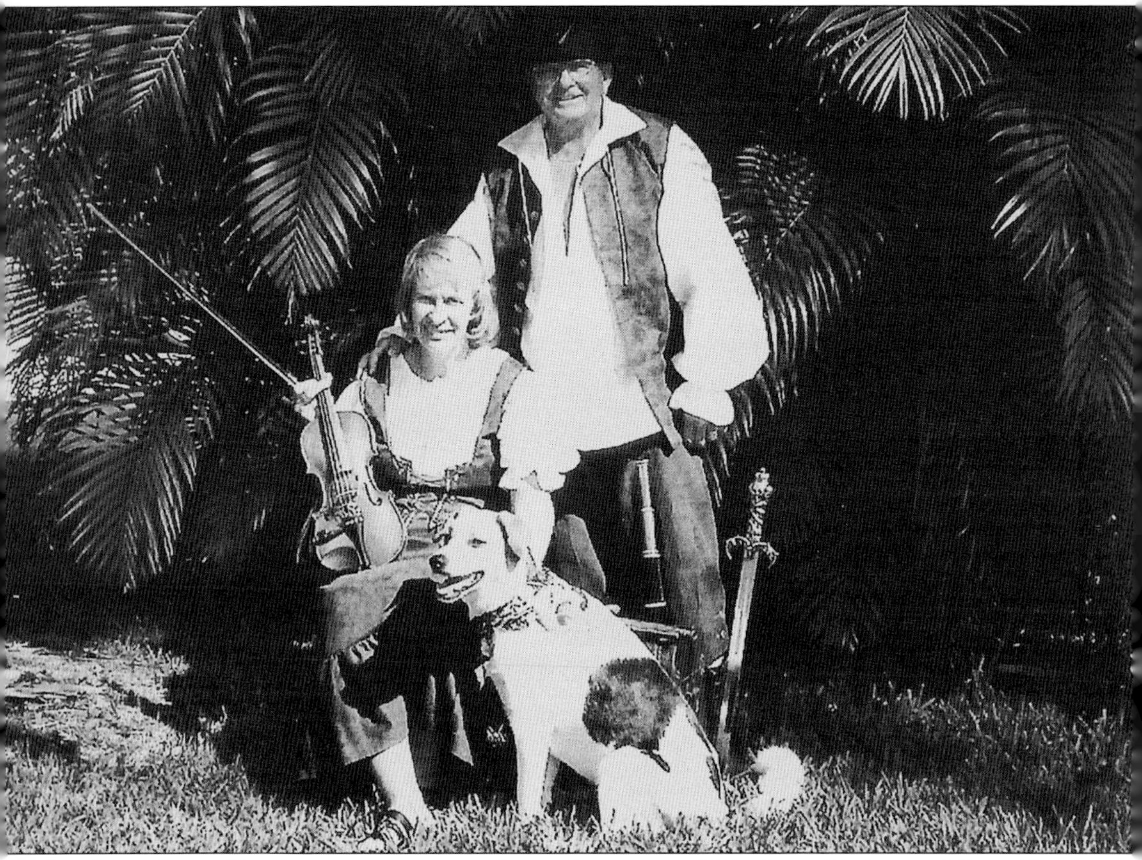

Pirate lore tells of a notorious pirate plying the waters of Charlotte Harbor and Pine Island Sound in the late 1700s. Supposedly, Brewster Baker ganged up with Jose Gaspar, also known as Gasparilla, for a period of time, making them the most feared pirates in Southwest Florida. After having a falling-out with Gasparilla, Baker ran his own successful pirate crew for a time. Making his home camp at Bokeelia, he abandoned the hideout when he heard the U.S. government had learned of his whereabouts and was sending law enforcement his way. In the rush to head out to open seas, it is said he and his men failed to dig up all of the buried loot. Soon afterwards, in a skirmish with native Indians, Baker suffered a fatal arrow wound. Never returning to Bokeelia to retrieve the treasure, it is believed to be still hidden away in Pine Island's sand. Keeping the Brewster Baker legend alive, James and Sarah Jane Kasserman reenact pirate stories and songs to the delight of anyone mystified with the thought of buried treasure. (James Kasserman.)

Two

ISOLATED LIVING

Don't fail to visit [Pine Island]. . . . Here your brow is fanned by the gentle breezes of Arcadian mildness, and which brings relief to the invalid and is a positive cure for catarrhal, bronchial, and rheumatic troubles. No swamps! No malaria! No Lagrippe!

—Florida Central and Peninsular Railroad advertisement, 1894

With the northern end of Pine Island resting in Charlotte Harbor, Northerners were unable to resist this advertisement by the Florida Central and Peninsular Railroad, which began the snowbird migrations still popular today. It is not surprising that for many the winter visit turned into a permanent residence. For the following 30 years, Pine Island relied on water transportation from fast, shallow boats know as "runboats," skiffs, steamers, and ferries.

Island residents lived in relative isolation from, not only the mainland, but also fellow islanders, as there were only trails of mud in the rainy season and sugar sand in the dry season. Yet even into the 1940s, impossible road conditions could not separate two young high school lovers. Many a weekend Ed Waldron would bicycle the 17-mile length of the island from Bokeelia to St. James City to visit with his girlfriend, Louise Pomeroy, and then bicycle back home in the dark.

Seeking a maintained north-south road on Pine Island, Dawson McDaniel is credited with a paved Stringfellow Road. He found that the county required a set number of dwellings along the road and the island had not met the quota. So he personally purchased the required number of empty sheds and placed them along the road. The county inspected the number and approved the paving. Later McDaniel laughed as he remarked on what he had done, saying, "Well, the county didn't say they had to be inhabited!"

Pine Island Road's completion in 1936 marked the end of a reliance on water transportation and the beginning of maintained roads and bridges connecting the island with the mainland. Additionally, the settlements' residents finally became acquainted with one another as their children shared bus transportation to schools in North Fort Myers and Fort Myers. With the bridge and road completions came the official end to Pine Island's isolation. It also brought an added sense of independence to the islanders. For the first time, they were no longer dependent on the constraining schedules of public transportation. It was with this new freedom that Pine Islanders adopted what became known as "island time."

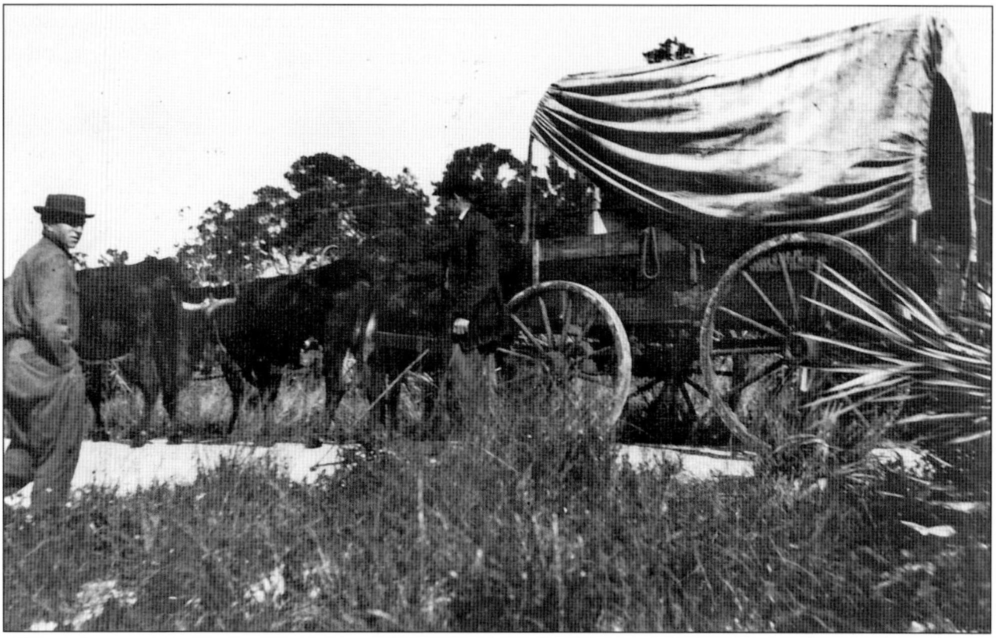

The earliest settlers arriving on Pine Island in search of homesteading land traveled by covered mule- or oxen-drawn wagons, much like this one from the late 1800s. Not only did the homesteaders face a rough terrain, but they also endured sweltering weather and swarming mosquitoes. Boarding their teams and supplies at a Punta Gorda, Fort Myers, Boca Grande, or Punta Rassa dock, they sailed by steamer to Pine Island. (Florida State Archives.)

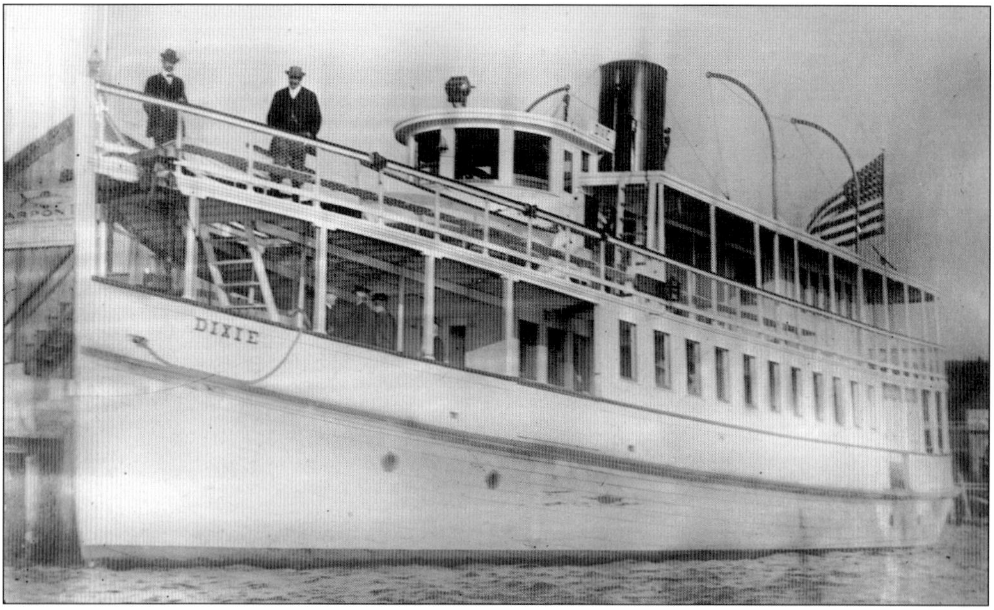

By the early 1900s, the Caloosahatchee River served as the main transportation artery between Fort Myers and locations along the river or the outer islands, including Pine Island. Several steamship companies vied for passengers, supplies, and mail delivery. At the time this photograph was taken, the Kinzie brothers served Pine Island residents and visitors with their steamships *Gladys* and *Dixie*. (Florida State Archives.)

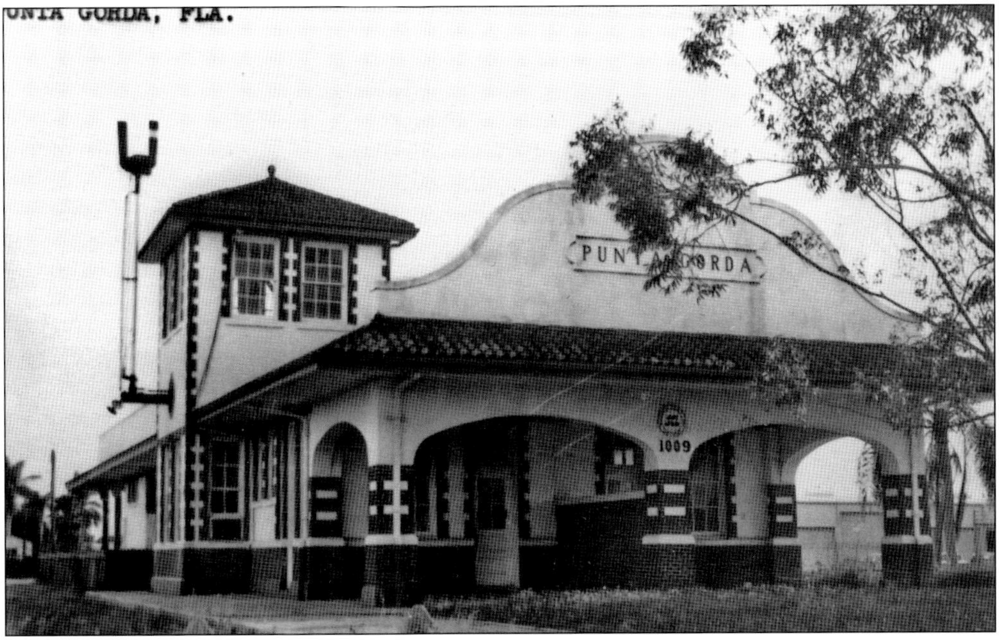

The Menge Brothers Boat Line carried mail, passengers, and produce from Punta Gorda to Fort Myers, stopping at Boca Grande and St. James City along the way. After being loaded into the ventilated boxcars, the vegetables and citrus were shipped north on the Atlantic Coast Line Railroad from this busy depot in Punta Gorda. (Fort Myers Museum of History.)

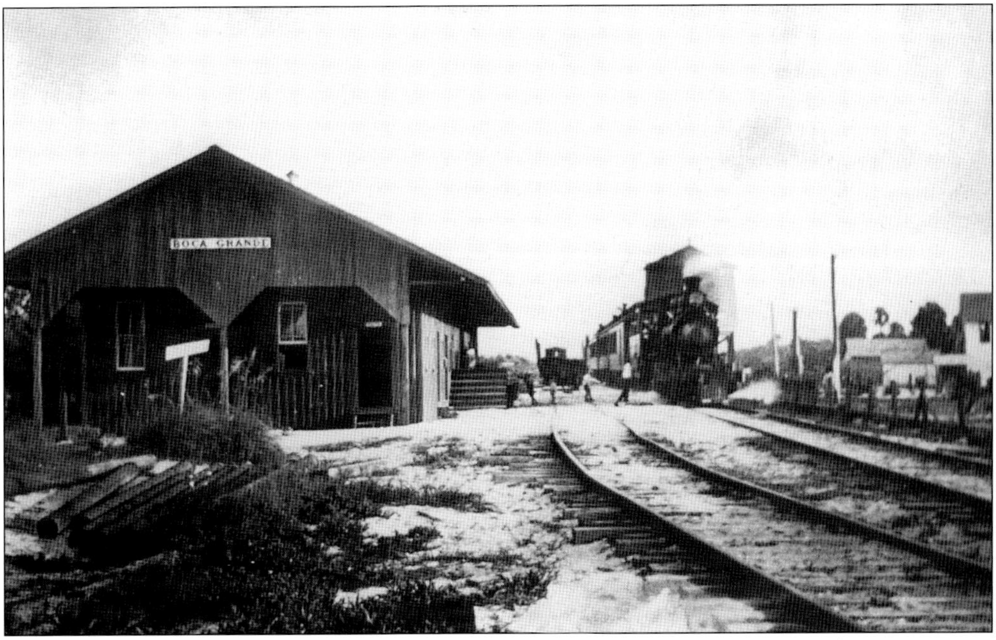

When the Charlotte Harbour and Northern Railroad (CH&N) began service between Punta Gorda and South Boca Grande, the depot was the end-of-the-road point for those needing transportation to the northern end of Pine Island or the neighboring islands of Useppa or Cayo Costa. In 1907, with the new rail service, came an additional mail route between Boca Grande, Bokeelia, and Pineland, six days a week. (Fort Myers Museum of History.)

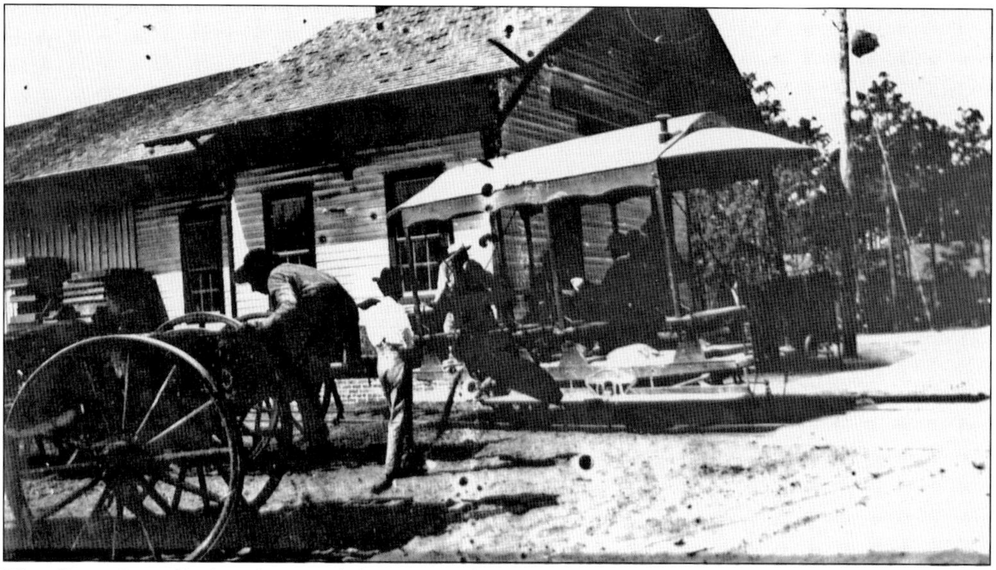

The Coast Line Railroad opened depots on the Fort Myers extension from Punta Gorda when regularly scheduled service began on May 10, 1904. Travelers could finally disembark the trains and board steamers bound for the islands from the downtown Fort Myers depot and docks. Omitting the long ride on dirt roads to Punta Rassa saved many hours in travel time. (Florida State Archives.)

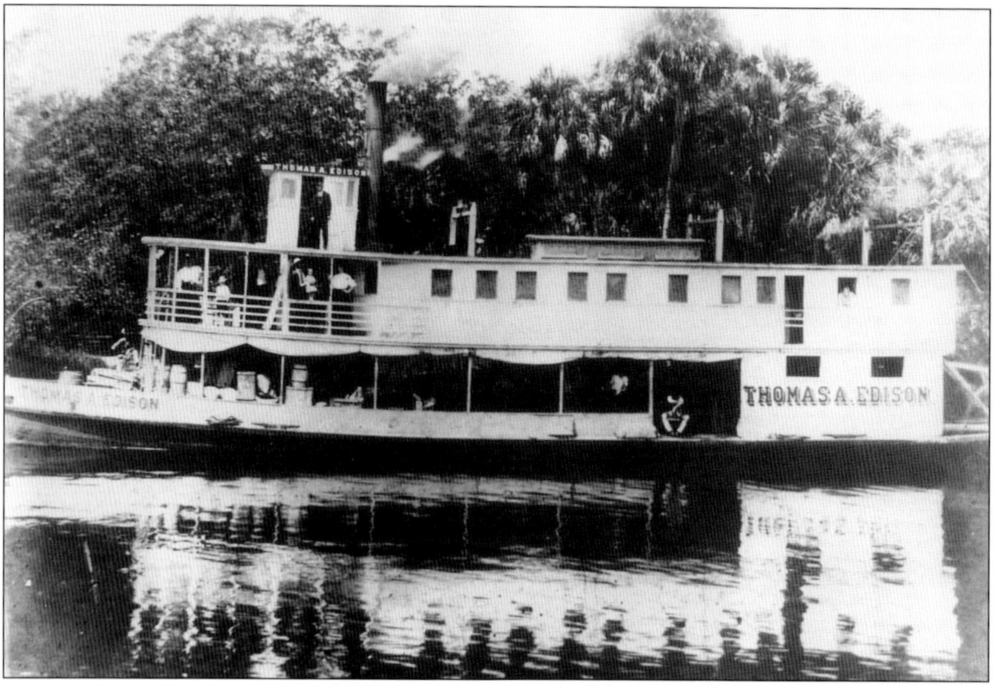

Built in Apalachicola in 1904, the *Thomas A. Edison* paddle steamer was a vital means of river transportation for island residents. Pictured here, the steamer rests at dock shortly before the big storm of 1910. Serving as both a supply freighter and a passenger boat for communities along the Caloosahatchee River, the *Thomas A. Edison* ran its scheduled route from 1904 until January 30, 1914, when it burned. (Florida State Archives.)

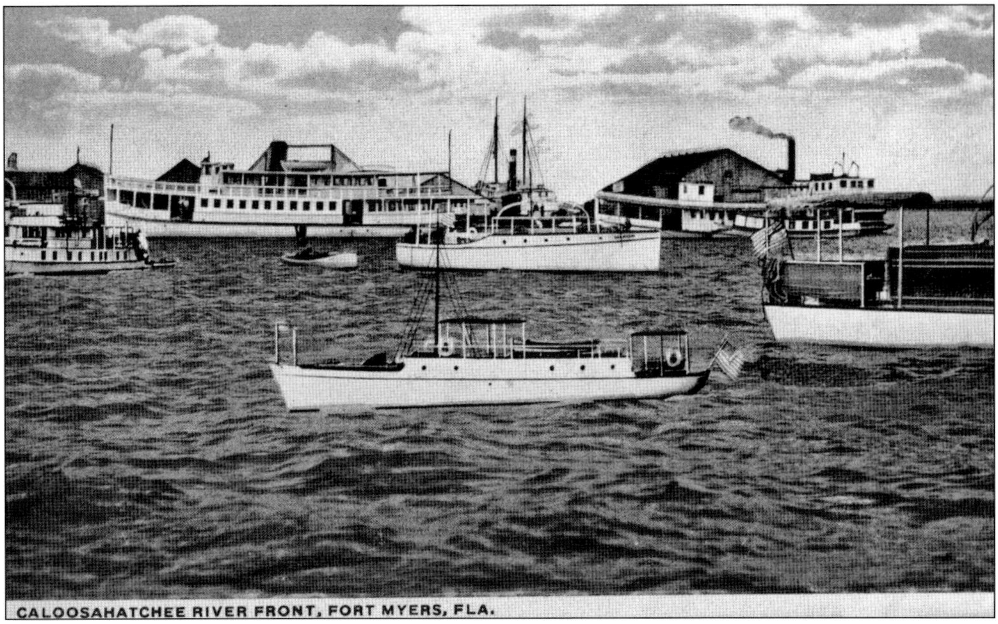

As the main artery of transportation between Fort Myers and the out islands during the early 1900s, the Caloosahatchee River was busy with boat and steamer traffic. Here the Fort Myers riverfront is alive with both river vessels and newly constructed landmarks. (Fort Myers Museum of History.)

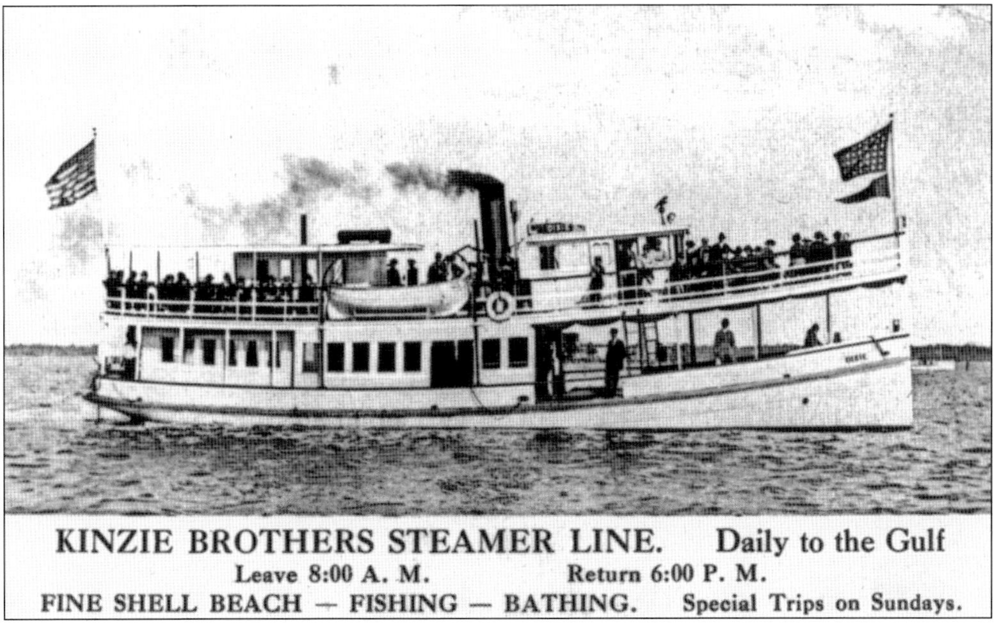

Brothers Andrew, Eric, and George Kenzie first contracted to carry mail from Fort Myers to the islands on their Kinzie Brothers Steamer Line in 1904. Except for a short period of time when they were underbid by Capt. Philip Valasquez in 1910, the brothers served the communities along the Caloosahatchee River well. Residents and visitors to the islands could depend on this river transportation every day of the week except Sunday, which was reserved for excursions. (Fort Myers Museum.)

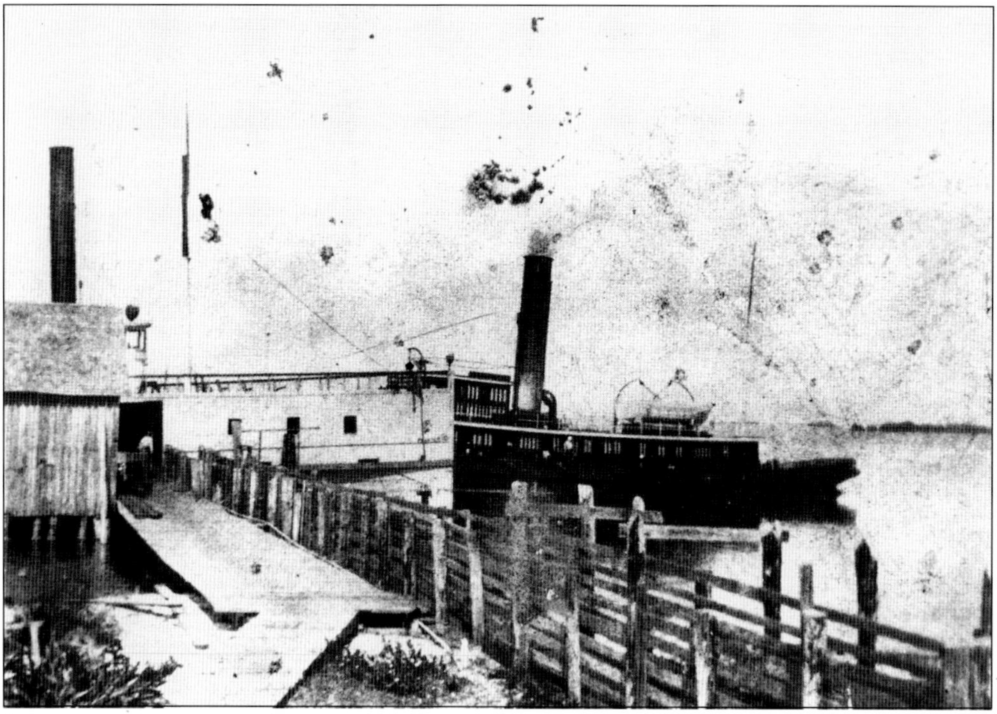

Passengers connecting with steamers from the Punta Rassa area discovered they were in for some excitement when, several times a year, the air would resound with loud "cracks" as cattlemen whipped their long leather whips in the air and jerked them into a startling crack—thus the nickname "Florida Crackers" originated. The crackers drove hundreds of cattle from Florida's uninhabited interior, pinning them up by the thousands in pins at Punta Rassa to await shipment by steamers. (Florida State Archives.)

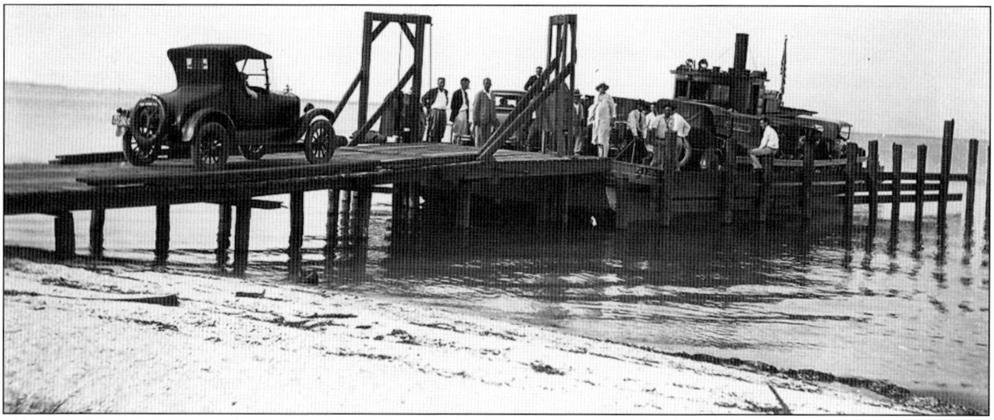

When the Kinzie Brothers Steamer Line opened ferry service between Punta Rassa and Sanibel in 1928, Pine Islanders had a new public transportation opportunity connecting them with the world beyond their shores. The *Best*, pictured here, ran four trips daily and additionally had the capacity to carry seven cars. The Kinzie Brothers operated the ferry service until 1963, when the Sanibel Bridge/Causeway opened. (Fort Myers Museum.)

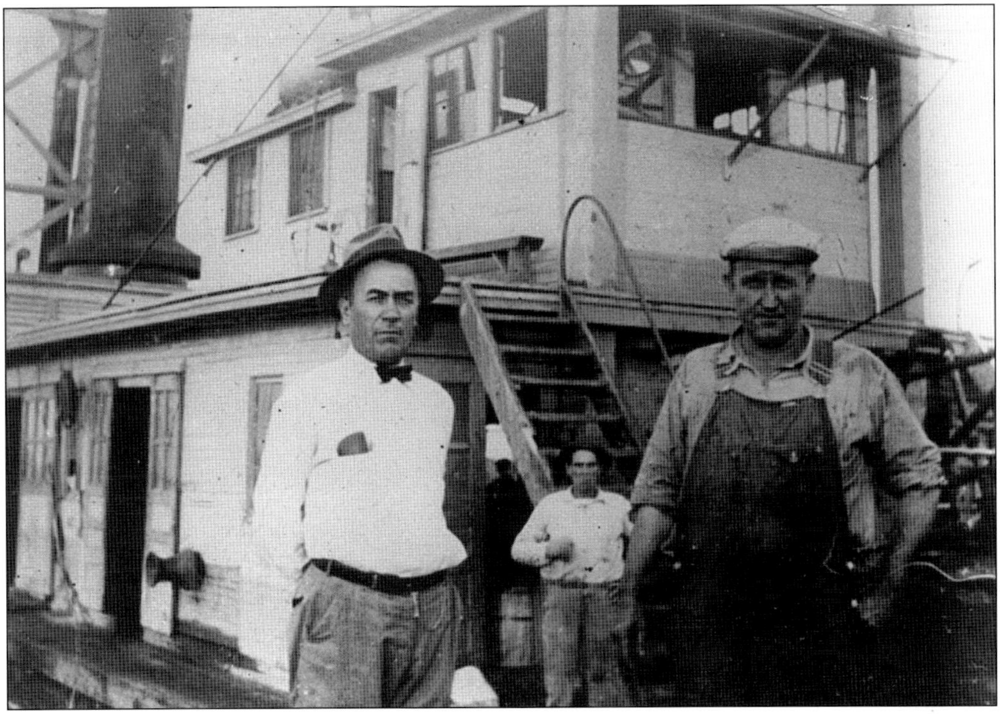

The crew of the dredge boat *Niagara* told of a night in 1935: "The mosquitoes, chizwink gnats, and other night-flying insects shut the *Niagara* down and killed seven cows, eleven hogs, and one mule." Dredging the waterways for steamer traffic was a test of endurance! (Fort Myers Museum of History.)

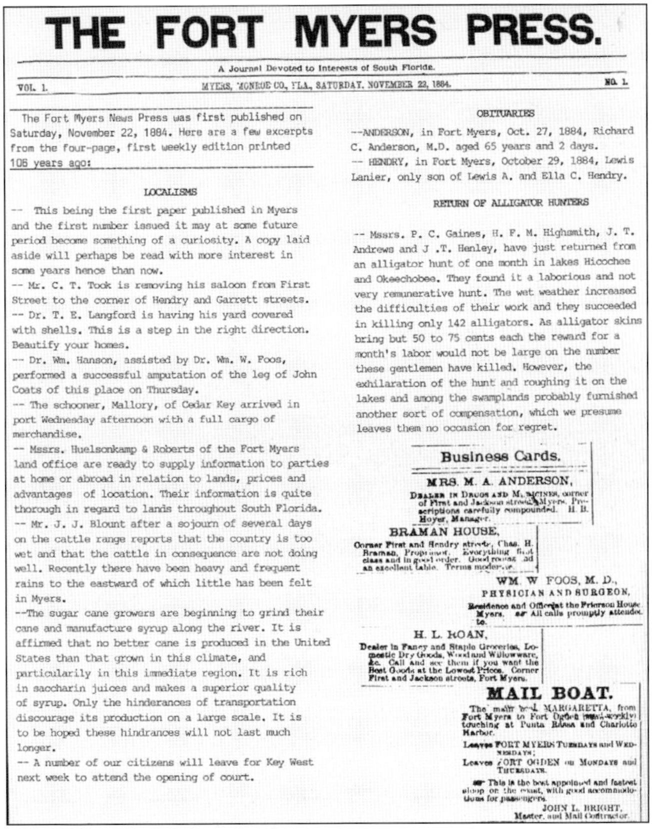

THE FORT MYERS PRESS.

A Journal Devoted to Interests of South Florida.

VOL. 1. MYERS, MONROE CO, FLA, SATURDAY, NOVEMBER 22, 1884. NO. 1.

The Fort Myers News Press was first published on Saturday, November 22, 1884. Here are a few excerpts from the four-page, first weekly edition printed 106 years ago:

LOCALISMS

-- This being the first paper published in Myers and the first number issued it may at some future period become something of a curiosity. A copy laid aside will perhaps be read with more interest in some years hence than now.

-- Mr. C. T. Took is removing his saloon from First Street to the corner of Hendry and Garrett streets.

-- Dr. T. E. Langford is having his yard covered with shells. This is a step in the right direction. Beautify your homes.

-- Dr. Wm. Hanson, assisted by Dr. Wm. W. Foos, performed a successful amputation of the leg of John Coats of this place on Thursday.

-- The schooner, Mallory, of Cedar Key arrived in port Wednesday afternoon with a full cargo of merchandise.

-- Mssrs. Huelsonkamp & Roberts of the Fort Myers land office are ready to supply information to parties at home or abroad in relation to lands, prices and advantages of location. Their information is quite thorough in regard to lands throughout South Florida.

-- Mr. J. J. Blount after a sojourn of several days on the cattle range reports that the country is too wet and that the cattle in consequence are not doing well. Recently there have been heavy and frequent rains to the eastward of which little has been felt in Myers.

--The sugar cane growers are beginning to grind their cane and manufacture syrup along the river. It is affirmed that no better cane is produced in the United States than that grown in this climate, and particularily in this immediate region. It is rich in saccharin juices and makes a superior quality of syrup. Only the hinderances of transportation discourage its production on a large scale. It is to be hoped these hindrances will not last much longer.

-- A number of our citizens will leave for Key West next week to attend the opening of court.

OBITUARIES

--ANDERSON, in Fort Myers, Oct. 27, 1884, Richard C. Anderson, M.D. aged 65 years and 2 days.

-- HENDRY, in Fort Myers, October 29, 1884, Lewis Lanier, only son of Lewis A. and Ella C. Hendry.

RETURN OF ALLIGATOR HUNTERS

-- Mssrs. P. C. Gaines, H. F. M. Highsmith, J. T. Andrews and J .T. Henley, have just returned from an alligator hunt of one month in lakes Hicochee and Okeechobee. They found it a laborious and not very remunerative hunt. The wet weather increased the difficulties of their work and they succeeded in killing only 142 alligators. As alligator skins bring but 50 to 75 cents each the reward for a month's labor would not be large on the number these gentlemen have killed. However, the exhilaration of the hunt and roughing it on the lakes and among the swamplands probably furnished another sort of compensation, which we presume leaves them no occasion for regret.

With the first issue of the *Fort Myers Press*, released on November 22, 1884, islanders and mainlanders alike finally felt connected through current news stories. The article on the right tells of an alligator hunt, and in the lower right-hand corner, there is an advertisement for the mail boat to the islands. (Fort Myers Museum of History.)

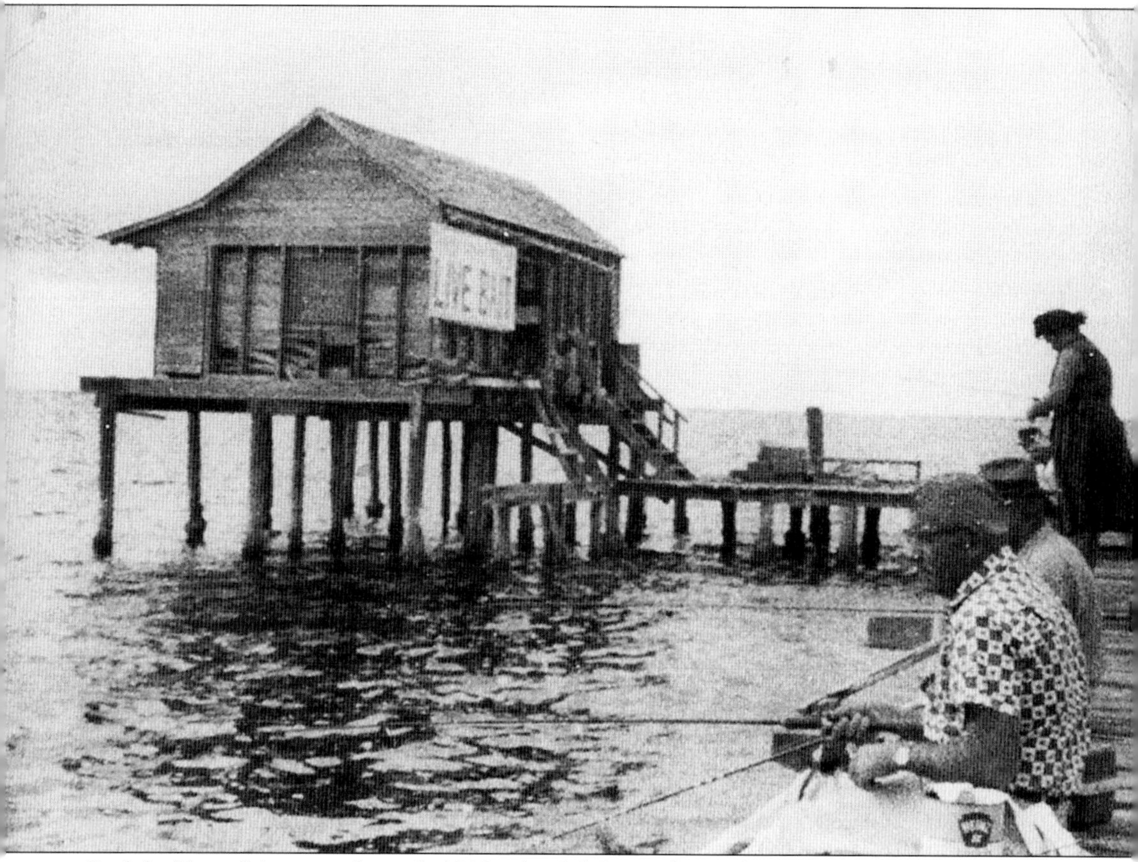

Built by Henry Martin in the early 1900s, this fish house, located at the end of Bokeelia's pier, was served by shallow draft "runboats" from Punta Gorda. Living in the back of the large fish house was the dock tender, who was available for loading or unloading provisions around the clock. Runboats would arrive from Punta Gorda bringing mail, supplies, and passengers. Commandeered by the U.S. government in 1941, the runboats were used in the war effort. In addition to the fish house and dock, Martin's wife, Minta, ran a boardinghouse and the first post office. Taken one month before Hurricane Donna destroyed the pier in 1960, this image shows fishermen enjoying the aging pier. (Nancy Brooks.)

Frank Adams of Pineland and Capt. John Smith from St. James City opened a sawmill in the 1920s. Located on the corner of Pineland and Roberts Roads, the sawmill supplied building materials to newcomers for several years. Logs from pine trees cut down in the Harbor Drive area were loaded onto wagons and hauled by oxen teams much like this one. (Florida State Archives.)

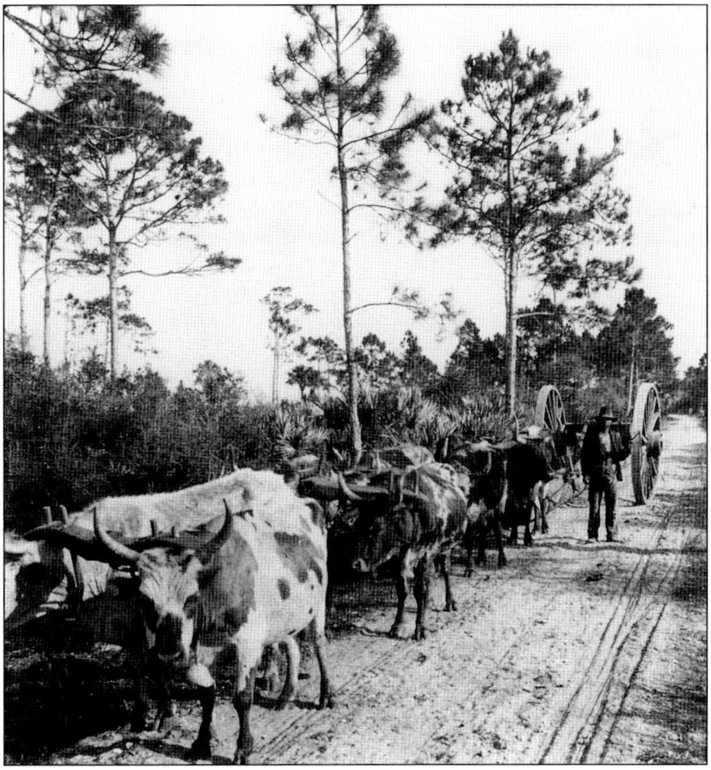

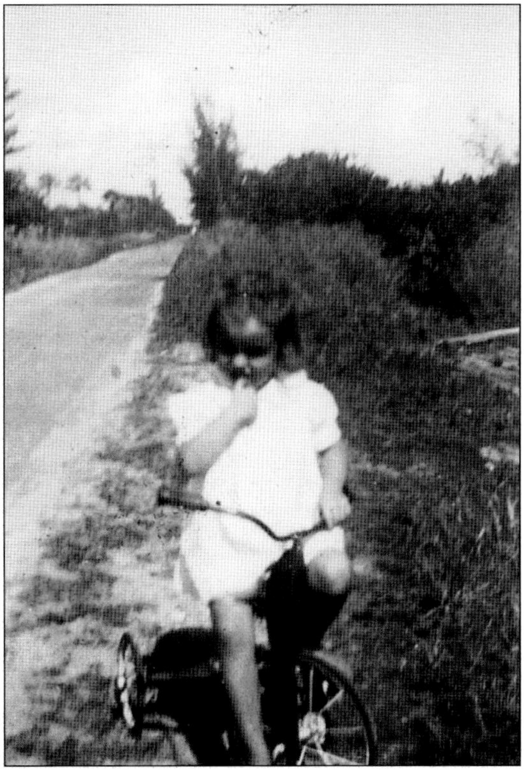

Before opening the Piner Seafood Company in Matlacha, Lewis Piner lived with his wife, Mary, and daughter, Corella, in St. James City. The roads in St. James City remained rough, as seen here in this image of Corella, at the age of three, taken in 1929. The road led to the fish house, with the rope factory located to the right of Corella. (Corella Stahl.)

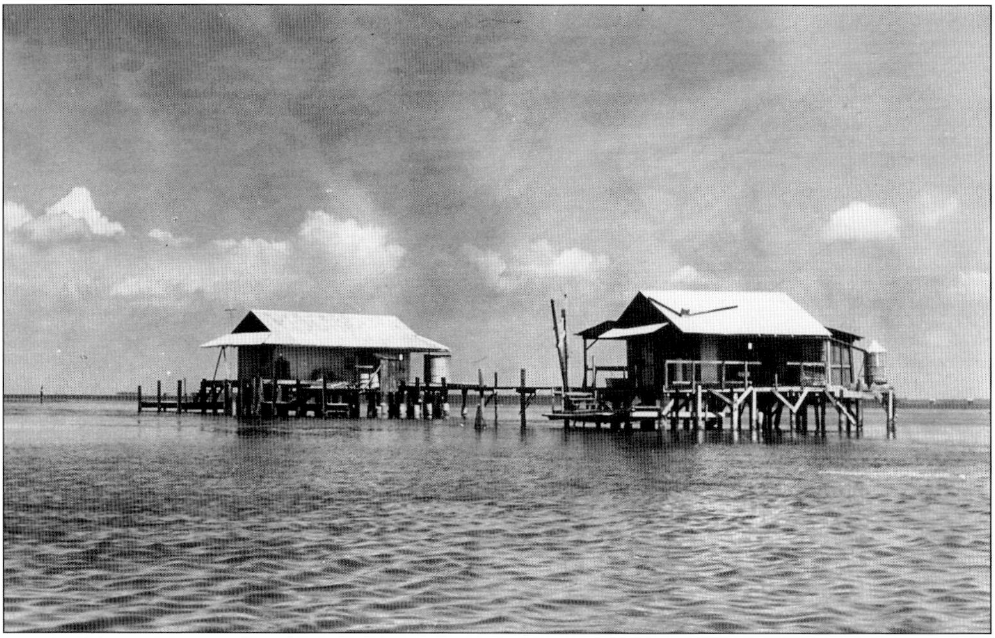

Stilt houses perched along the island's shores or in the shallow waters of Pine Island Sound provided a practical, yet isolated, housing solution for fishing families. Labeled as Historic Fish Cabins in the National Register of Historic Places, there are only nine stilt houses left in Pine Island Sound. By law, no new fish cabins may be built. (Florida State Archives.)

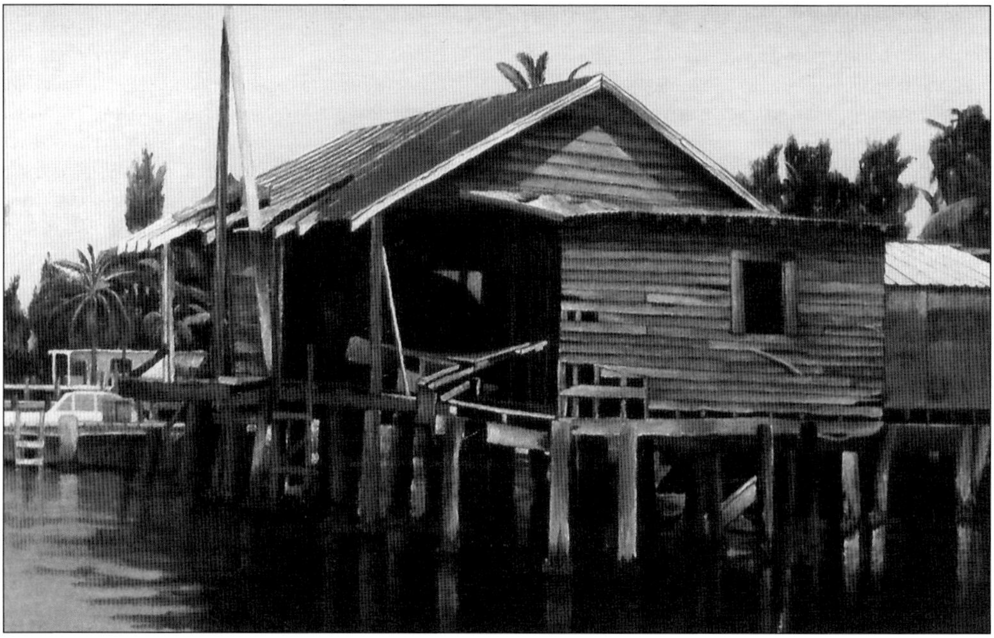

According to Kay (Caputo) DellaBitta, "When I was about four years old, I wanted to join my brothers fishing from the porch. Fearing I would fall off the porch and drown, Mama had me fish through the outhouse toilet seat that opened over the open water beneath. I can remember fishing and catching fish so big I couldn't get them up through that hole!" Pictured is the stilt house she grew up in. (Kay DellaBitta.)

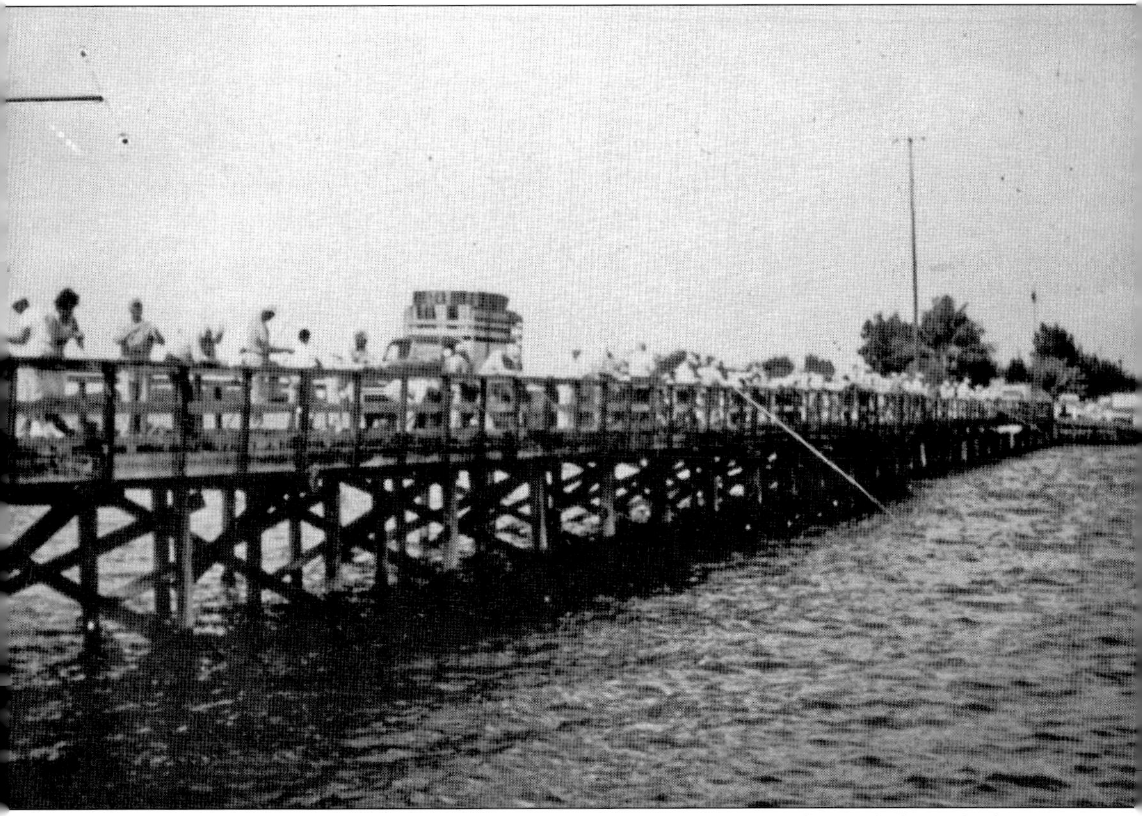

Before the construction of the Matlacha Bridge, mid-islanders had to walk or ride by mule-drawn wagons from home to St. James City to pick up mail and supplies. This all-day trip was eliminated when Harry Stringfellow, along with Bruce Scott, succeeded in convincing Lee County to build a bridge connecting Pine Island with the mainland. The story goes that when Stringfellow was elected as county commissioner, he wearied of the routine of leaving his home near Pineland for a three-hour ride by mule-drawn wagon to St. James City. Then it was a round-trip steam boat ride to Fort Myers and back. In 1927, the convenience of a bridge and road to Pine Island became a reality. It was not long before people discovered good fishing from the Matlacha Bridge. Sometimes it was so crowded on the bridge that people were actually pushed off into the water—thus the "Fishingest Bridge in the World" label. (Fort Myers Museum of History.)

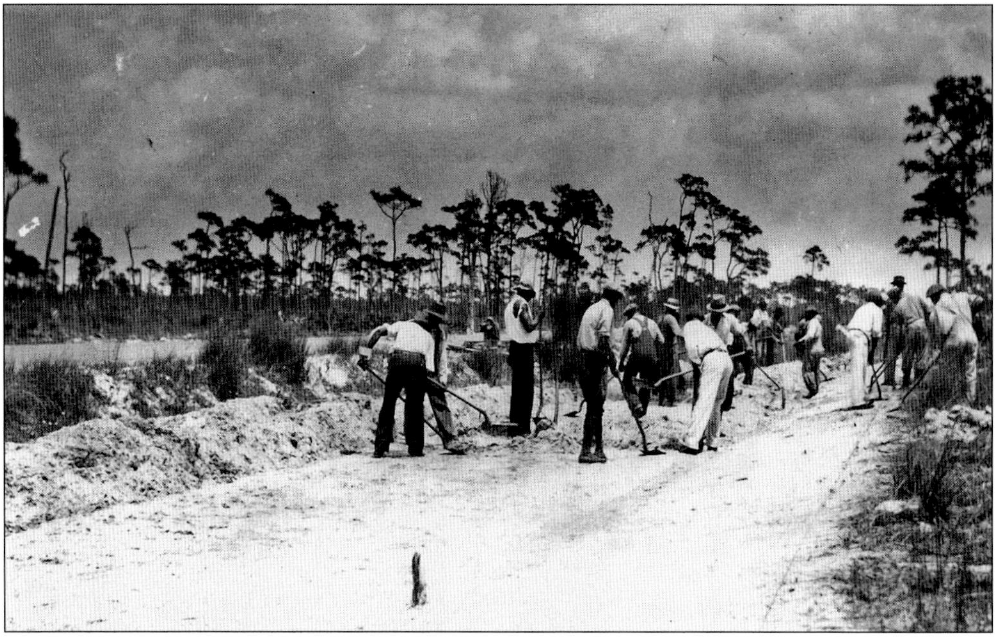

Before the completion of the Matlacha Bridge in 1927, the roads leading toward Pine Island were nothing more than trails. Here a road construction crew works by hand on the then county-maintained Pine Island Road on April 27, 1935. (Florida State Archives.)

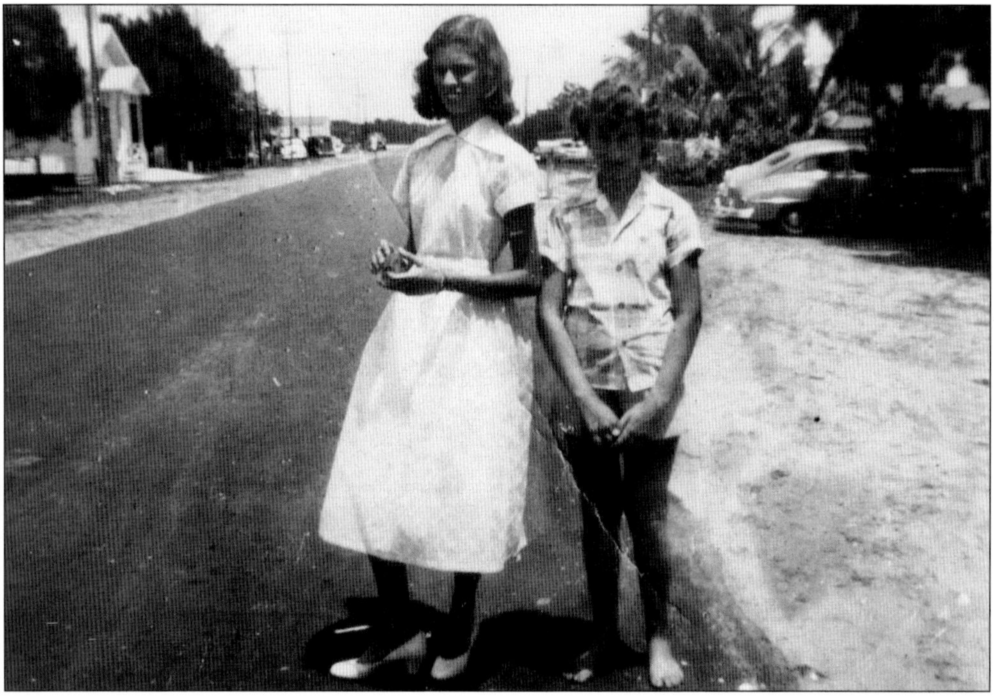

Traffic congestion was never a problem on Pine Island Road in the early 1950s. Virginia and Susie Padilla laugh as they tell of how everyone in Matlacha chose to stand in the middle of the road for pictures. The road also made a perfect place to play or ride bikes. Here, as the girls pose, there are no visible signs of moving cars in either direction. (Padilla Family.)

Piner's Seafood Company served as Matlacha's largest employer in the early 1940s. Here Lewis Piner, owner and operator of the plant, stands beside the bus he ran between Fort Myers and Matlacha, providing transportation for city women seeking employment. Underage girls needing spending money would also work at the tables, causing the implantation of a practiced "drill" for when the inspector showed up. The bell would ring, and the girls would all run out the back door and jump into Matlacha Sound, splashing and yelling like they had been there all along. As soon as the inspector left, the "all clear" was sounded, and the girls got out of the water, dried off, and returned to picking crabs. (Corella Stahl.)

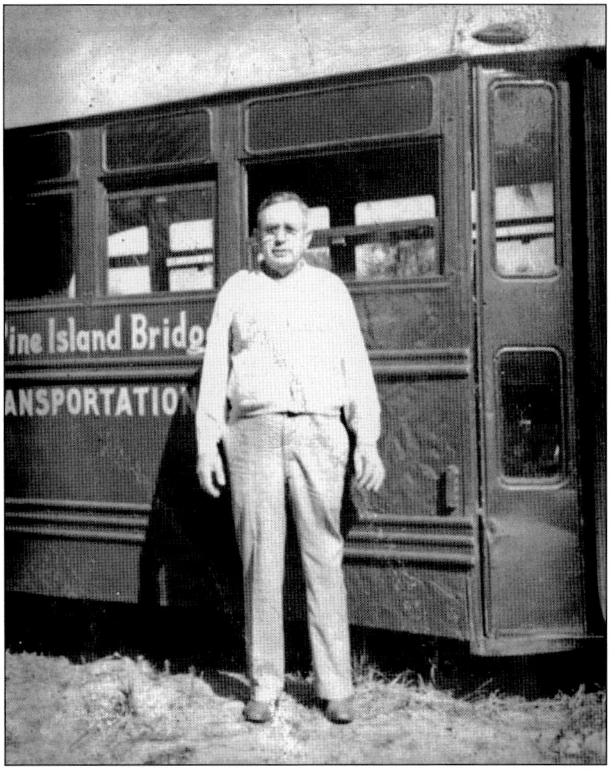

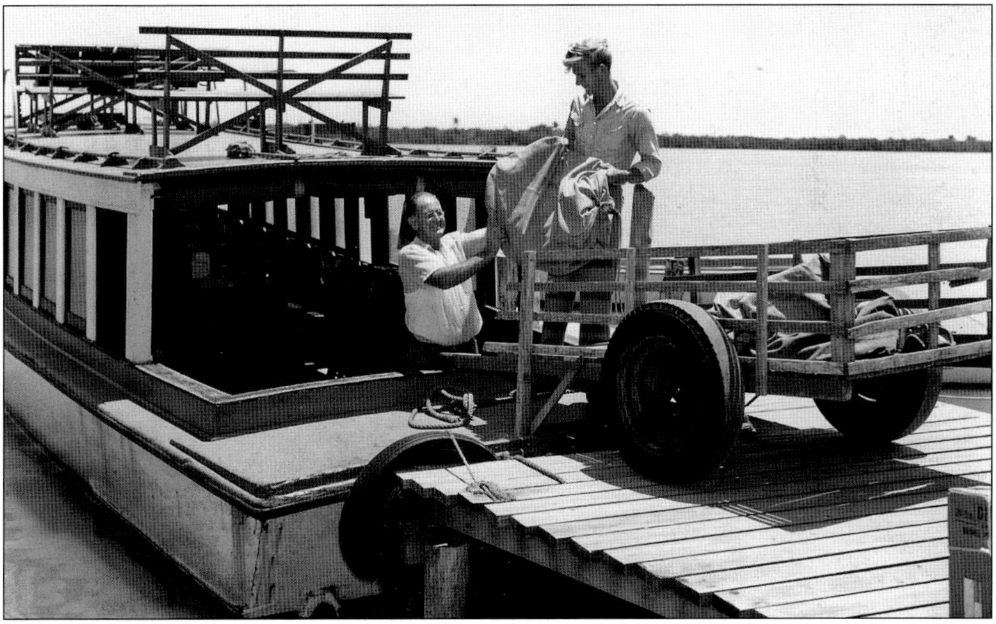

The Singleton brothers, Ray and Cleon, were responsible for some of St. James City's early mail service. Punctuality was the brothers' motto; during the 16 years of mail service to the islands, they were never late. Taken on March 15, 1948, this photograph shows not only the mail boat, but also the large white canvas mailbags and the dock cart used to transport the mail from the boat. (Florida State Archives.)

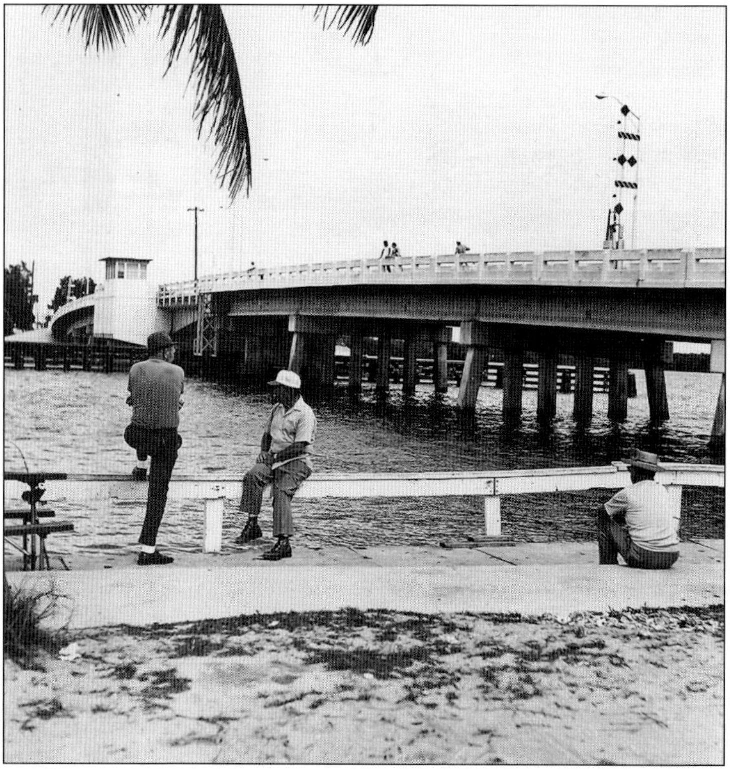

Opening to traffic in July 1968, the new bridge spanning Matlacha Pass was built at the cost of $738,000. At 10 feet wider than the old bridge, it could accommodate a double-lane of the newer, wider automobiles. A 5-foot-wide catwalk along both sides allowed for fishermen to continue their quest of catching a "big one" from the new "fishingest bridge in the world." (Fort Myers Museum of History.)

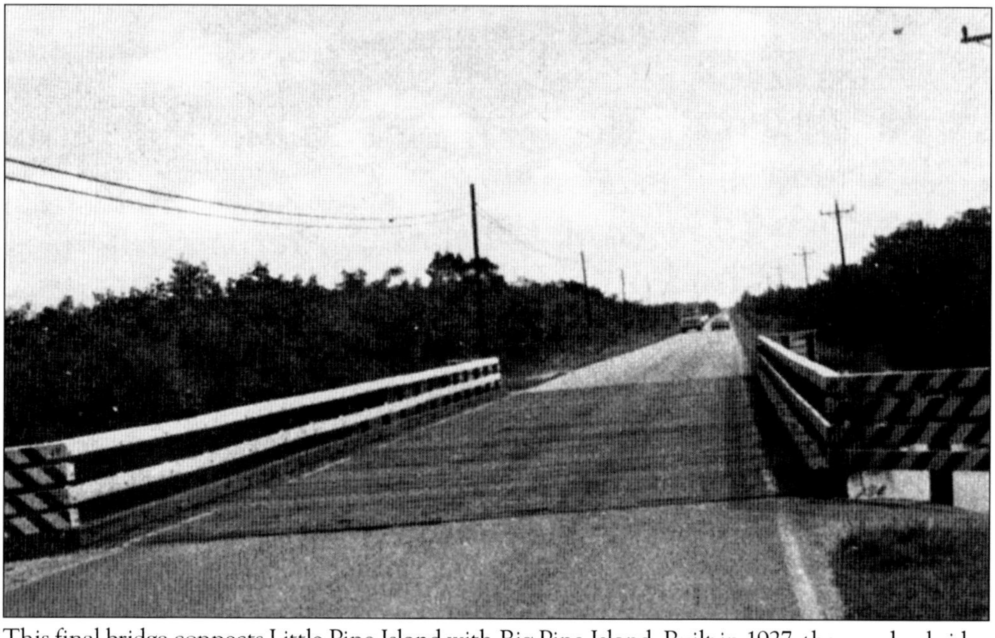

This final bridge connects Little Pine Island with Big Pine Island. Built in 1927, the wooden bridge was replaced with a concrete bridge in 1978. During the project, Maurie and Dan Stevens stopped and made a deal with the department of transportation. The men purchased the old bridge and had it delivered to the Stevens property for $500. The planks still rest on the property. (Museum of the Islands.)

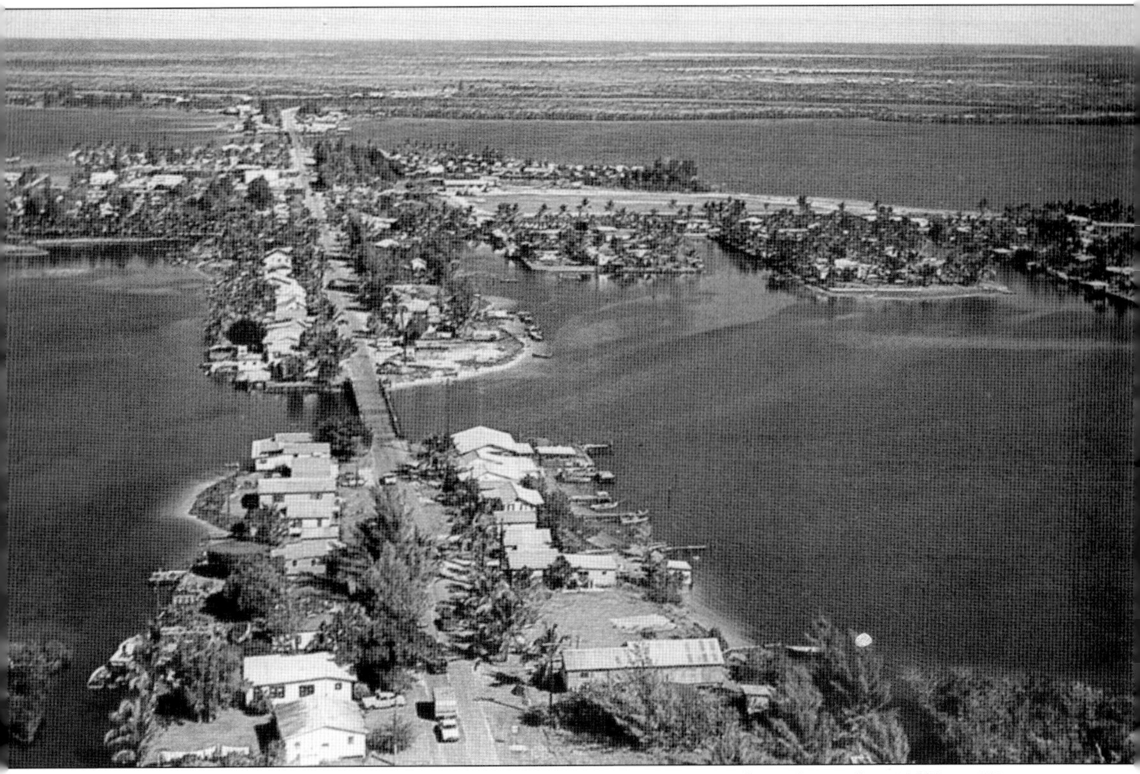

By the 1950s, "Matlacha" was the official community name, rather than the "fill" or "Pine Island Bridge." Velma Padilla recalls how the loud rattling of the bridge planks as vehicles crossed could be heard from one end of town to the other. Many of these original squatter homes are standing in Matlacha today, thanks to an organized effort for historic preservation by the community. (Padilla Family.)

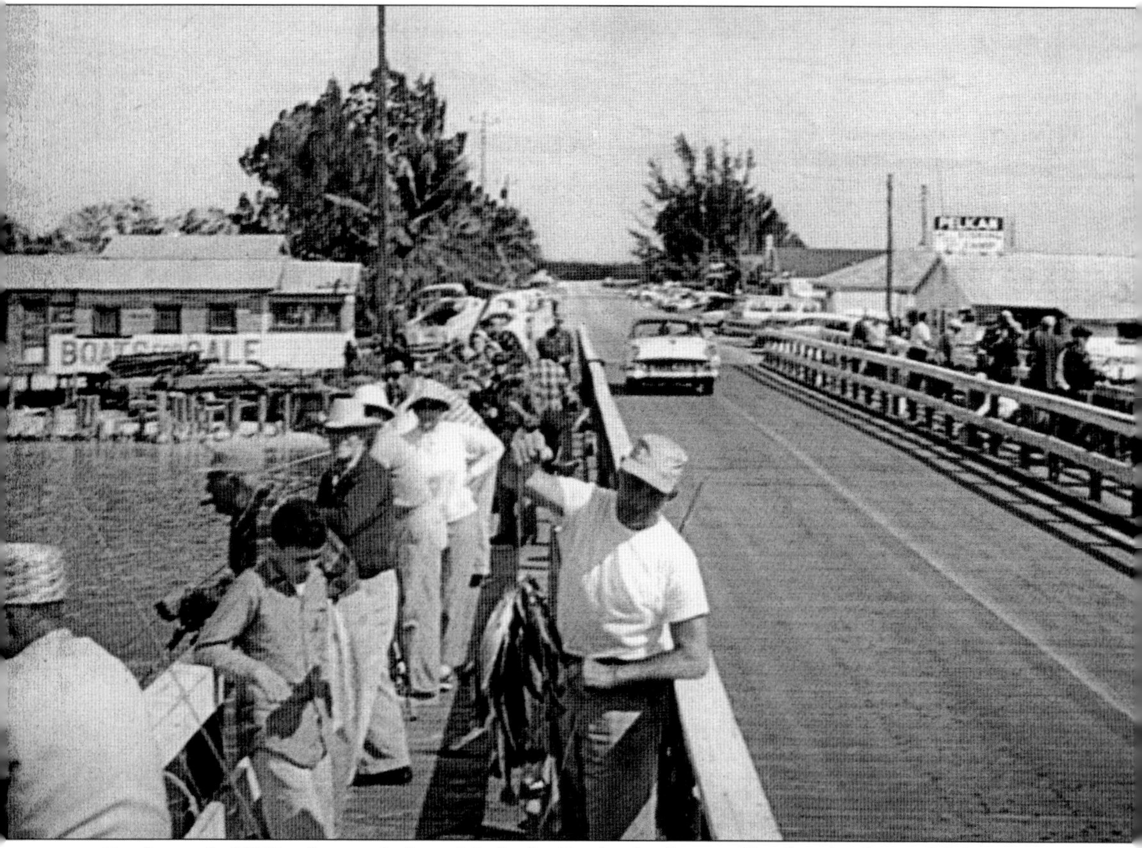

By the early 1960s, the single-lane Matlacha Bridge had served both vehicles and fishermen well for 31 years. According to Elaine Jordan in *Pine Island, the Forgotten Island*, the numerous repairs to the wooden planks and side rails could not prevent the bridge from being replaced Jesse Padilla, a Matlacha resident, commented, "The wooden bridge was a fine span when it was built, but it failed to keep up with the size of autos over the years. In 1928 that bridge was to the Model T what the new bridge is to a modern car. It had to be replaced." (Fort Myers Museum of History.)

Three

Five Quirky Communities

Although some have compared Pine Island to "Mayberry surrounded by water," in reality, Pine Island is comprised of five separate, unique communities, all resembling 1960s small Southern towns. The remoteness of the island originally attracted tough, independent settlers and fishermen. Later, after the Matlacha Bridge connected the island with the mainland, a new wave of freethinking, hardworking, somewhat antiestablishment individuals found the island and made it home.

Surprisingly, Miami was still just a mosquito swamp when the hemp capitol of St. James City was incorporated in 1885. It is generally believed the community received its name from Jesuit missionaries setting up a garrison, called Saint James, under the command of Pedro Menendez DeAviles in the 1500s. The mission was abandoned by the time Capt. John Smith arrived in 1873, yet the name remained.

Originally called Batty's Landing, Minta Martin is credited with bestowing the name Pineland to the community when she applied for a post office. Carrying on a Calusa tradition, most evenings find novelist Randy Wayne White blowing an ancient conch, sending the shell's mournful notes across Pineland into the sunset on Pine Island Sound.

Bokeelia, pronounced "Bo-keel-ya," is located on the northern shore, resting in Charlotte Harbor. Whelks and conchs were so plentiful in the early 1900s that the first schoolteacher, Josie Henderson, used them as part of the landscaping, including conch shell-lined paths. As in its earliest days, Bokeelia's residents, commercial fishermen, and transplanted Northerners alike, enjoy an easy-going social foundation.

Now referred to as the Center, the area was originally called "Tom's Town" after the owner of several hundred acres in the area. Today it is the island hub for churches, the library, a school, a fire station, and retail stores. With a four-way stop, it is the closest thing to city living on the island.

According to Frank L. Padilla Sr., Matlacha was still called Pine Island Bridge in 1937. As told by his grandfather, Frank shares the name's origin: "They had Indians [Seminole] there then. One got into a fight with a man named Jose. While they were fighting, another fellow was shouting 'killin' Joe'—Mata-la-Jose in Spanish."

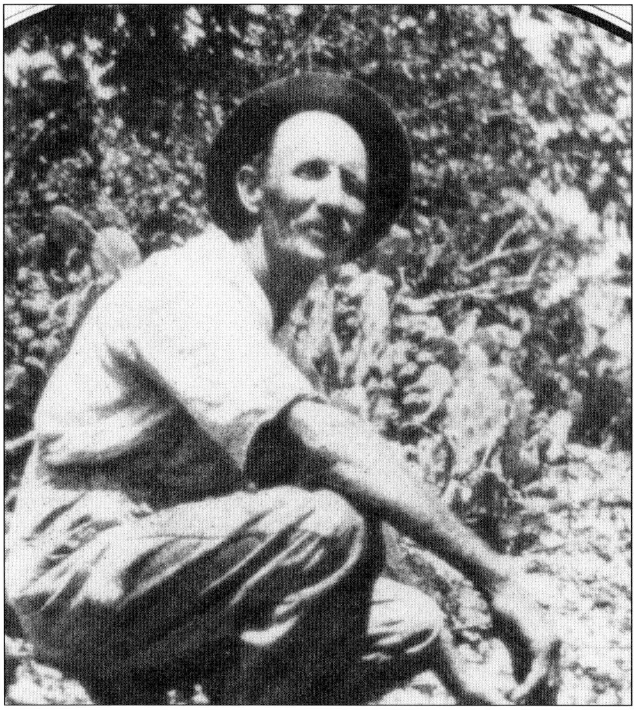

A Finnish sailor by the name of Capt. John Smith was the first permanent settler of St. James City following the destruction of his family home at Punta Rassa in the hurricane of 1873. First, Smith provided for his family through catching and selling fish. Later, when the tarpon fishing "boom" years of the 1880s hit the community, he became a noted tarpon guide. In addition, Smith opened a business, building and renting rowboats used for popular tarpon expeditions. (Museum of the Islands.)

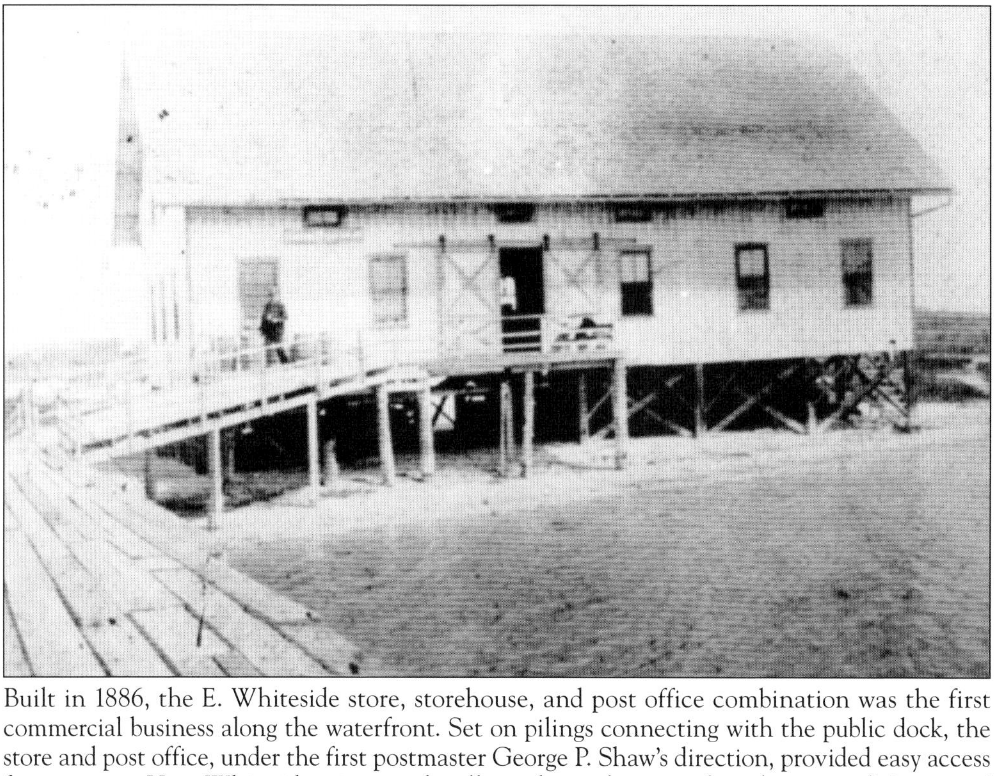

Built in 1886, the E. Whiteside store, storehouse, and post office combination was the first commercial business along the waterfront. Set on pilings connecting with the public dock, the store and post office, under the first postmaster George P. Shaw's direction, provided easy access for everyone. Here Whiteside is pictured walking down the ramp from his store. (Museum of the Islands.)

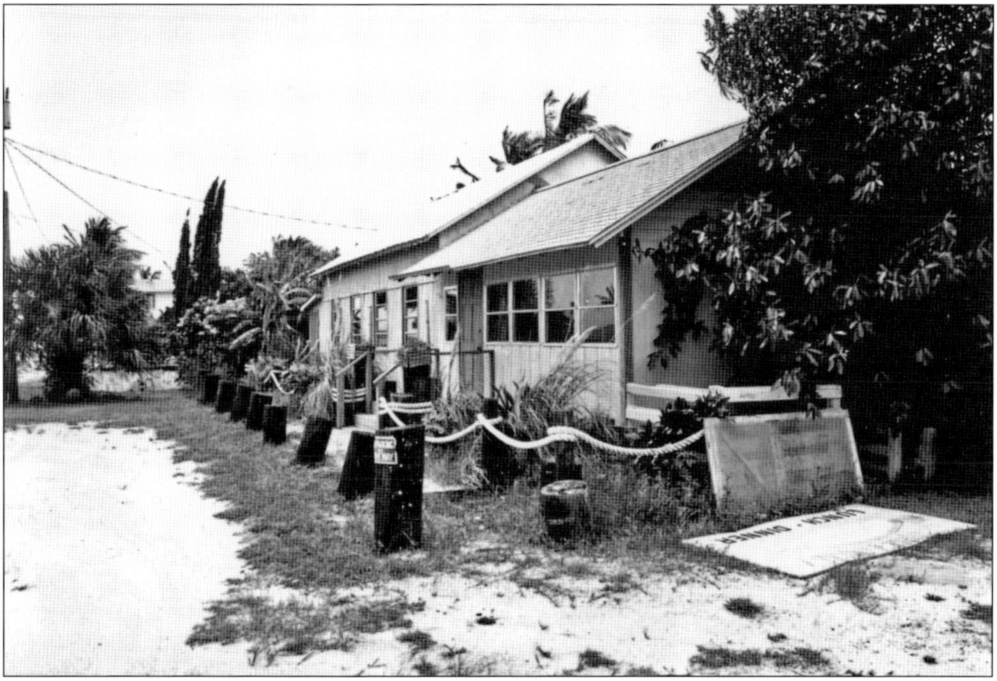

Twenty children attended the town's first school, built in 1887 by the St. James-on-the-Gulf Company. When the company filed for bankruptcy and families moved away, the school was all but abandoned, and was destroyed by fire in 1896. The Sisal Hemp and Development Company built another school in 1912. Abandoned by the early 1940s, the building was sold and moved several times. Known as the Sea Belle Fish Camp and later the Rum Pointe Inn, today it is home to the Waterfront Restaurant on Oleander Street near Hopkins Point. (Fort Myers Museum of History.)

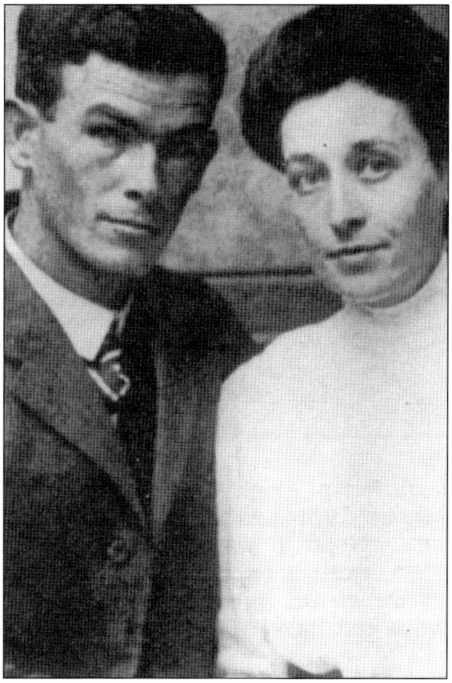

Ernest and Eunice Hord, pictured here, joined Hord brothers Fred and James in settling in St. James City in 1908. They were instrumental in building the Sisal Hemp Plant and the second school, where Eunice served as teacher. The reputedly haunted Hord Mansion, built by James, burned to the ground in 1980. (Museum of the Islands.)

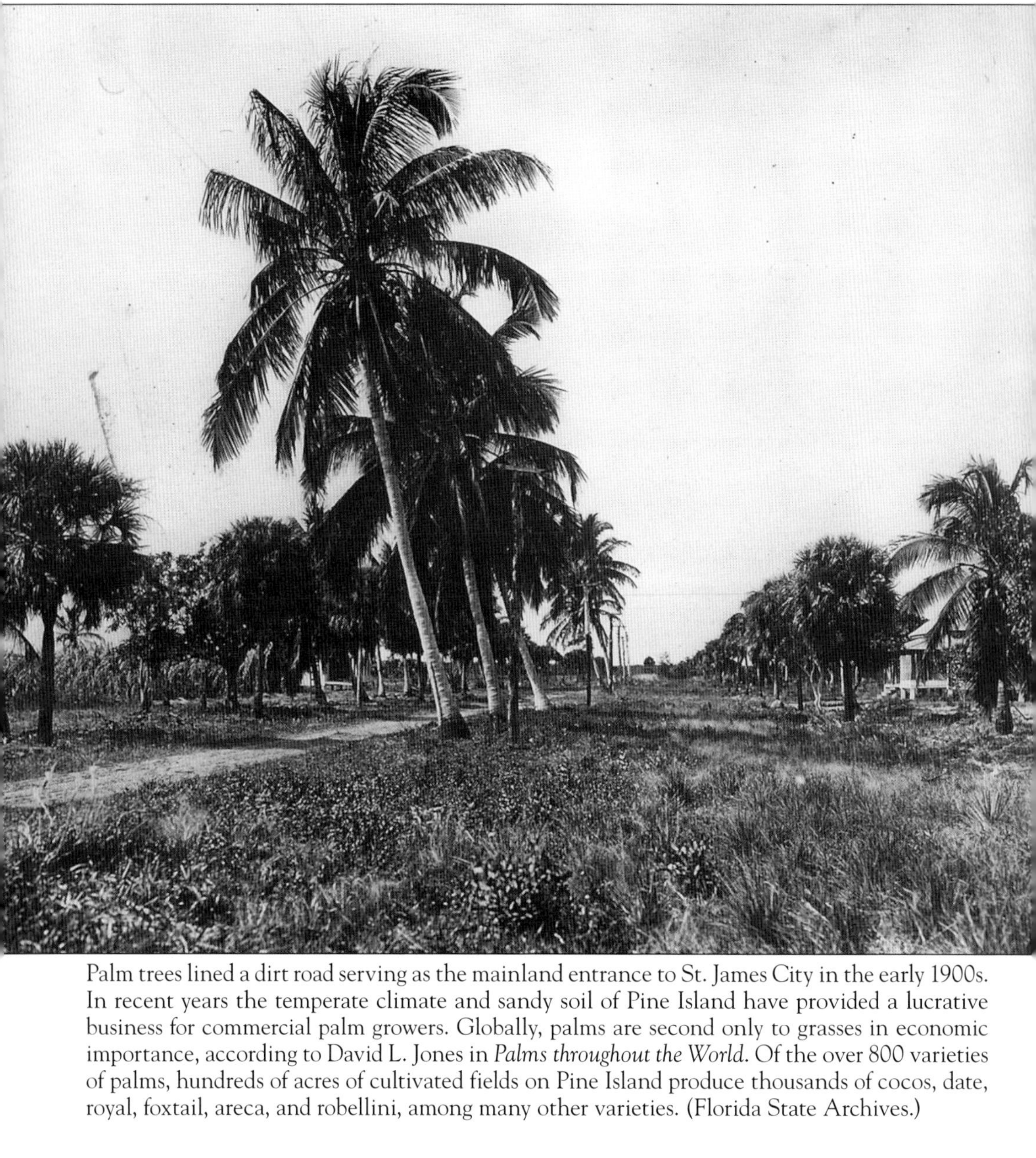

Palm trees lined a dirt road serving as the mainland entrance to St. James City in the early 1900s. In recent years the temperate climate and sandy soil of Pine Island have provided a lucrative business for commercial palm growers. Globally, palms are second only to grasses in economic importance, according to David L. Jones in *Palms throughout the World*. Of the over 800 varieties of palms, hundreds of acres of cultivated fields on Pine Island produce thousands of cocos, date, royal, foxtail, areca, and robellini, among many other varieties. (Florida State Archives.)

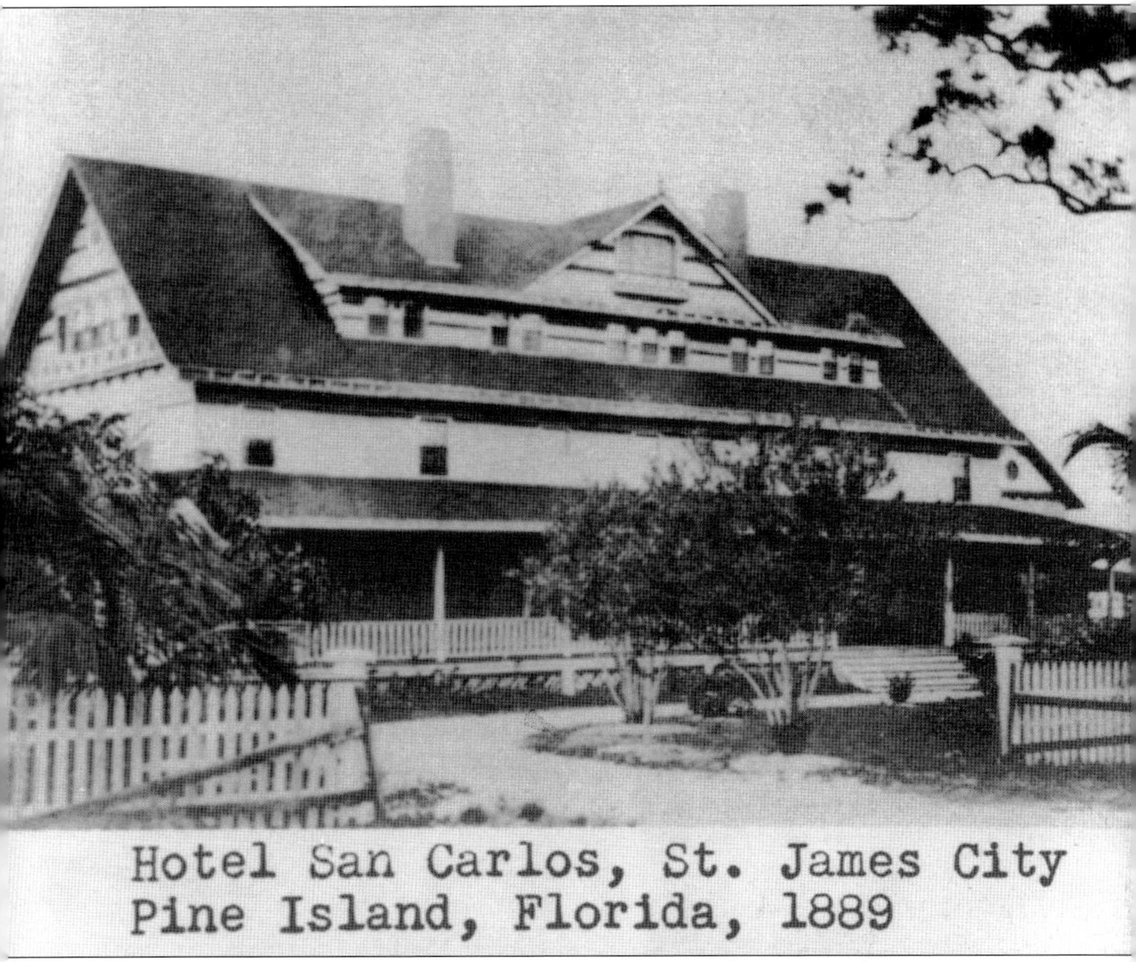

Famous guests staying at the impressive three-story San Carlos Hotel included Thomas Edison, Henry Ford, and Sam Colt. Built in 1886, by the St. James-on-the-Gulf resort company to attract tarpon fishermen, the hotel, along with the company, went bankrupt in the early 1900s. (Florida State Archives.)

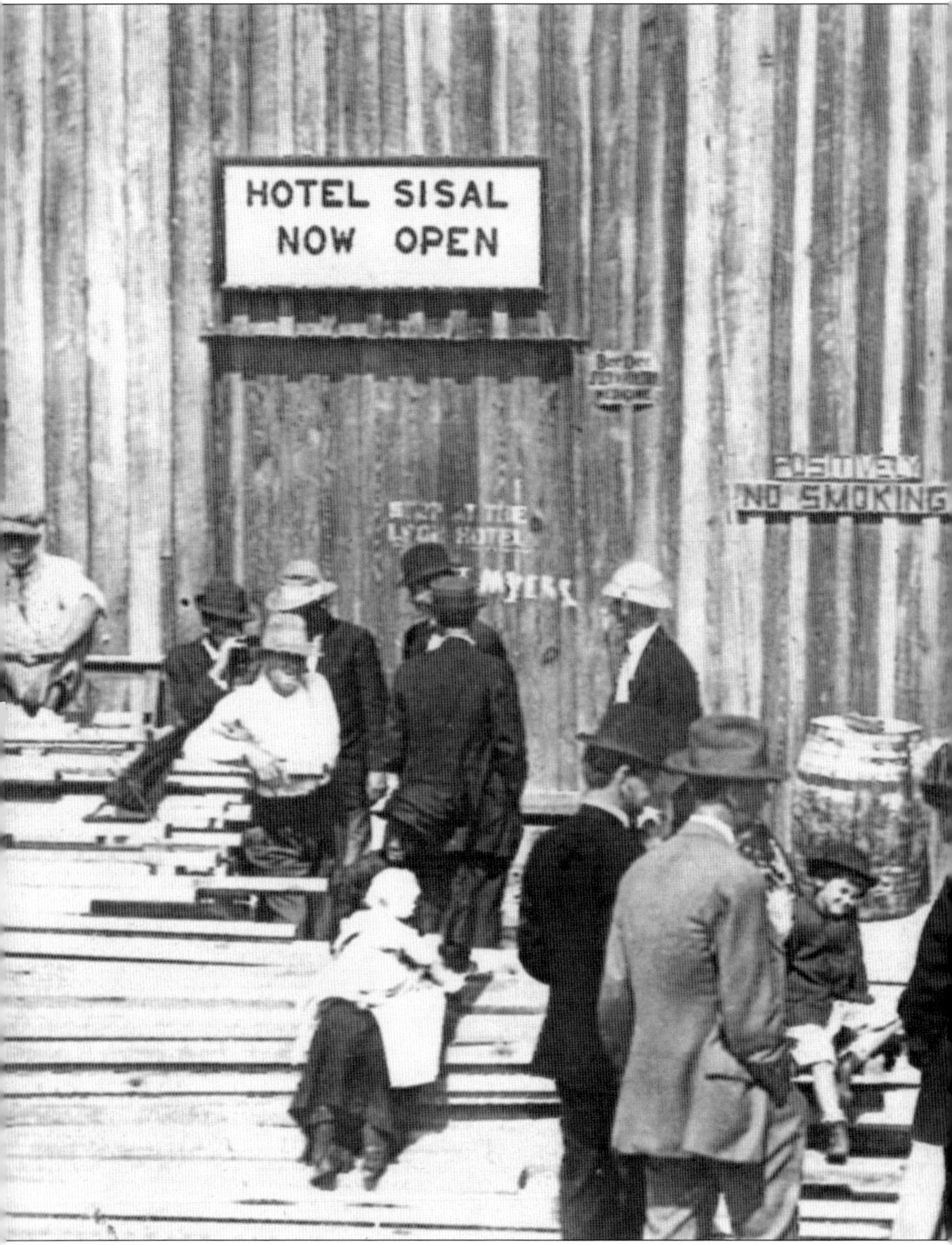

After arriving by a Kinzie steamer, passengers mill around downtown St. James-on-the-Gulf, a tourist development, around 1912. The Hotel Sisal was built after the San Carlos was destroyed by

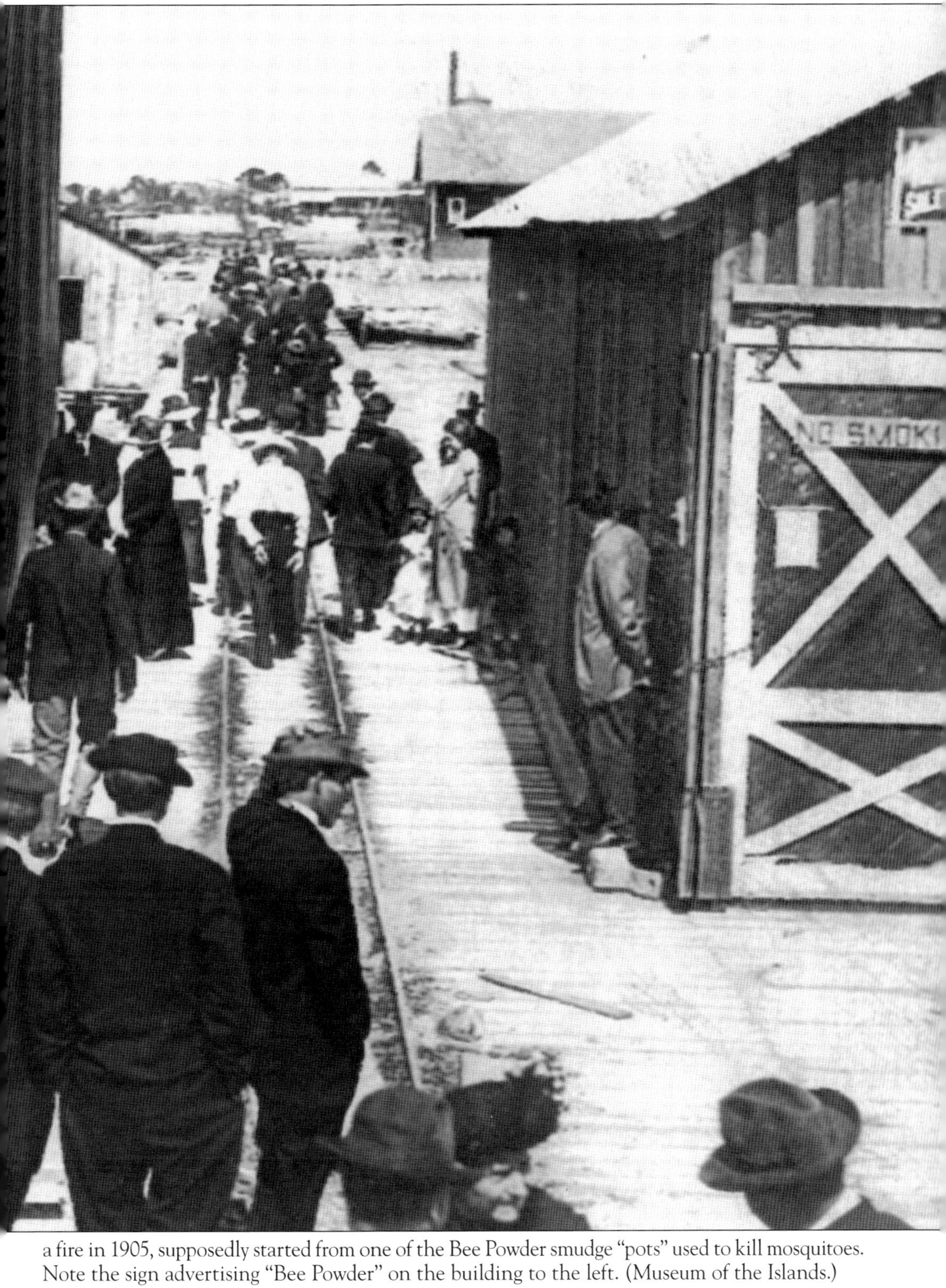

a fire in 1905, supposedly started from one of the Bee Powder smudge "pots" used to kill mosquitoes. Note the sign advertising "Bee Powder" on the building to the left. (Museum of the Islands.)

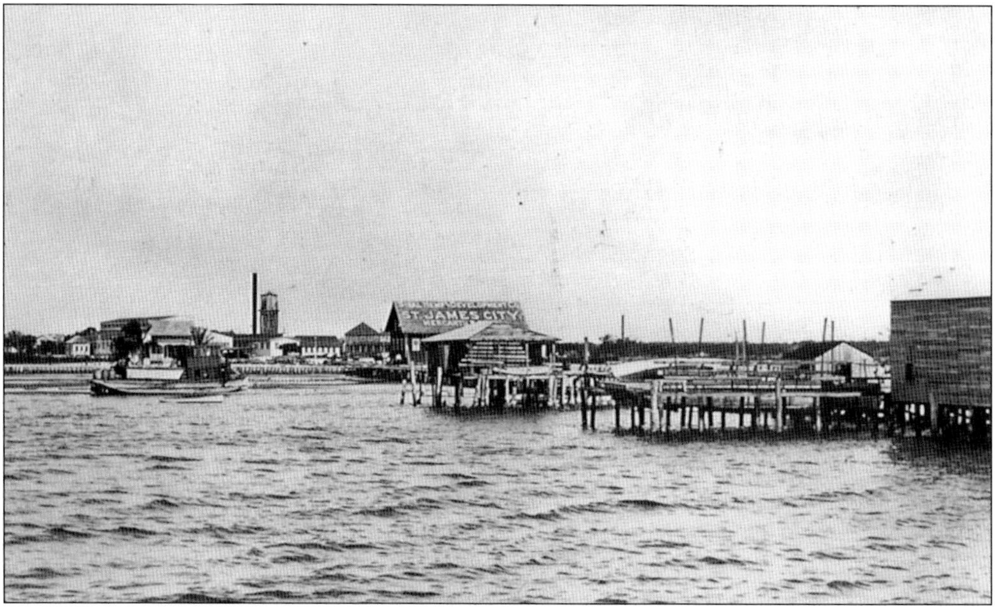

Approaching St. James City aboard a Kinzie steamer in 1911, one would see a 600-foot dock, the E. Whiteside store on the right, the Sisal Hemp Company water tower and factory, plus a private home located on the left. (Museum of the Islands.)

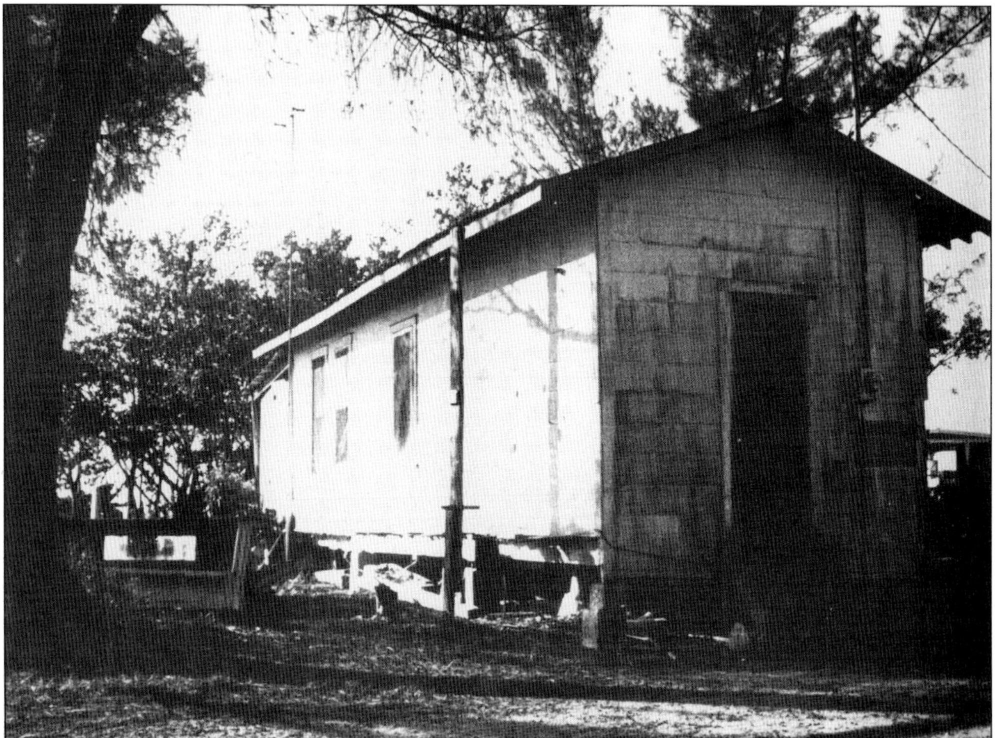

Serving St. James City until 1962, this post office was located at the end of Palm Avenue and was built by lumber salvaged from the Whiteside store/post office building destroyed in the hurricane of 1926. (Museum of the Islands.)

Consisting of about 4,000 acres on the southern end of Pine Island, the Sisal Hemp and Development Company produced this map in early 1910. A portion was subdivided into building lots, constituting St. James City. Sisal fields lay to the east of what is now State Road 767. The remainder (shown as numbered blocks) "was divided into Sisal Plantations and suburban and villa plats and tracts for truck gardening," per the brochure pitch. (Museum of the Islands.)

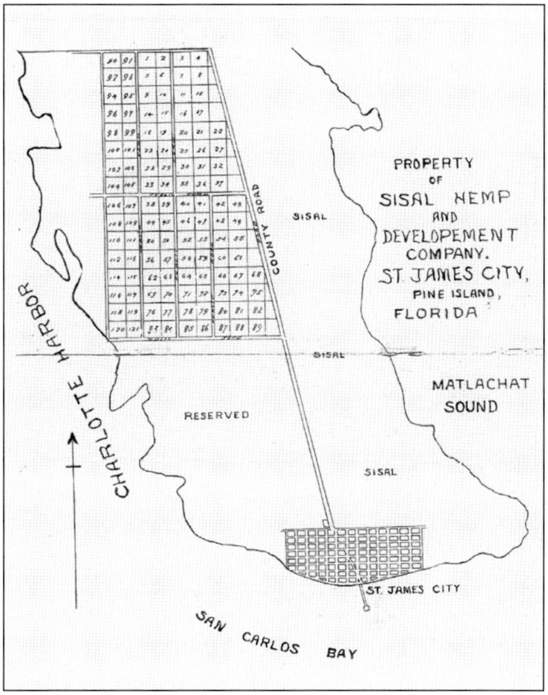

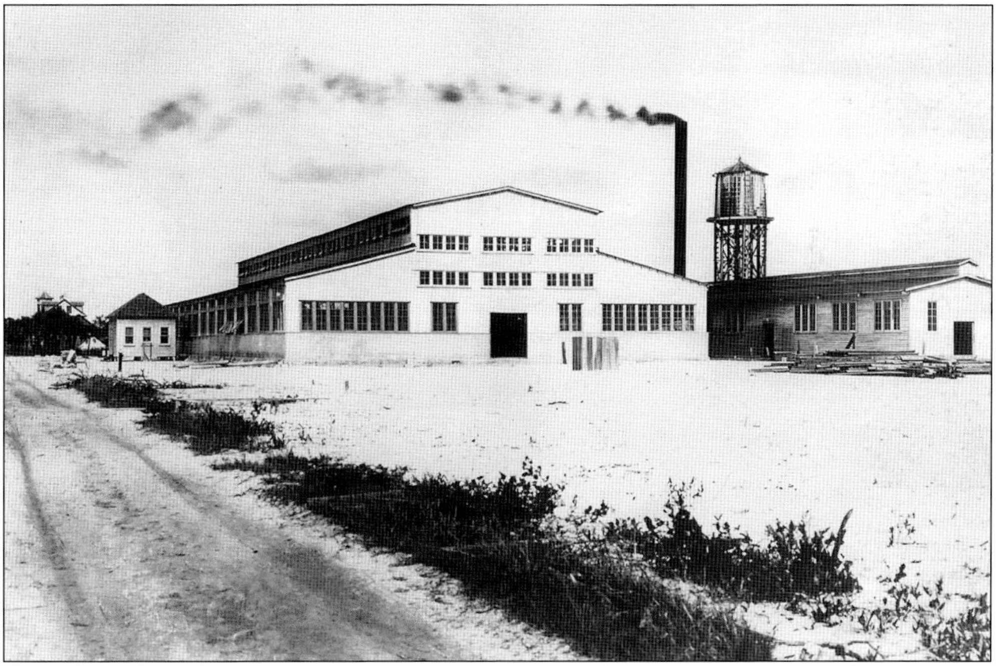

In 1911, investors from Maine purchased property once owned by the bankrupt St. James-on-the-Gulf Company. Under the direction of Arthur Knowles, this rope factory, a new dock, and additional warehouses were built. With a concrete block foundation, sloping sides, and many high windows for ventilation, the factory was impressive. After the building was abandoned, the community women would go there on Mondays, using the artesian well water and other facilities to do the week's laundry while the children played. (Florida State Archives.)

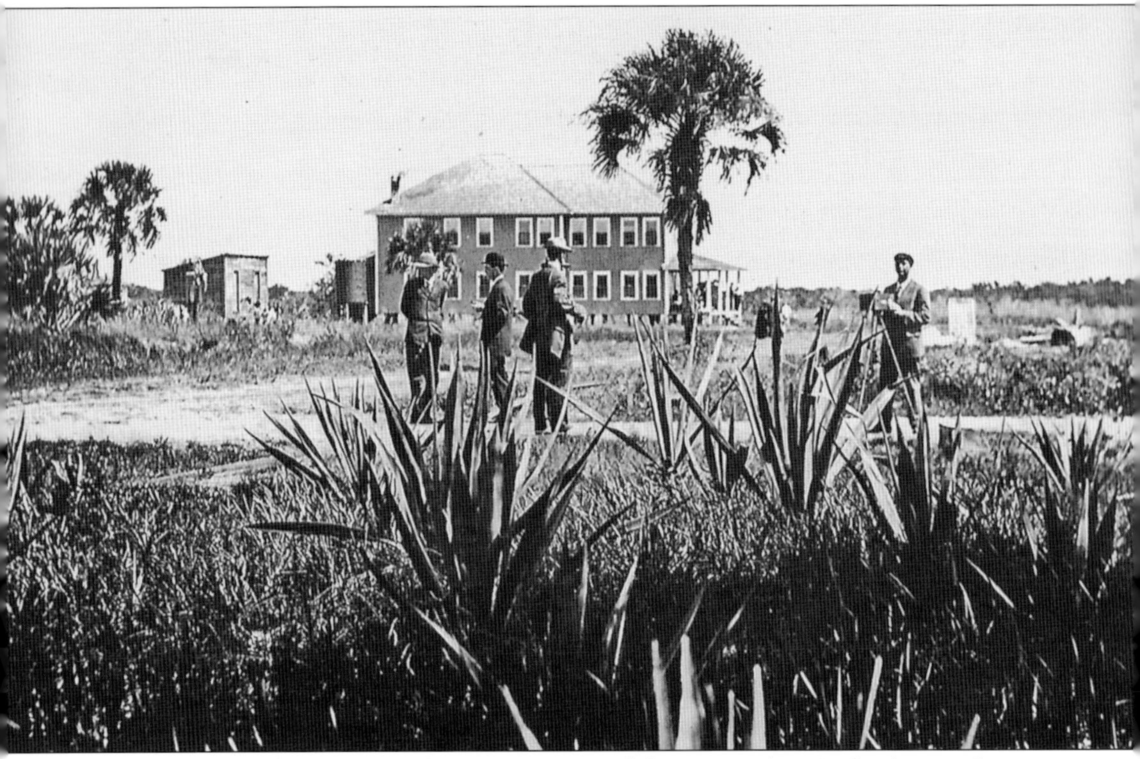

Contrary to local lore, the Sisal Hemp Company did not grow thousands of acres of marijuana plants. The sisal hemp plant (pictured in the foreground) is not really a variety of hemp, but was named so because hemp was for centuries a major source for fiber. The thick leaves of the sisal plant are sword-shaped and about 18–24 inches tall. Posing for a photograph, these men stand between a sisal hemp field and the Annex, a boardinghouse for the factory workers. (Florida State Archives.)

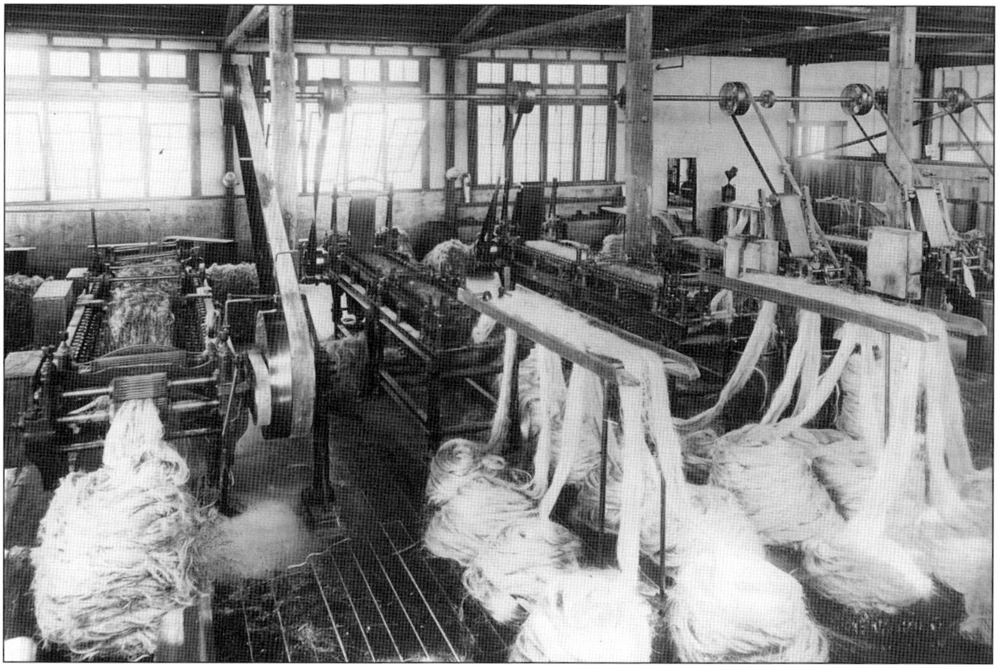

Spinner machinery in the interior of the Sisal Hemp Factory made for a state-of-the-art operation. The factory was built to meet the eventual demands of some 2,250 acres in sisal production. Sadly, the factory was abandoned a short time after full production began. (Florida State Archives.)

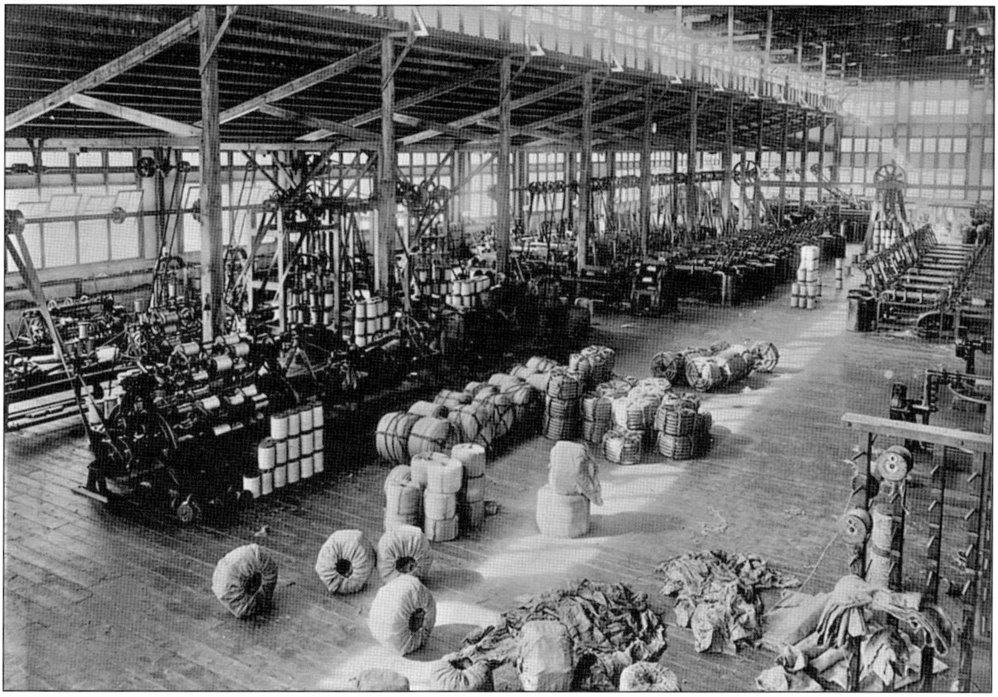

The final step in sisal rope production was wrapping huge wooden spools with the finished rope product. The burlap-wrapped spools were then loaded onto heavy-duty trollies and rolled down railroad ties to the pier. (Florida State Archives.)

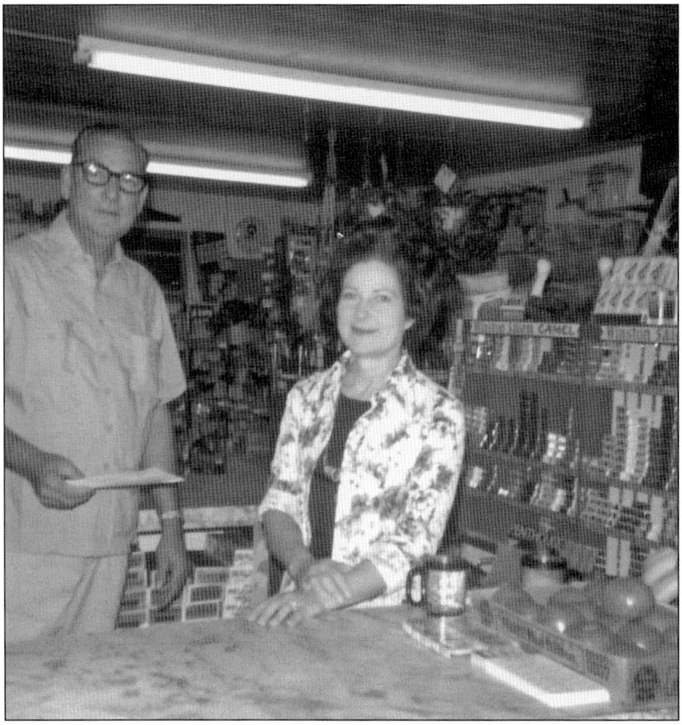

Bob and Dorothy Muske purchased the General Store in 1972. As the only store south of Pine Island Center, customers were thankful the Muskes' business was open every day, closing at noon on Christmas Day. Living in the back of the store, they provided a bell for customers to ring for service. They also sold bait shrimp for 50¢ a dozen, $1 for three dozen, or $3 for 100. (Dorothy Muske.)

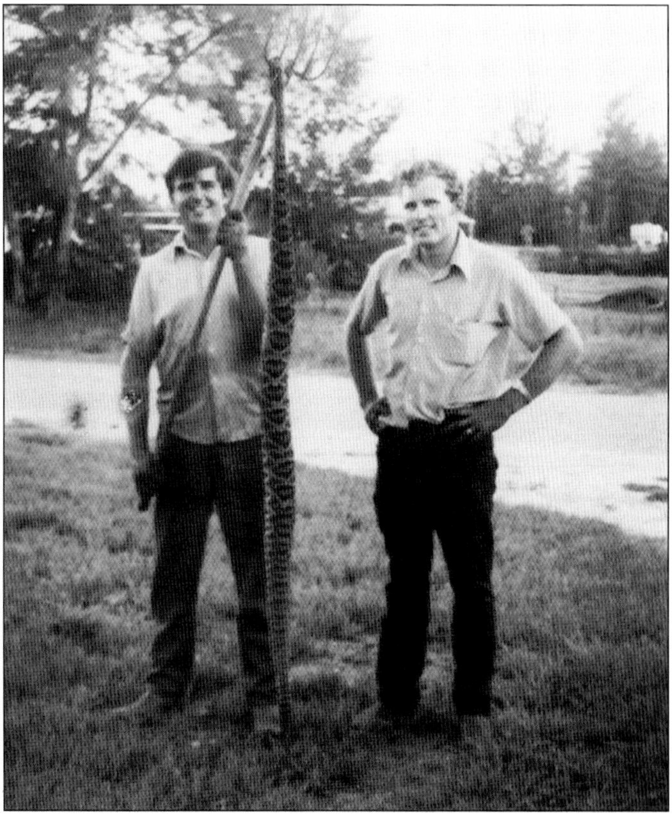

On Quail Run Nursery's shell road in about 1975, Ladonna Peterson drove around what she thought was an alligator lying halfway on the road. Dan Stevens and Ladonna's husband, Jim, investigated and found this 7-foot-long rattlesnake! (Photograph by the author.)

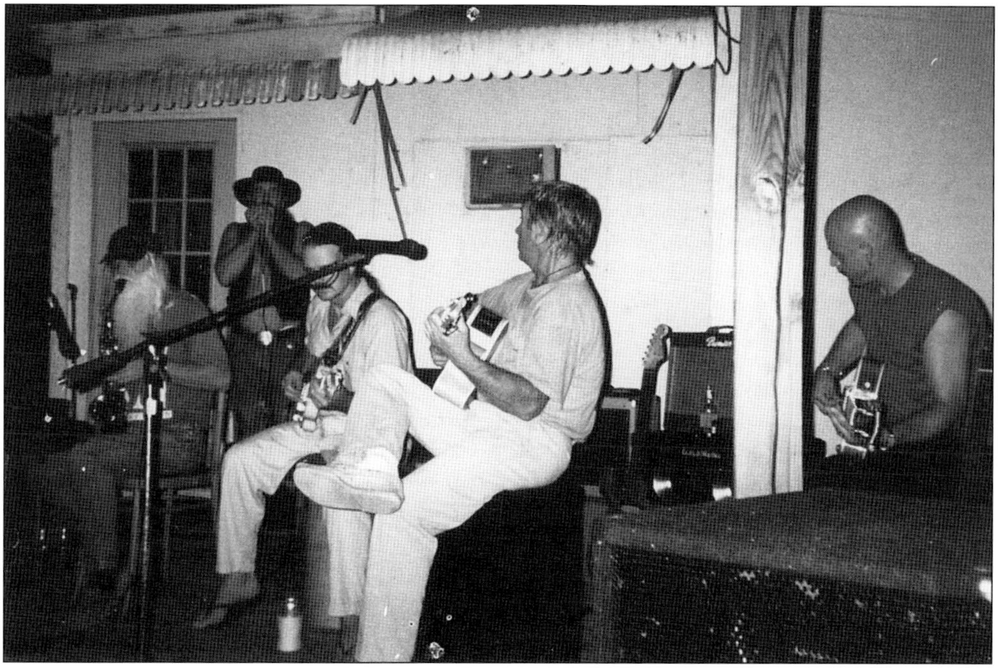

Downtown Larry Brown jams on the saxophone with local band, Corky and the Troublestarters, and John Mooney at Island Hardware and Marina Supply in St. James City in March 1999. Thanks to hardware owners Collette and Bob Hawkins, the parking lot concerts were popular fare in the 1990s. A favorite musician, Mooney compared the concerts as similar to years ago in New Orleans when everyone would get together outside and play. (Colette Hawkins.)

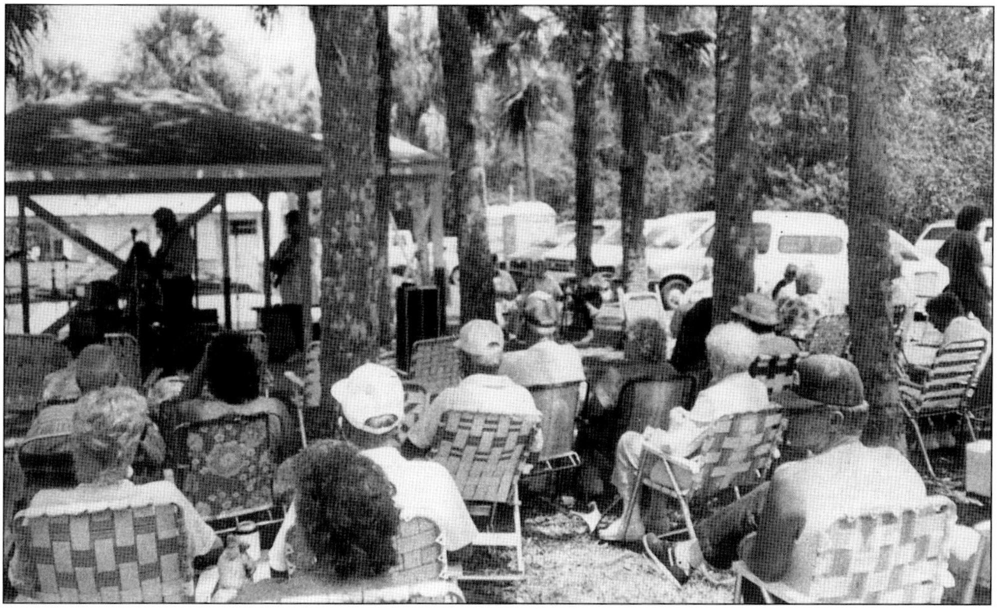

Community events, such as the Spring Festival held in 1993, have been enjoyed by all ages. The casual atmosphere of "bring your own chair" adds to the down-home feeling. Holiday parades, concerts, boat races, and fishing tournaments have all strengthened the community spirit of St. James City. (Museum of the Islands.)

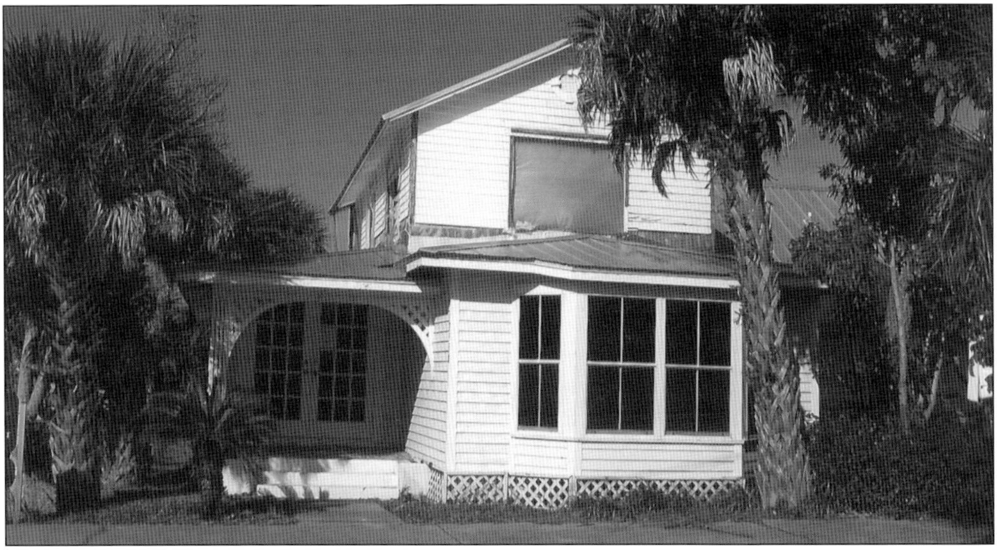

Built in 1922 by Percy and Ruby Gill, the Ruby Gill House is one of Pineland's oldest buildings. Moving to Pineland with her husband at the age of 22, Ruby succeeded James Wheeler as postmaster in 1924, serving until 1957. Also serving on the county electric board, she was instrumental in bringing electricity to Pineland in 1941. Following her death in the 1960s, the house has had a reputation for being inhabited by Ruby's ghost. Now owned by the Randell Research Center, it is fitting that her ghost should be present as researchers study the past. (David Overholt.)

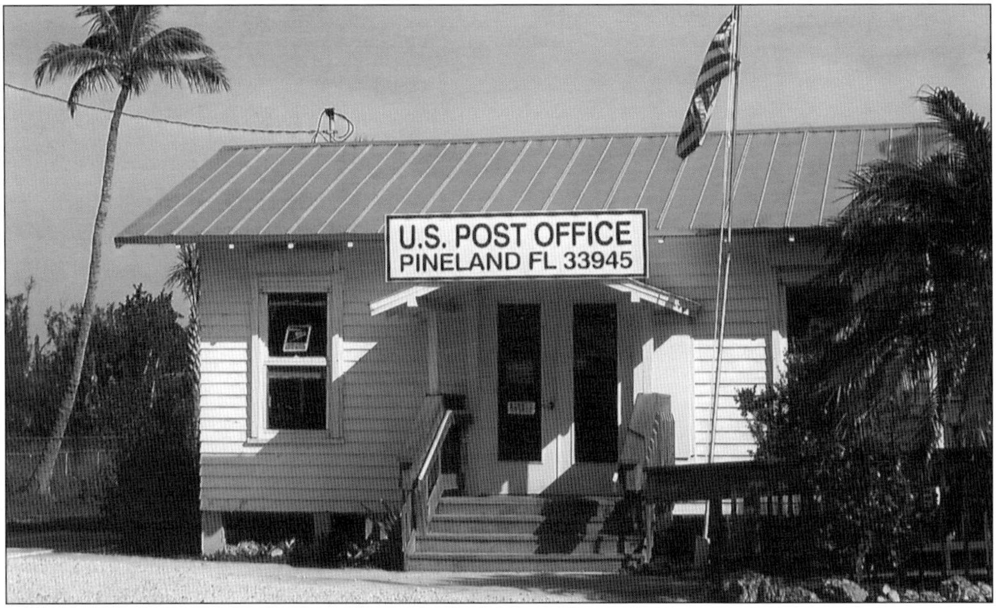

Located on the same property as the Ruby Gill House, the Pineland Post Office remains an enduring symbol of Pineland's identity. Thinking it would be more protected, Ruby Gill built the new post office next to her home after a storm swept away the previous post office in 1925. Pineland residents have managed to convince the government to keep it open, despite plans by the U.S. Postal Service to close it by merging it with the Bokeelia Post Office. Possibly Pineland's most famous resident, John L. Lewis led one such effort in the 1950s. Lee County is the current owner, renting the building to the U.S. Postal Service. (David Overholt.)

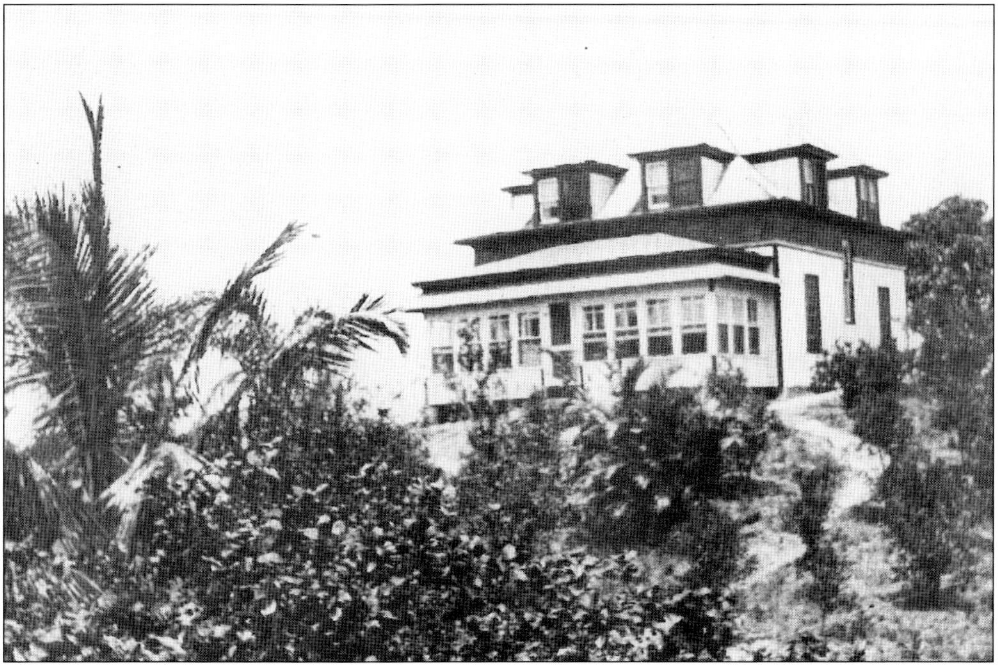

Located on what is said to be Lee County's highest point is the home of Pennsylvania coal magnate Frank Adams. Built in 1911, with windows on all four sides, vistas of tropical vegetation greeted the residents. (Museum of the Islands.)

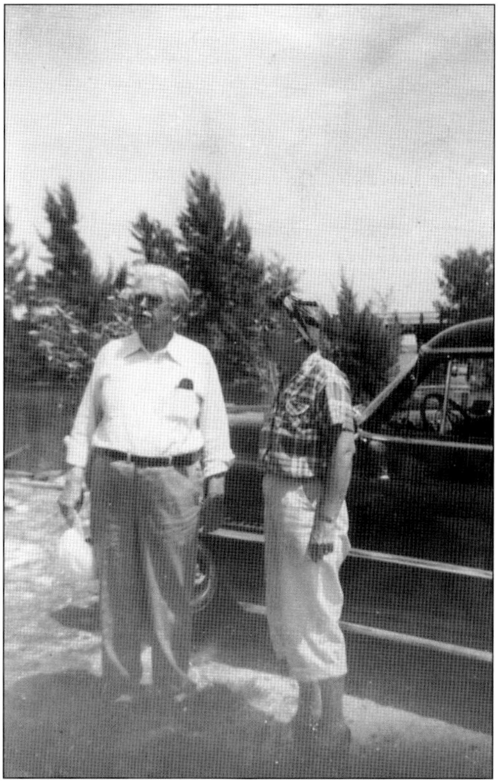

After staying at the Pine-Aire Lodge in the 1950s, United Mine Worker's Union president John L. Lewis purchased a Pineland guesthouse for winter vacations. Lewis often brought along his sister Hattie, pictured here. Kay DellaBitta recalls his compassion for the island children, often expressed anonymously with necessities or luxuries given to Pine Island children. Purchasing First Communion clothes for twin island girls was one such gesture. Sharing his vice of smoking expensive cigars with a friend was one of his enjoyments. Sadly, upon Hattie's death, Lewis left Pineland for the last time in 1963. (Kay DellaBitta.)

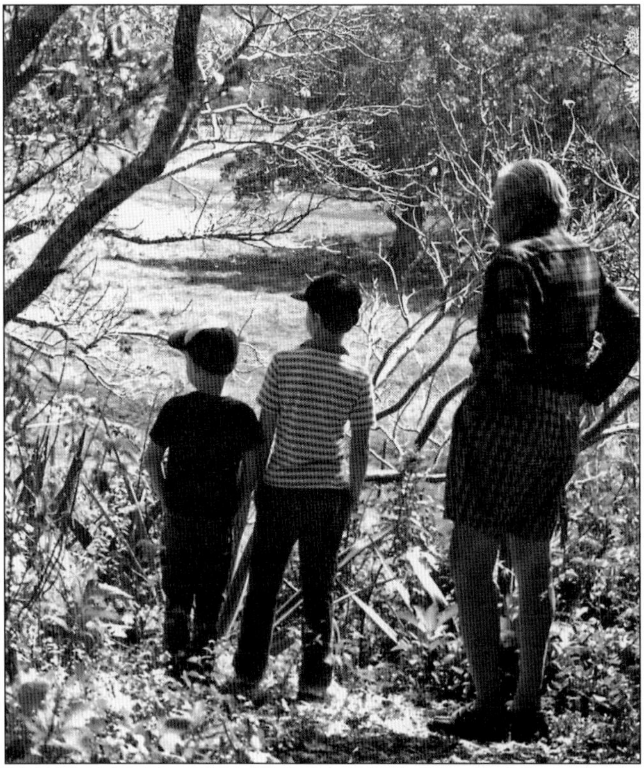

Shortly after his retirement at his 1930s Florida-style home in Pineland, Col. Donald Randell proudly surveys his "Rocking 'R' Ranch." Sharing the view of Santa Gertrudis cattle and a Honey Bell Orchard are Aaron and Nathaniel Burman. Randell later bequeathed the bulk of the property to the University of Florida with preservation stipulations, and it is now the location of the Randell Research Center. (PineIslandNews.com.)

Patricia "Pat" Randell, pictured here in the late 1940s, was the daughter of Charles Crandon, the well-known entrepreneur and philanthropist for which Crandon Park in Miami is named. Pat and Donald Randell were married for more than 50 years and had three children. Even though Donald rose to the level of colonel in the Army Intelligence Corp and was a Princeton-trained money manager, overseeing large market funds, Donald often remarked that Crandon made it known that he thought Pat had not married particularly well. (Debra Randell.)

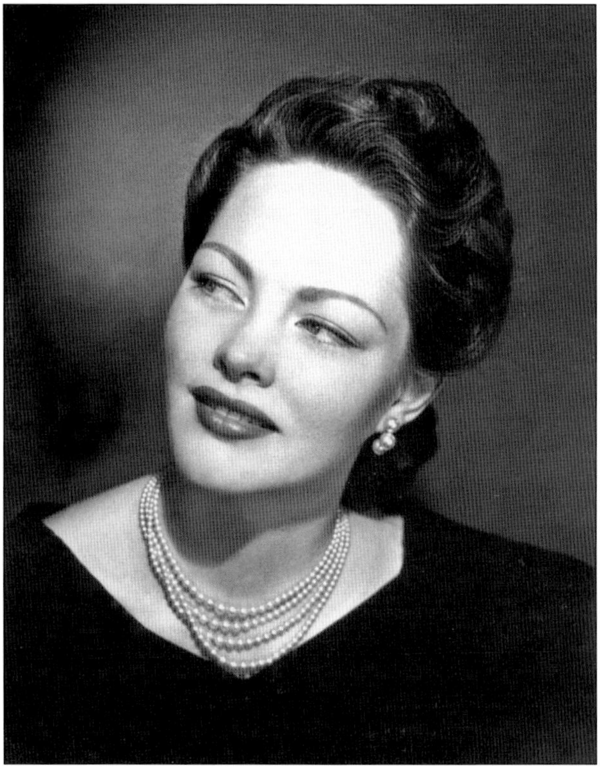

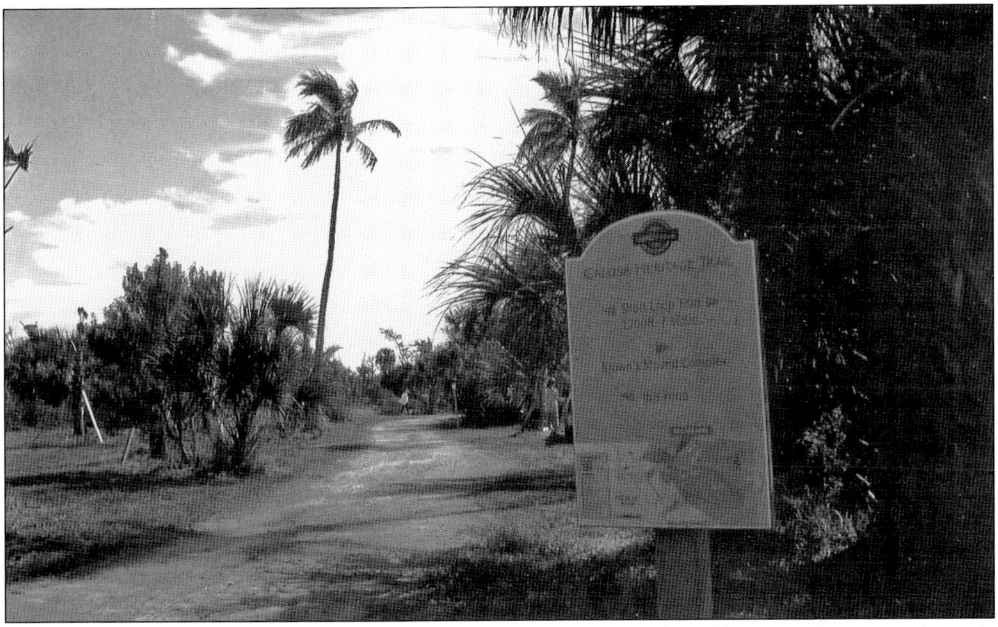

As part of the Randell Research Center, the 3,700-foot interpretive walkway leads visitors through the shell mounds, canals, and other highlights of the Pineland archaeological site. Sponsored by Dwight and Susan Sipprelle, and funded in part by the Florida Department of State, the informative signs provide visitors with fascinating information regarding the Calusa settlement. (David Overholt.)

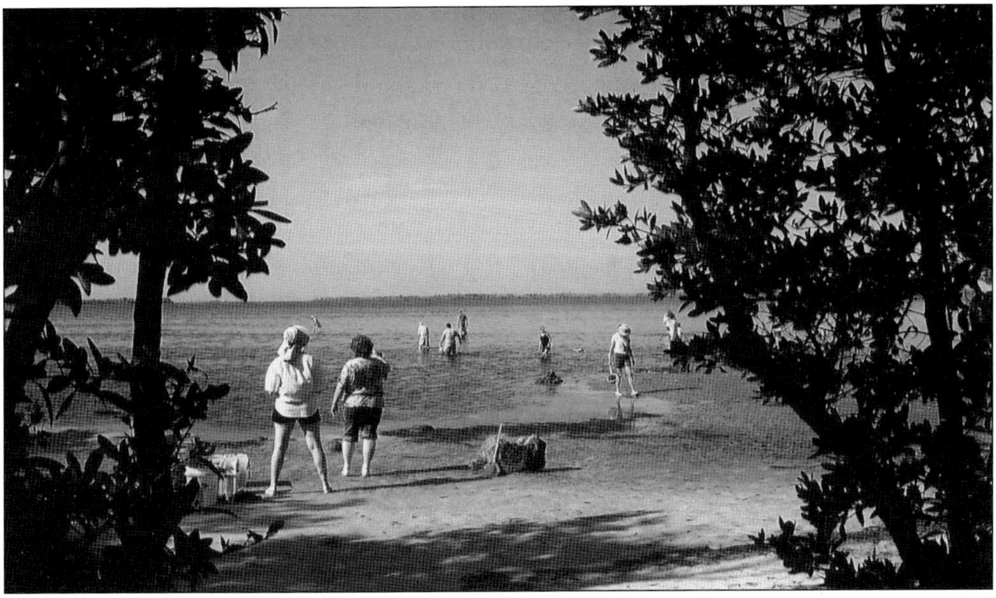

Monitoring and protecting Charlotte Harbor and Pine Island Sound estuaries is a primary goal of the Department of Environmental Services. Although the Mote Marine Lab facilities, located at Pineland, were destroyed in Hurricane Charley, marine studies continue on a regular basis. Here volunteers participate in collecting marine specimens under the direction of Mary McMurray in the spring of 2008. On the horizon to the left lies Useppa Island, home to the Collier Inn and the Bay of Pigs training site. (Photograph by the author.)

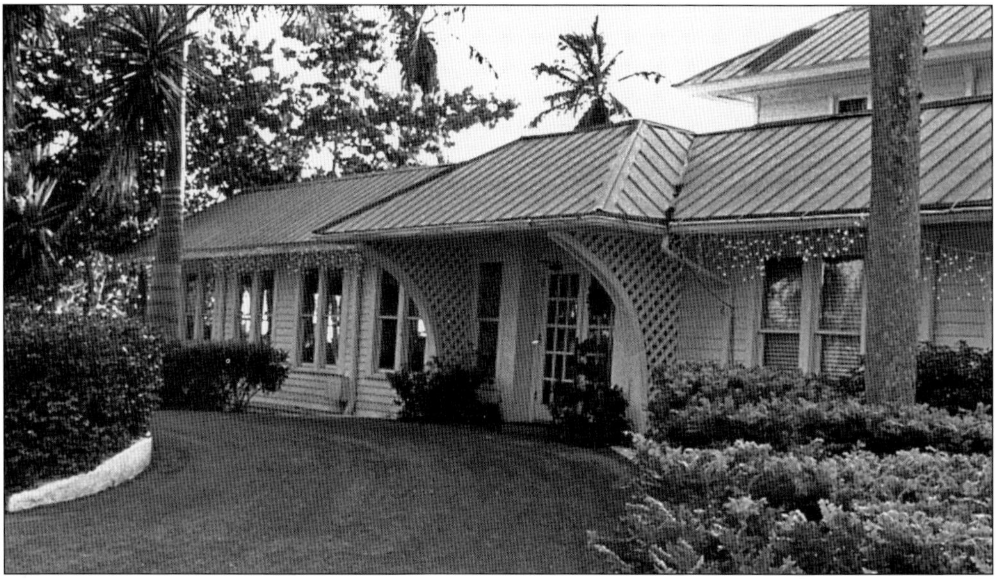

In the early 1920s, Graham and Mary Wilson built Gramar Villas, now known as the Tarpon Lodge. An avid fisherman, Wilson is credited with hiring a crew to dig, by hand, a channel from his property out to deep water, more than a mile away. Into the 1990s, the property was home to The Cloister's, an upscale drug rehabilitation clinic. Now owned by the Robert Wells family, the lodge is a popular year-round sports fishing lodge. (Robert Wells.)

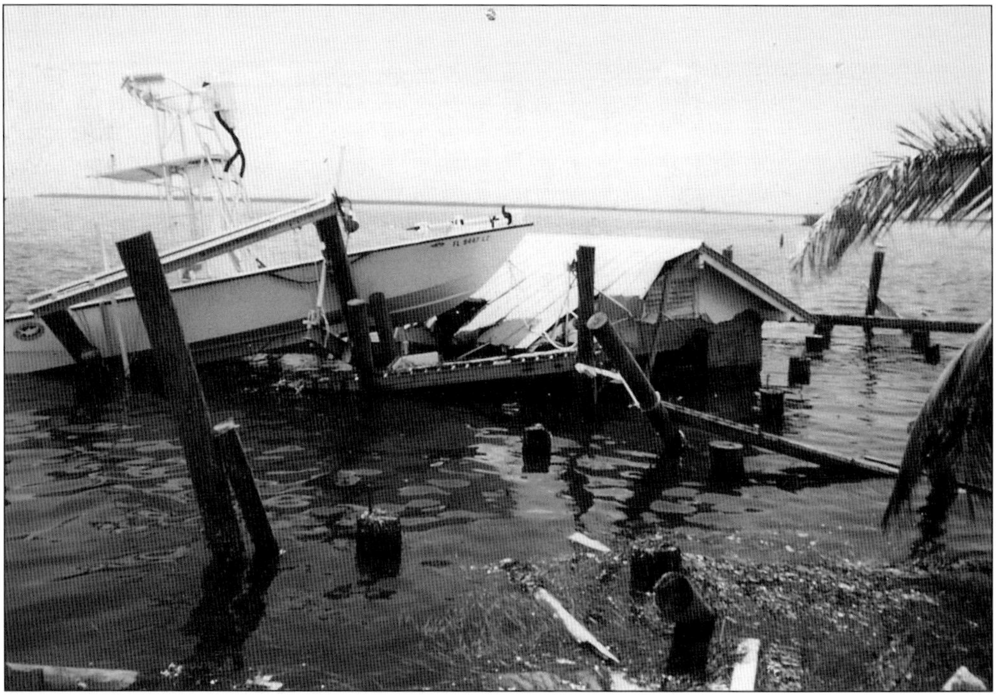

Thinking there was a good chance his boat would sink during the landfall of Hurricane Charley, Robert Wells III, manager of the Tarpon Lodge, placed all of the boat's electronic equipment in the boathouse. How ironic to find his boat high and dry atop the sunken boathouse in the storm's aftermath. (Robert Wells.)

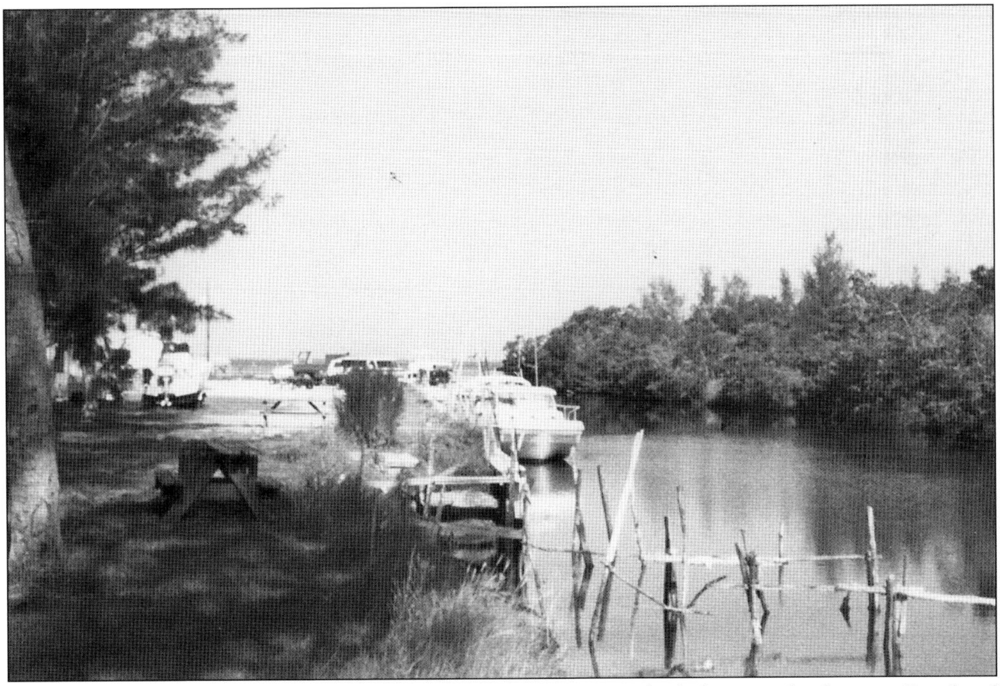

Moving to the area in 1981, Bob and Collette Hawkins parked their trailer here at Pineland Marina. Not much more than a dug-out channel and small ramp at the time, it has since grown into one of Southwest Florida's largest marinas. (Colette Hawkins.)

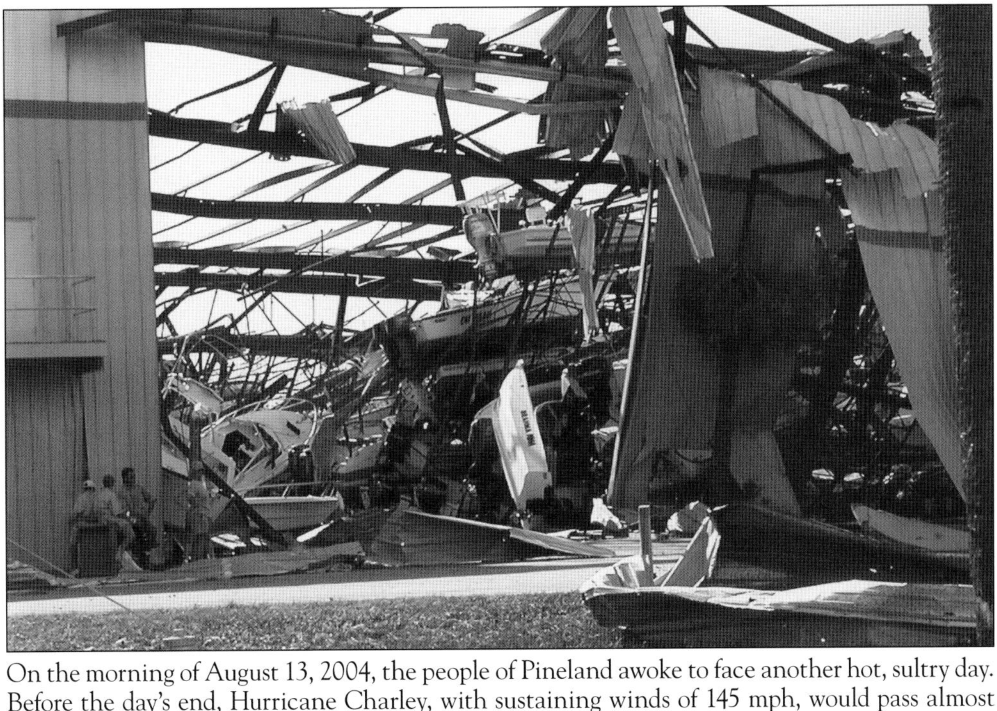

On the morning of August 13, 2004, the people of Pineland awoke to face another hot, sultry day. Before the day's end, Hurricane Charley, with sustaining winds of 145 mph, would pass almost directly over Pineland. Here Pineland Marina's main dry-storage building lies in ruin. Surprisingly, no lives were lost. (Courtesy of Deb Wedeking.)

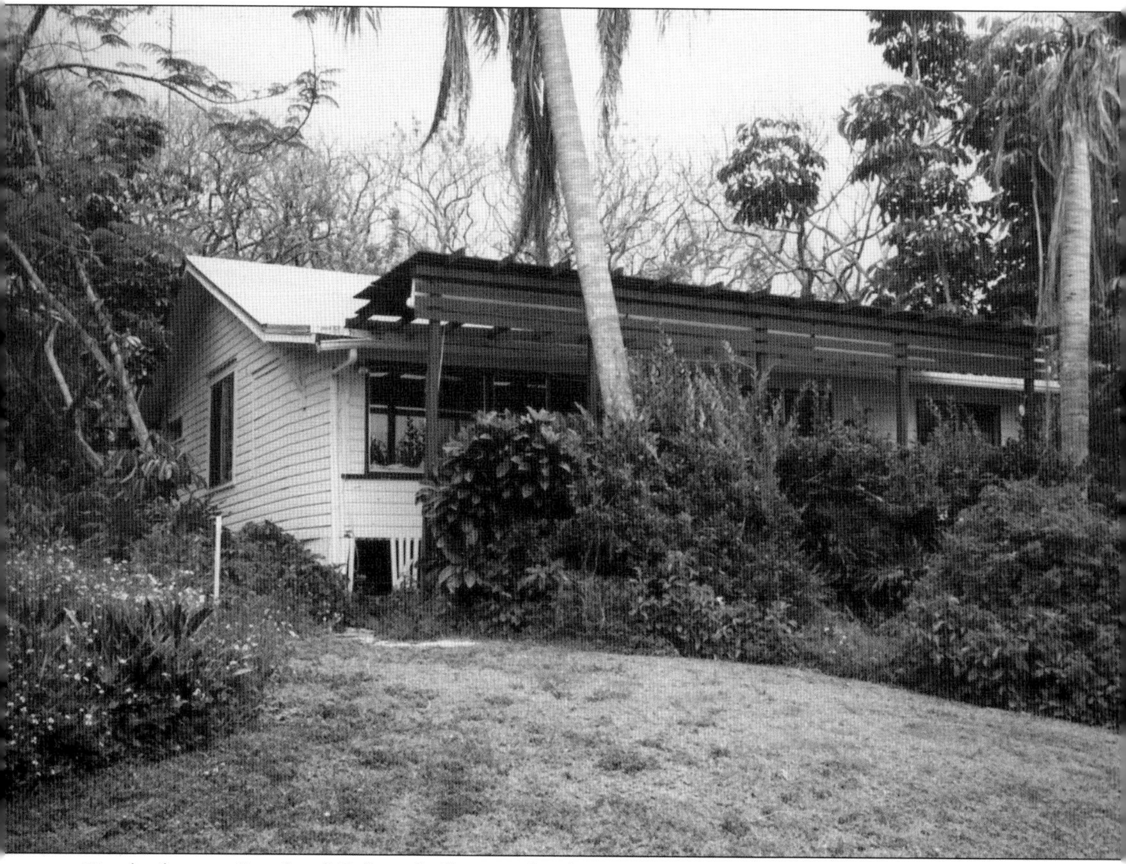

Perched atop a Pineland Calusa shell mound, John L. Lewis's winter cottage provided spectacular views, while still granting the labor leader the seclusion he sought. He once drove to Punta Gorda just to give a mechanic "a piece of his mind" to speed up the repairs on an islander's outboard engine." Thanks to Lewis, the commercial fisherman had the repairs completed and the engine returned on the very next runboat. (William McNagny.)

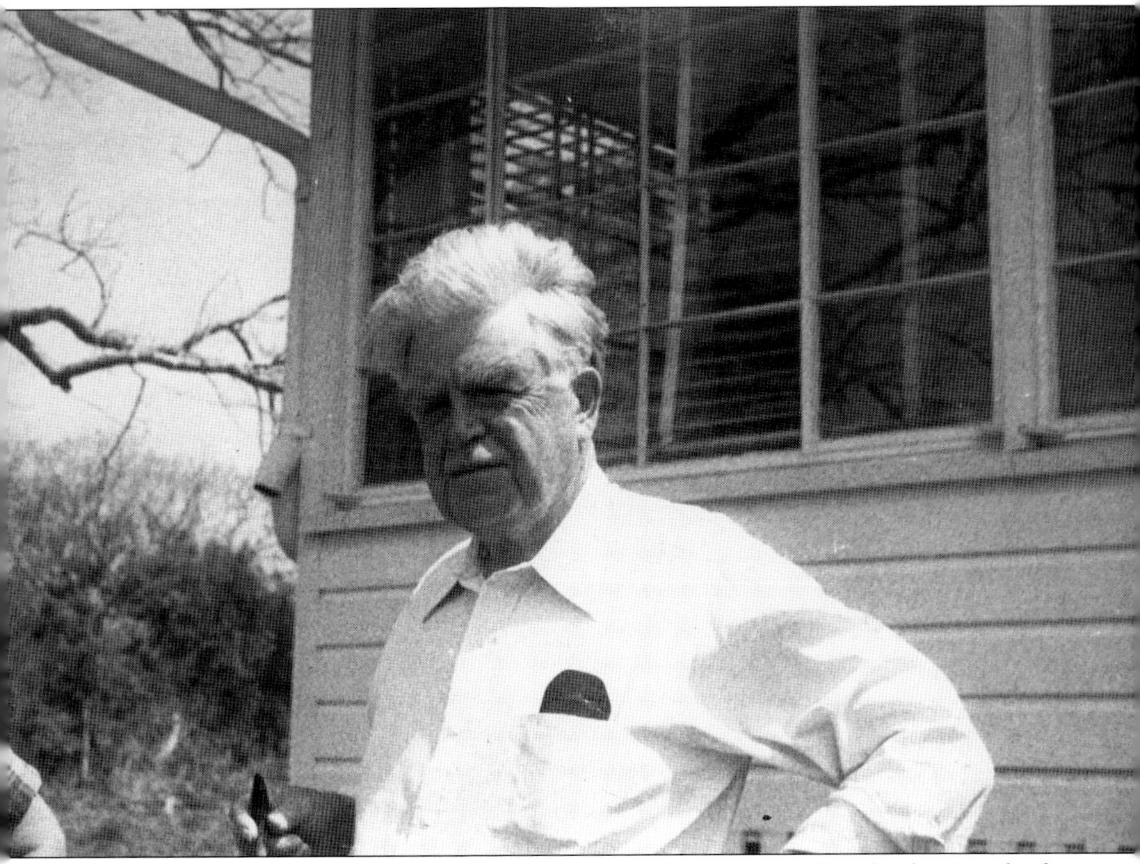

According to Lewis's Pineland neighbor, Clagget Dorsey, in Elaine Jordan's book, *Pine Island, the Forgotten Island*, "I heard him say many a time that it was love at first sight when he first came to Pine Island. He originally stayed at the Pala Mar Lodge, [now the Tarpon Lodge] there along the waterfront on the curve. Whenever things got too 'hot' for Lewis in the outside world, he'd have his chauffeur drive him to Pineland." (William McNagny.)

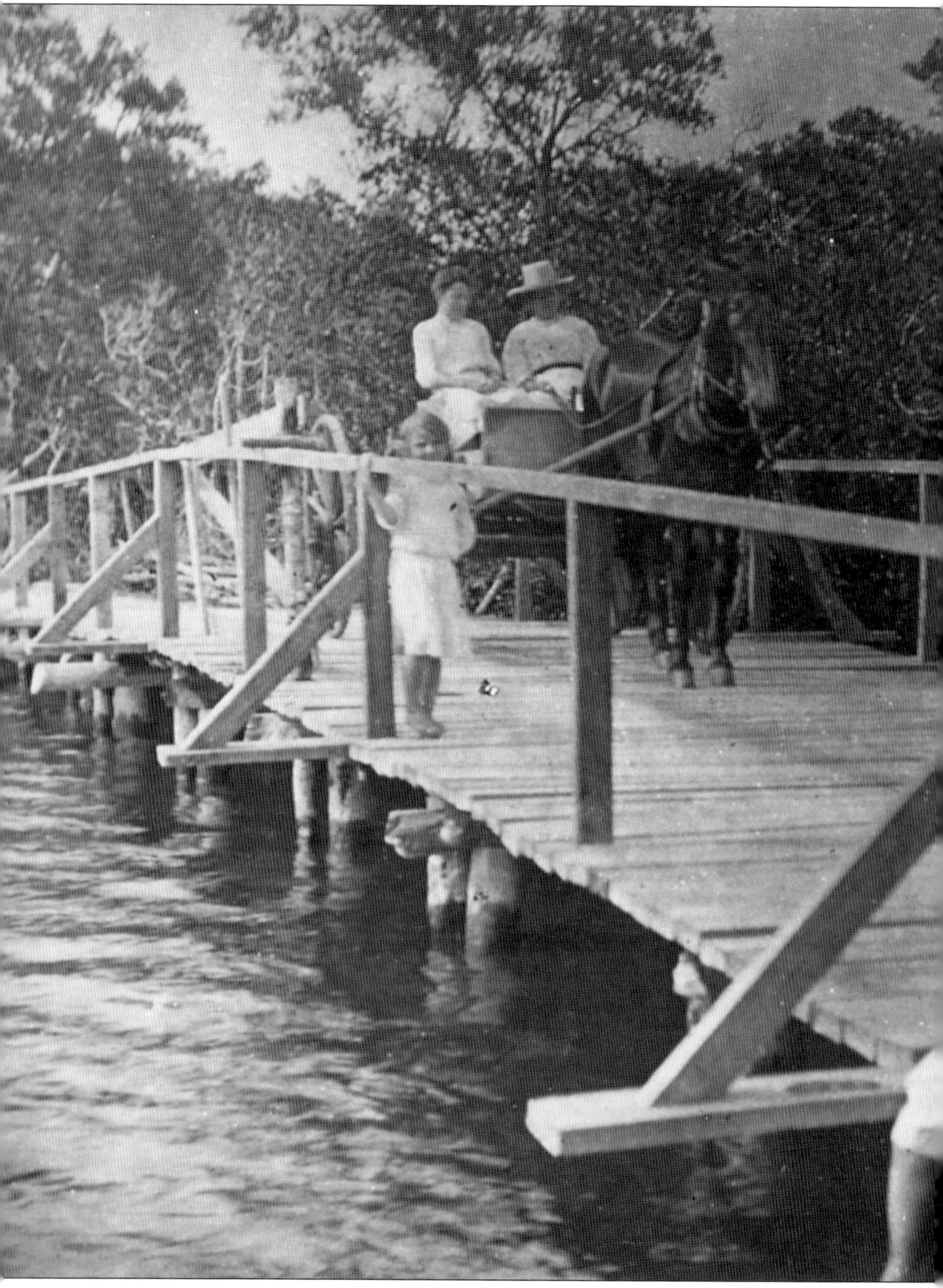

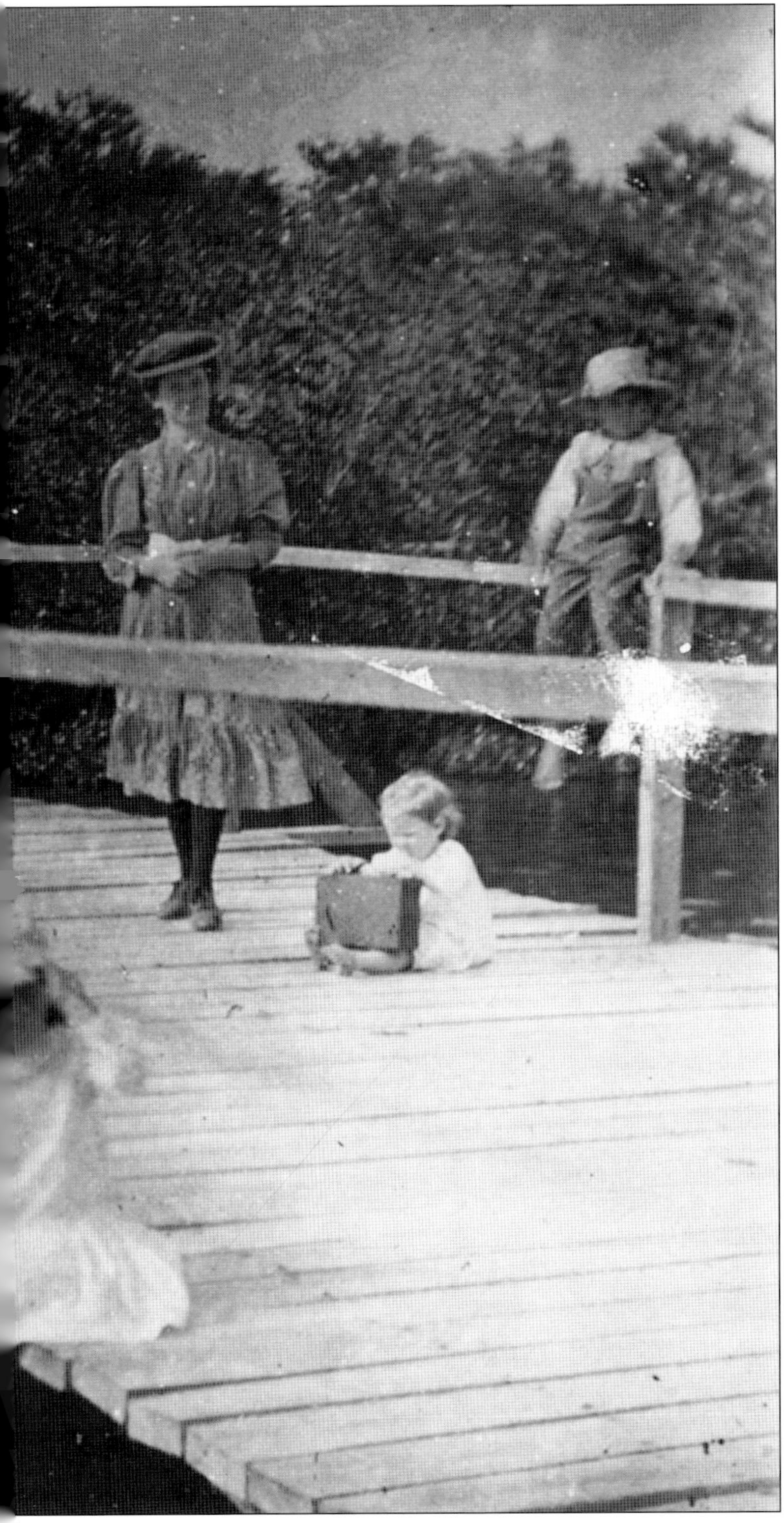

The first bridge across Jug Creek at Bokeelia is shown along with the Martin family: Minta, Henry, Jamie, Pattie, John, Ann, and Robbie Lee. The creek was so named by locals knowledgeable in the rumrunners' practice of tying ceramic jugs of "aguardiente" (rum) to the bridge supports, allowing the water to cool the rum, while keeping it safe, away from the ever-watchful eyes of federal agents. (Museum of the Islands.)

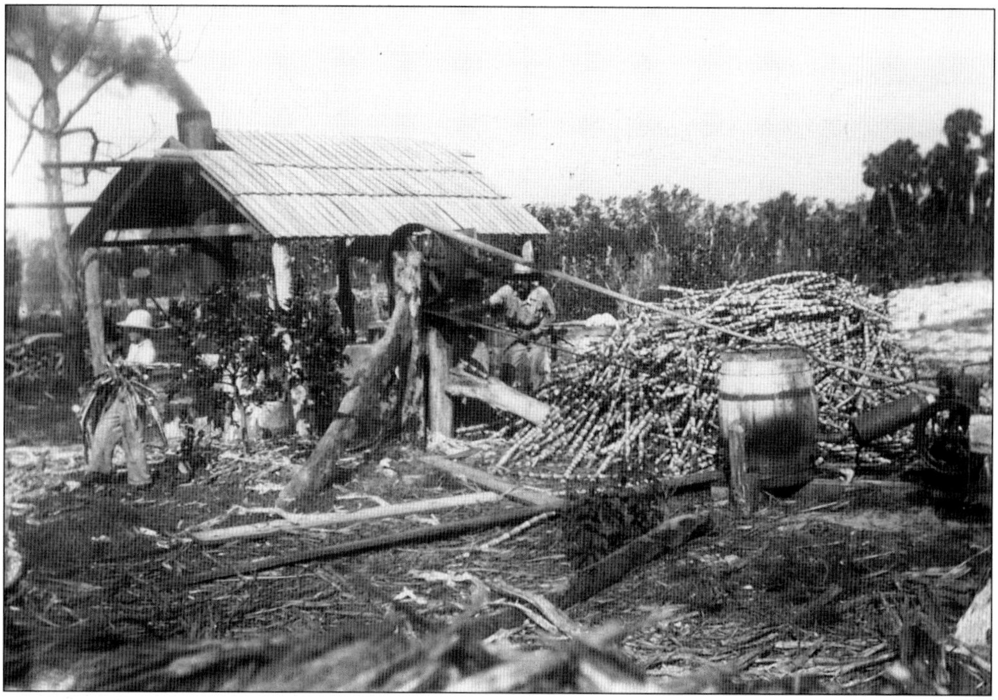

Cane-grinding time at the Henry Martin Grove, located about one mile south of Bokeelia, often turned into a party while providing a necessary food item. Here the sugar cane grinding is being done by a gasoline engine, a fairly modern method in 1910. After the cane was ground, it was boiled, and the syrup was canned in mason jars. (Museum of the Islands.)

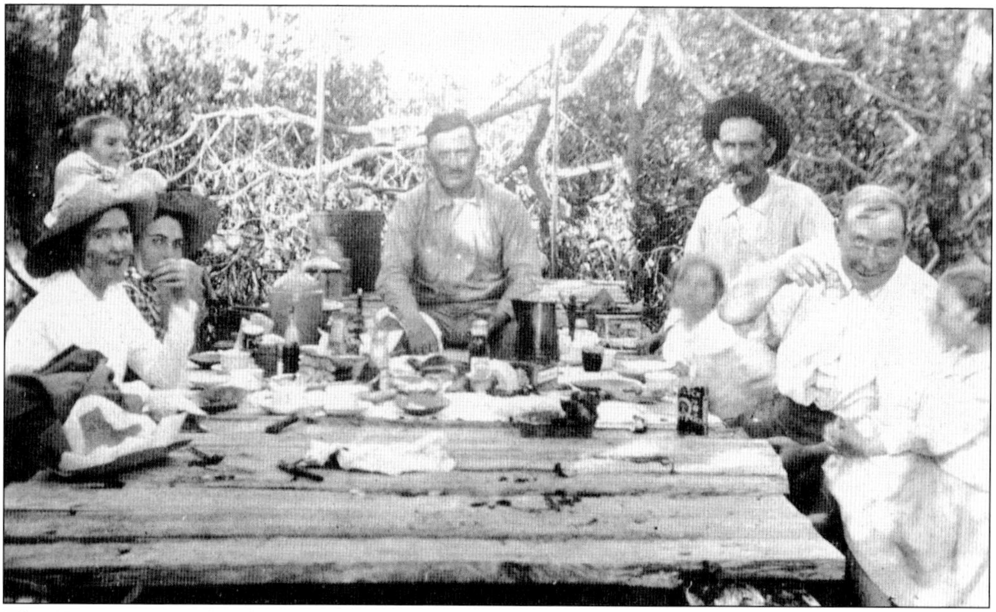

The Henry Martin family and friends enjoy a picnic. Taken in 1909, they may have been eating some of the fresh oysters or scallops gathered from the outing pictured on the cover of this book. Although they were probably swarmed with mosquitoes, everyone is smiling and seemingly oblivious to the heat and insects! (Museum of the Islands.)

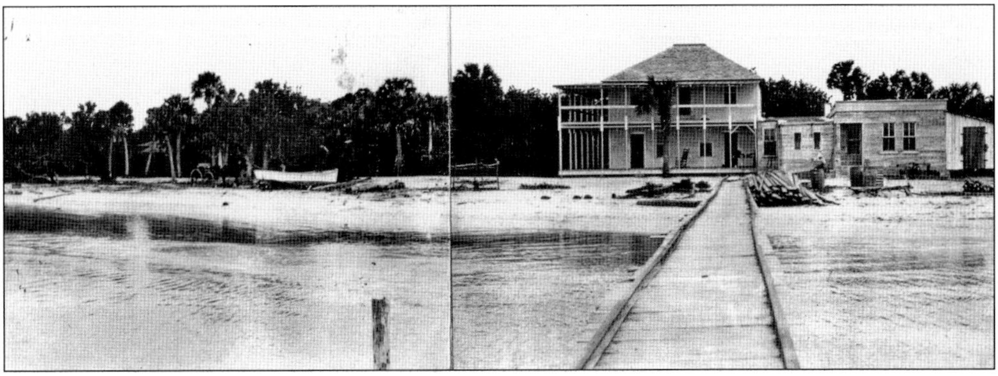

In 1909, the Bokeelia waterfront was barren, but for the Minta Martin Boarding House and long pier. A portion of the boardinghouse was used as a store, as well as the community's first post office. The historic landmark building is home to a restaurant today. (Museum of the Island.)

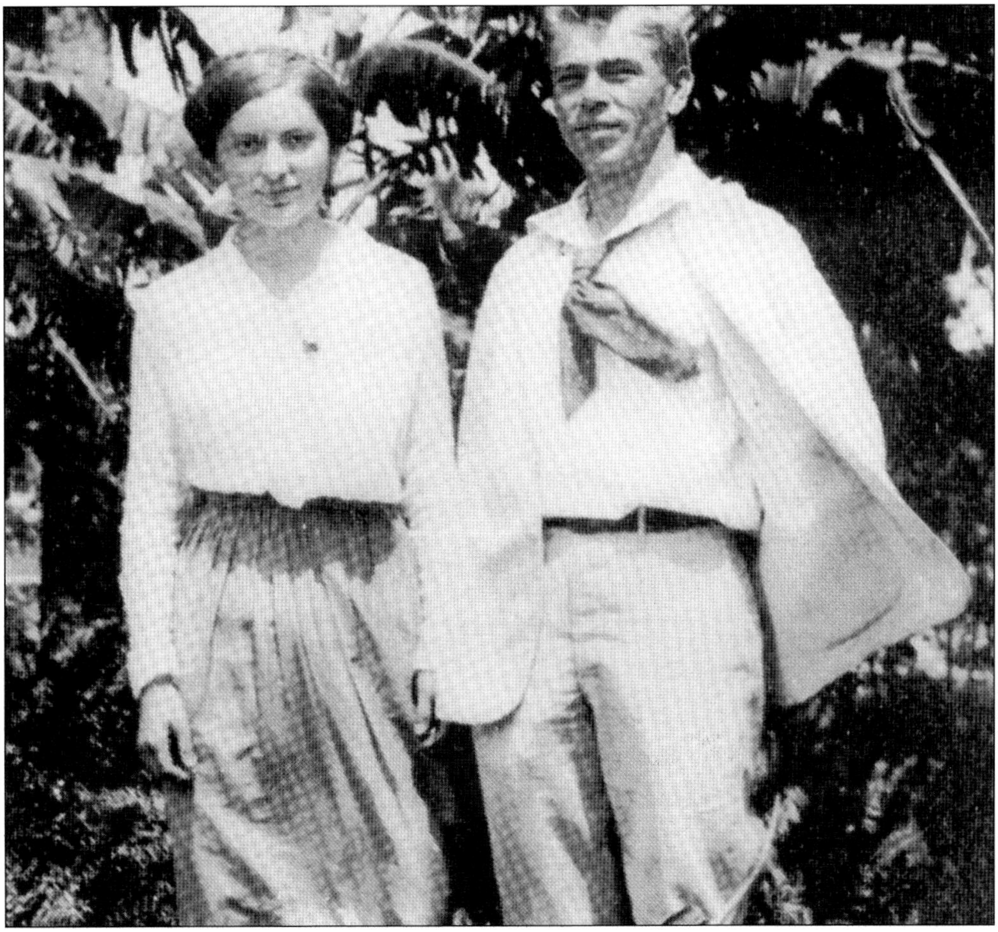

Honeymooners Vincent and Ludmila Honc Sr. decided to move to Pine Island after a visit in April 1918. From Czechoslovakia, Honc is credited with grafting the first mango trees on the island. Ludmila was known for her canned mangoes, which she sold. She reserved an entire tree for one loyal customer, John Ringling, of Ringling Circus fame. Today the island is known for its mango crop, and celebrates the Mangomania Festival each year. (Museum of the Islands.)

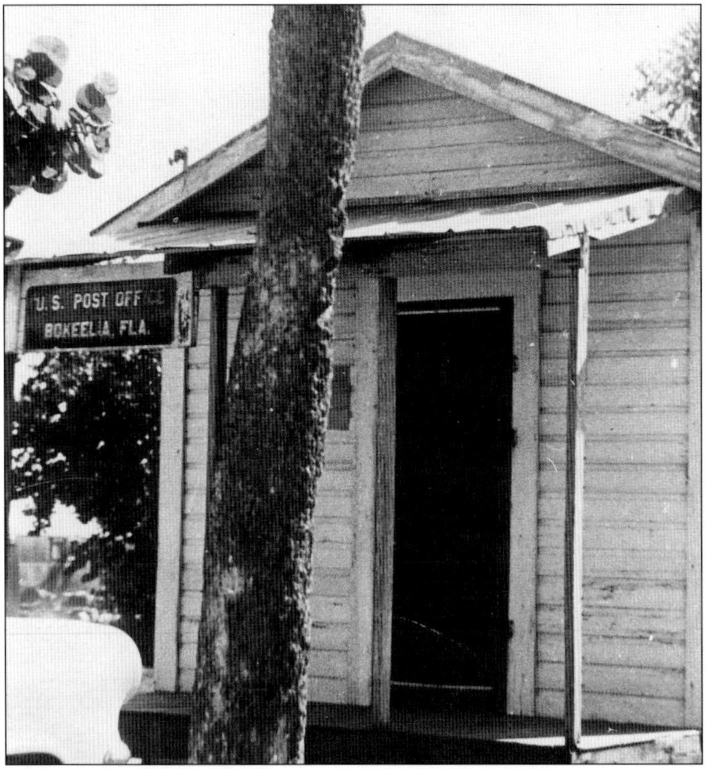

When the original post office built by Henry Martin opened in Bokeelia, business was minimal. According to records, only 12 letters were received during its first year of operation in 1906. By 1922, the community had outgrown the so-called "smallest post office in the nation" and was replaced with this slightly larger one, built by Joe Caputo. (Kay DellaBitta.)

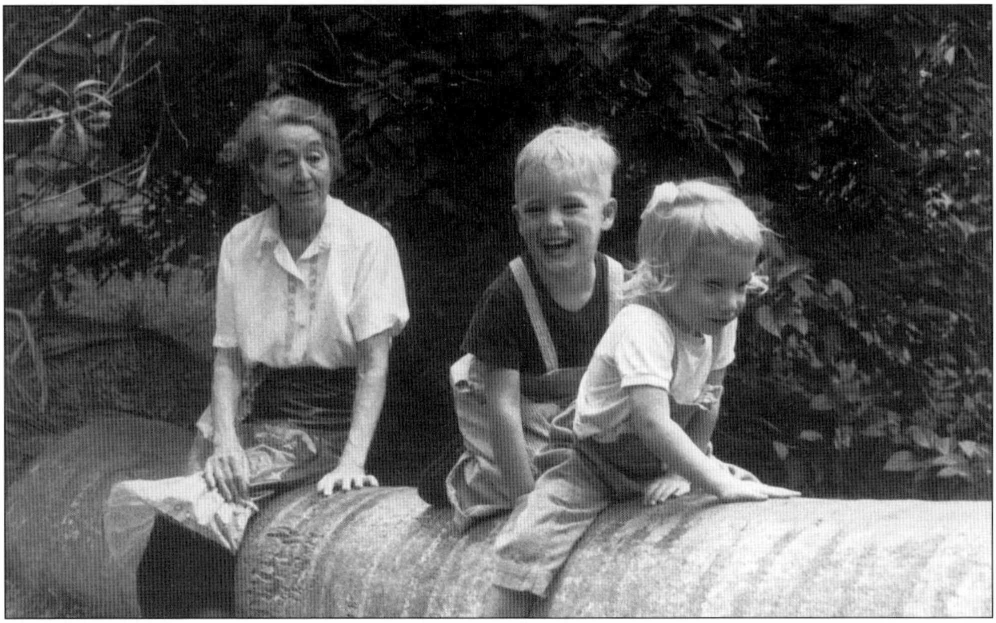

The Bokeelia postmistress from 1937 to 1952, Grace N. Chipley sits on a downed palm tree while watching Charles McNagny, age four, and Joyce McNagny, age two. The children's grandmother Lucy McNagny served as Chipley's substitute postmistress at the post office, which was the size of an outhouse. Chipley and her husband, Ed, arrived in 1914 and called their place "Chipley's Sand Patch." (William McNagny.)

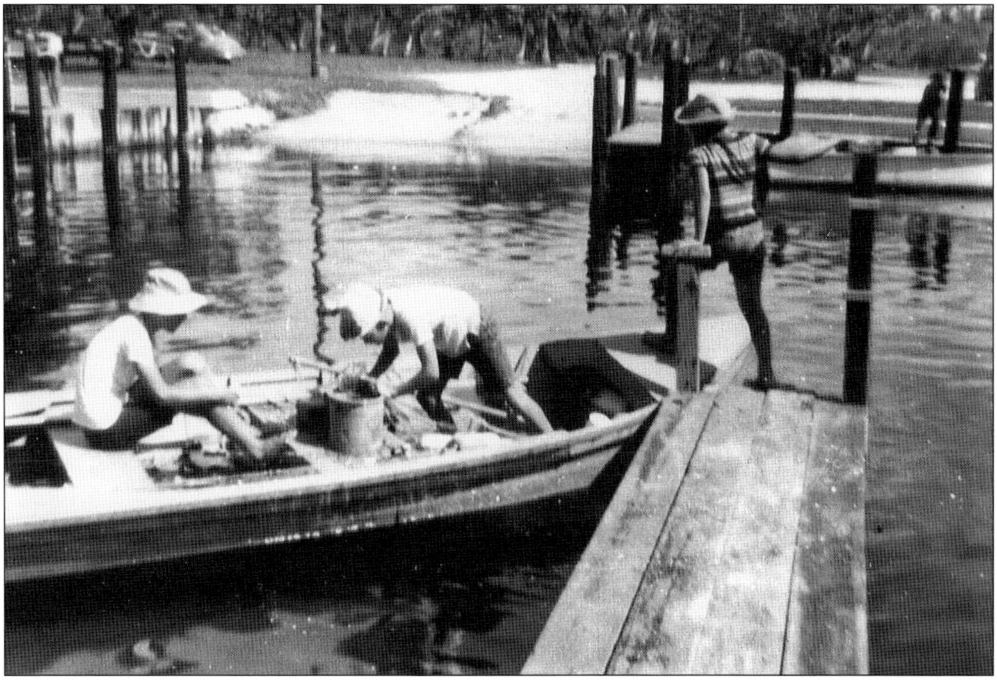

Members of Dot Goodwin's family (above) launch their boat in Jug Creek in the 1950s. (Dot Goodwin.)

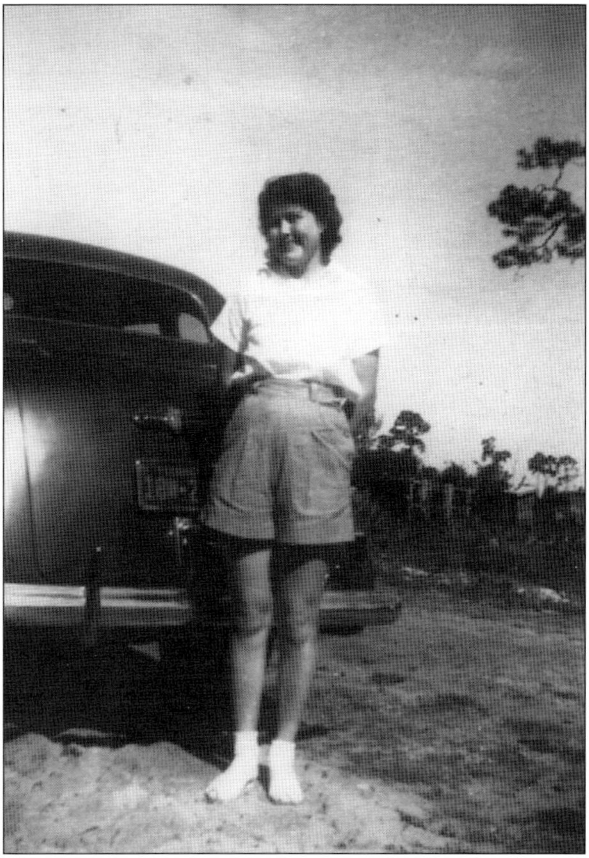

Dorothy "Dot" Hall Goodwin lived in the old schoolhouse on Bokeelia in the 1920s. As a safety precaution when the hurricane of 1926 struck, her father tied her to a tree so she would not blow away! During her childhood, the Whidden family ran Carl's General Store and Bar in the original Minta Martin's Boarding House, where they also lived. Dot remembers socializing with the Gladdings, Sterns, and Greers families. With a grin, she said, "those were good days!" (Dot Goodwin.)

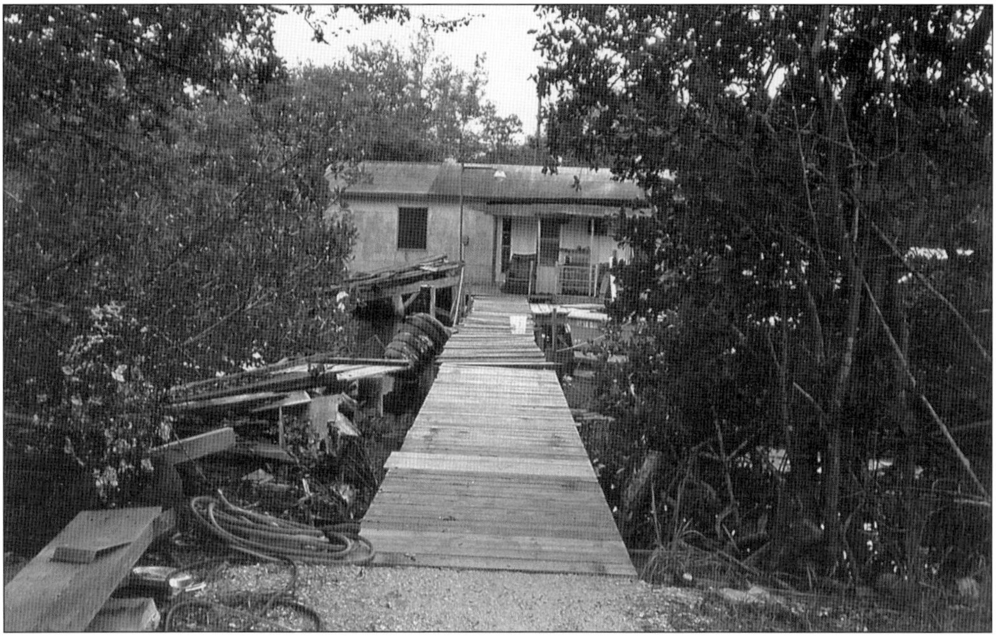

Dorothy "Dot" Hall Goodwin's father pulled a houseboat up on the island at Jug Creek and Stringfellow Road so he could scrape the bottom, removing the barnacles. While he was using a hatchet to scrape, the hatchet slipped and badly injured his knee. Dot and the family eventually fixed and added on to the original houseboat, making it home. Her children, Jackie and Jesse, were two of the first children to attend Pine Island Elementary School. (Dot Goodwin.)

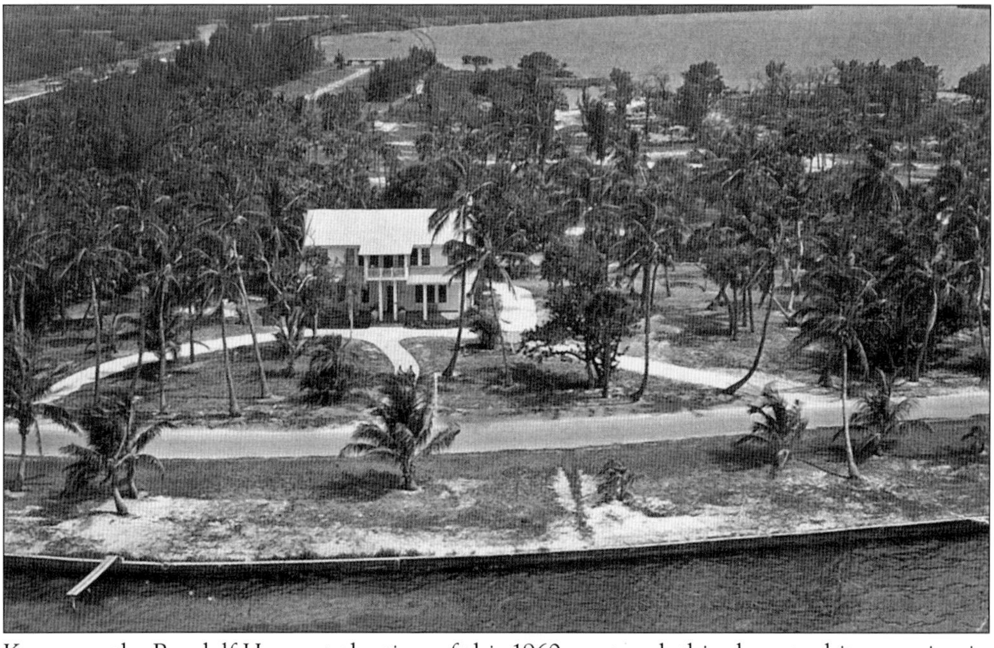

Known as the Randolf House at the time of this 1960s postcard, this elegant white mansion in Bokeelia was built by Harry Poe Johnson in 1914. Later it was owned by Sen. Mark R. Bacon, followed by the Hixsons. After a complete restoration, the stately white clapboard is now the Tarpon Inn Bed and Breakfast. (Nancy Brooks.)

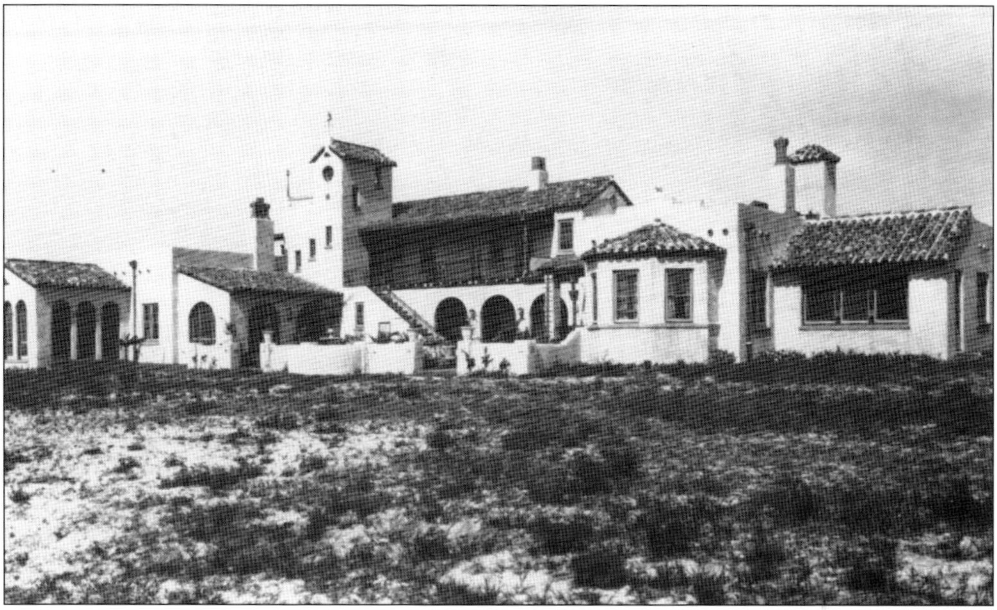

Originally named Little Bokeelia Island, the property was renamed Burgess Island after owner Charles F. Burgess, inventor of the dry-cell battery and flashlight. With a sprawling 28 rooms and a full laboratory, this Spanish-style mansion was built by Burgess in 1928 and was occupied by him until 1945. (Museum of the Islands.)

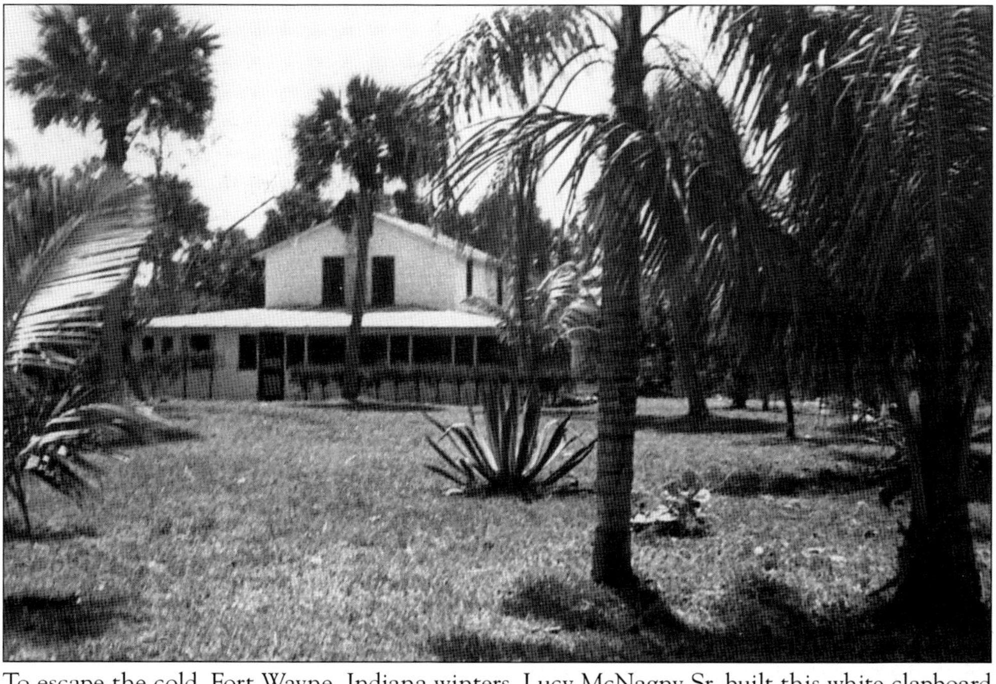

To escape the cold, Fort Wayne, Indiana winters, Lucy McNagny Sr. built this white clapboard cottage in Bokeelia in the 1930s. While strolling the grounds with Vince Honc Jr., her teenaged gardener, Lucy commented, "I don't understand why this palm seems to be thriving so much more than the others." Vince replied, "Oh, I buried Miss Nettie's cat in the hole before I planted that palm; that's why." (William McNagny.)

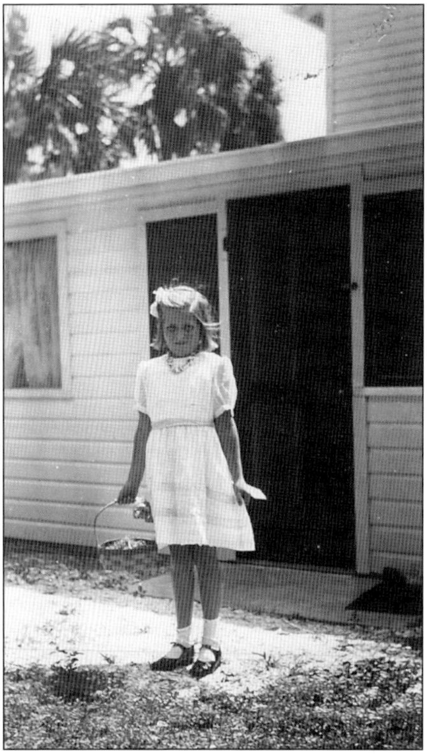

Lucy McNagny (Lucy Sr.'s daughter), at the age of eight, is pictured (left) on Easter Sunday in front of her Bokeelia home in about 1946. Lucy was one of the youngest original snowbirds, wintering on Pine Island and riding the bus to town for school. The rest of the year she lived with her family in Fort Wayne, Indiana. (Nancy Brooks.)

Although John L. Lewis was known for his boisterous, no-nonsense persona, here (below) he takes a moment to pay attention to two-year-old Joyce McNagny at his Pineland winter home. His sister, Hattie watches Lewis put a cigar-wrapper ring on Joyce's finger. (William McNagny.)

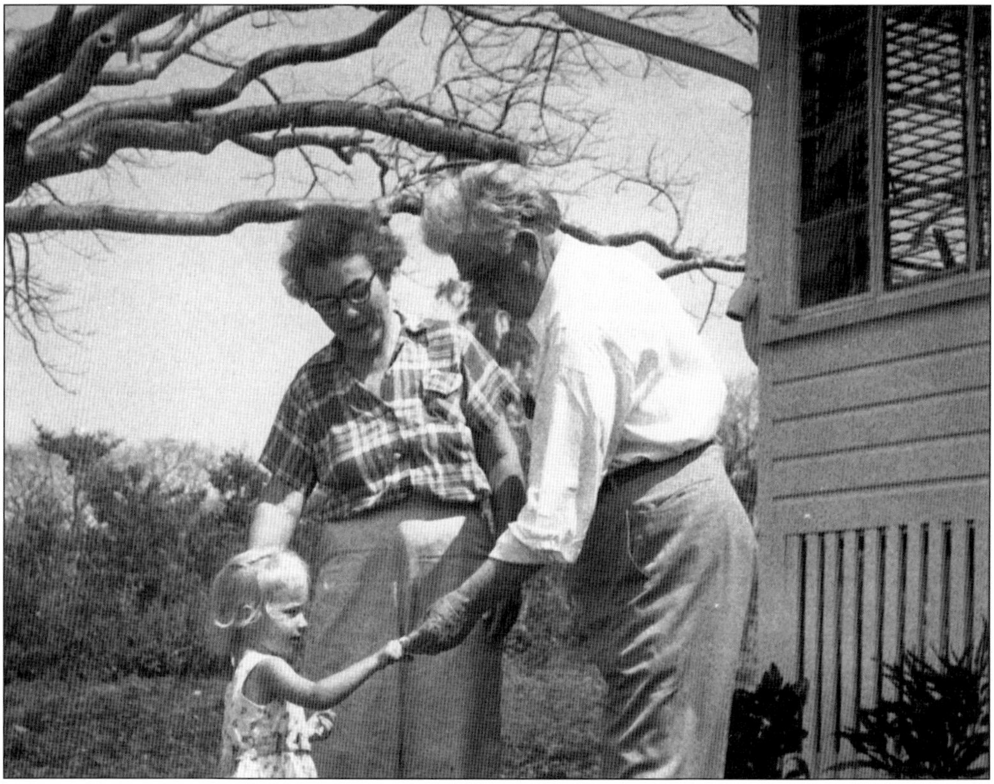

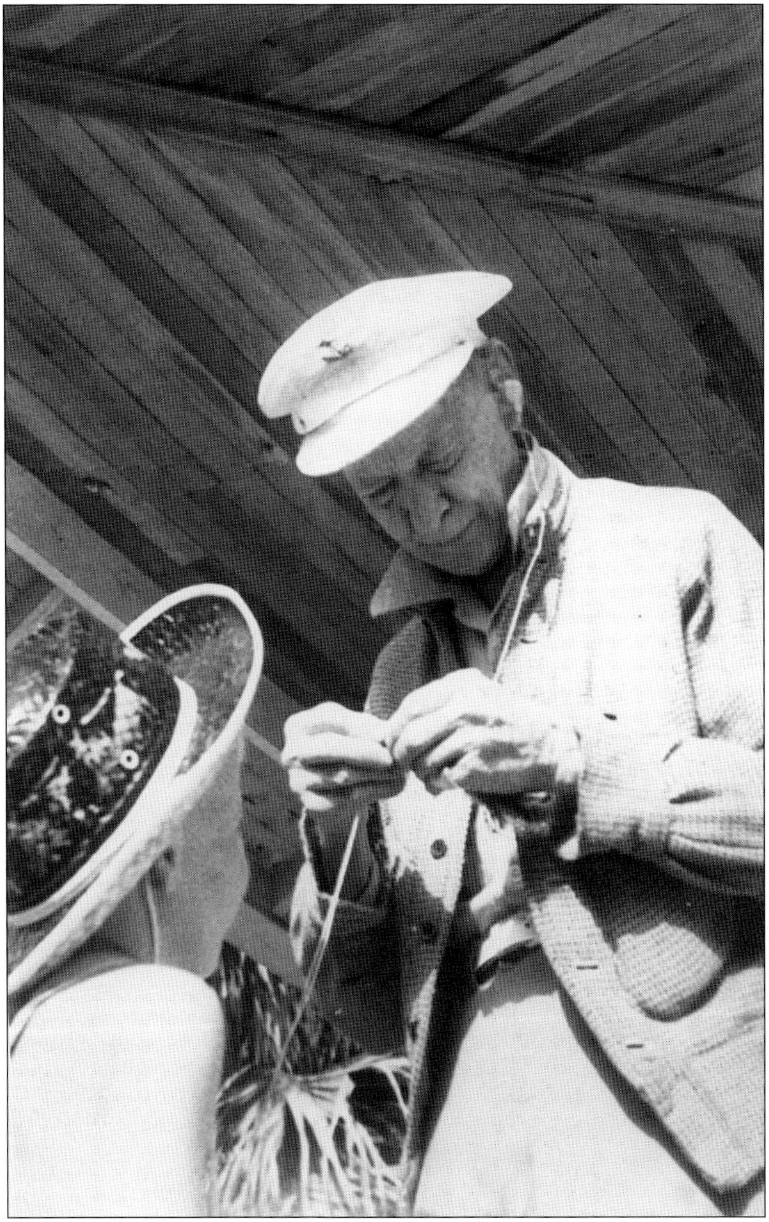

Legendary Bokeelia resident Capt. Peter C. Hains Jr. arrived with a mysterious past. The captain moved to Bokeelia after serving time for murdering a man in a fit of jealous rage. Here Hains ties a hook to a line for Charles McNagny, aged four, a short while before Hains's death in the mid-1950s. Neighbor Joan McNagny said, "Captain Hains was a sweet man. He loved listening to Caruso on the Victrolla while he bathed upstairs with all the windows open. Caruso's voice could be heard all over Bokeelia during Hains's lengthy soaks. We'd all get a concert and know the Captain was bathing!" When his daughter made plans to place Hains in a nursing home, he told Joan McNagny he would kill himself before he would go. He instructed McNagny that if the porch light was on in the morning, he would be found dead inside. One morning after McNagny and family shared some of her homemade fudge and conversation with him the night before, the light was on and, true to his word, his body was found inside. (William McNagny.)

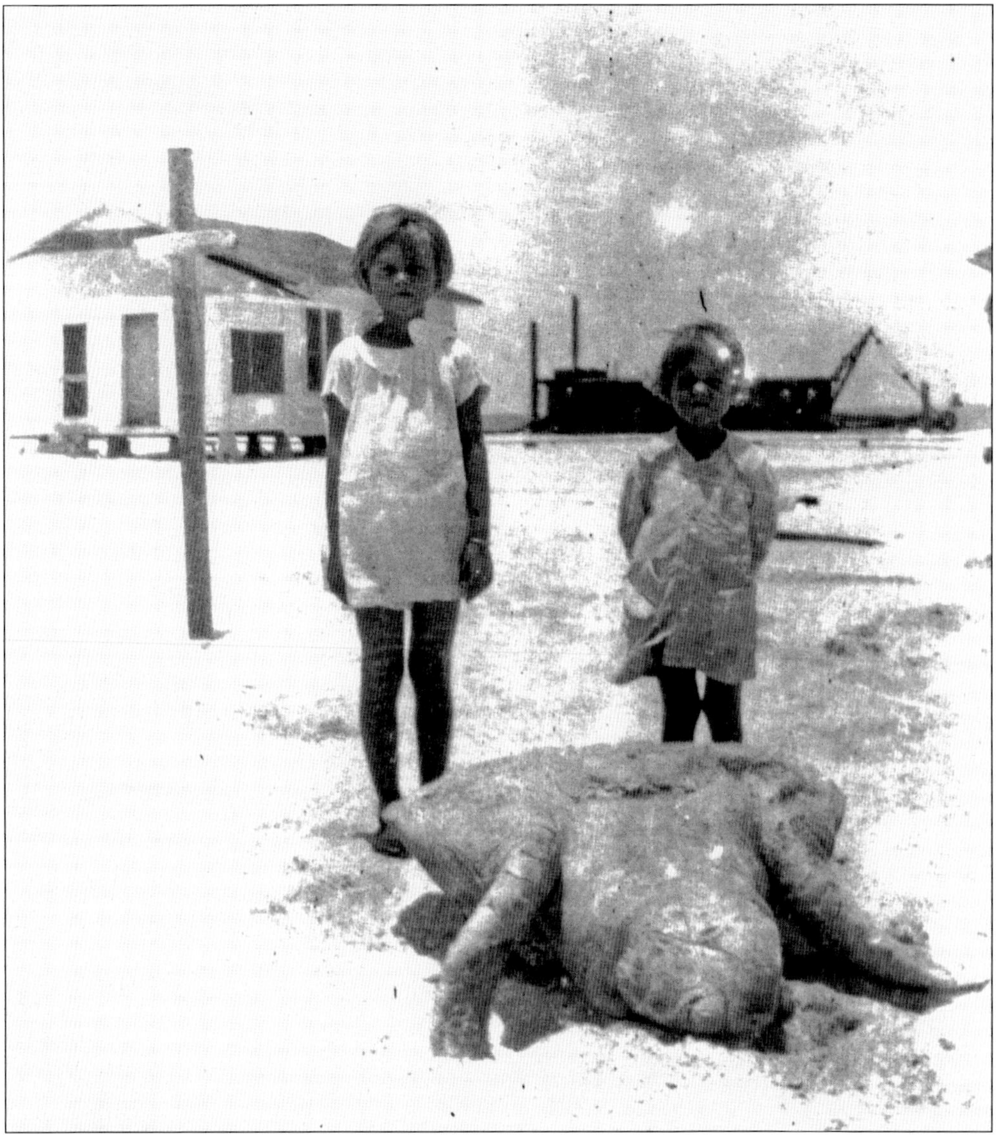

In the early to mid-1900s, loggerhead turtles were plentiful in the waters surrounding Pine Island. Laying their eggs in nests dug in the sand, the turtles visited Bokeelia's beach annually. Early settlers were known to gather the loggerhead eggs and prepare them as a menu delicacy. Here two unidentified children pose beside a beached loggerhead. Sometimes weighing in at over 300 pounds, a stewed or roasted turtle like this one could feed all of Bokeelia. By law, all sea turtles are now protected. (Museum of the Islands.)

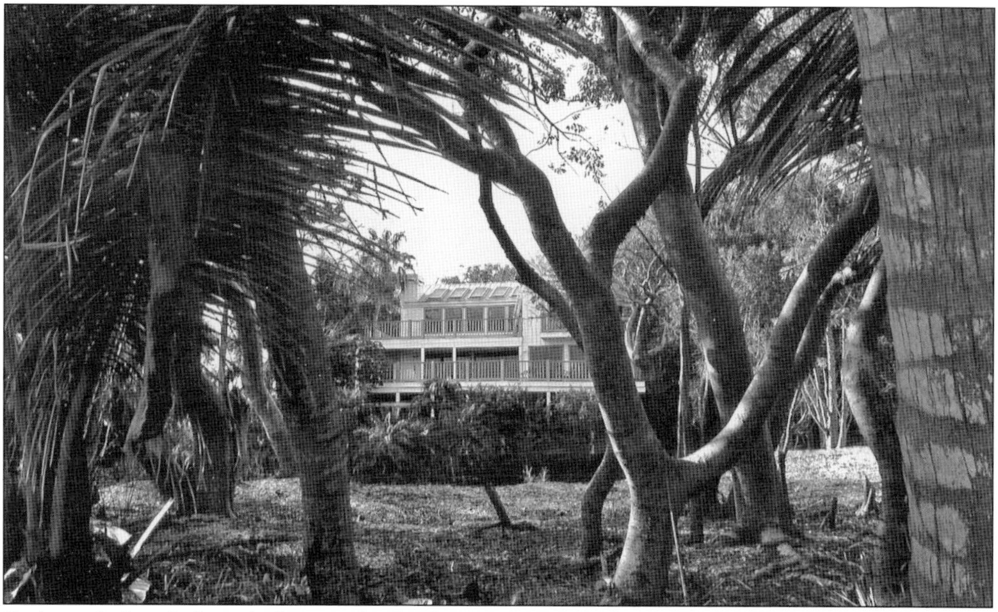

Built on Calusa Indian shell mounds, the former Dr. DeVris/Edd Dean property (above) is heavily landscaped with palms. Bill McNagny tells of visits to DeVris's home in the 1940s: "After picking us up at the train station, Dr. DeVris would stop along the drive back to Pine Island, picking up "road kill." When all of the guests were settled, the guests would gather around the ring of a shallow amphitheater (below) built by the Calusa Indians during their island reign. Dr. DeVris would dump the road kill in the middle of the area and step back. The sky would turn black and with a rustle of wings, turkey buzzards would swoop in and start fighting over the rotting varmints. Soon the shadow of a bald eagle's approach would circle and then land, scattering the buzzards to tree perches. After allowing the eagle a few minutes to himself, the buzzards would return to make their claim on the road kill. The eagle would take on one and all, always winning what was left of the road kill." That is what is called Roman gladiator entertainment, Pine Island-style! (William McNagny.)

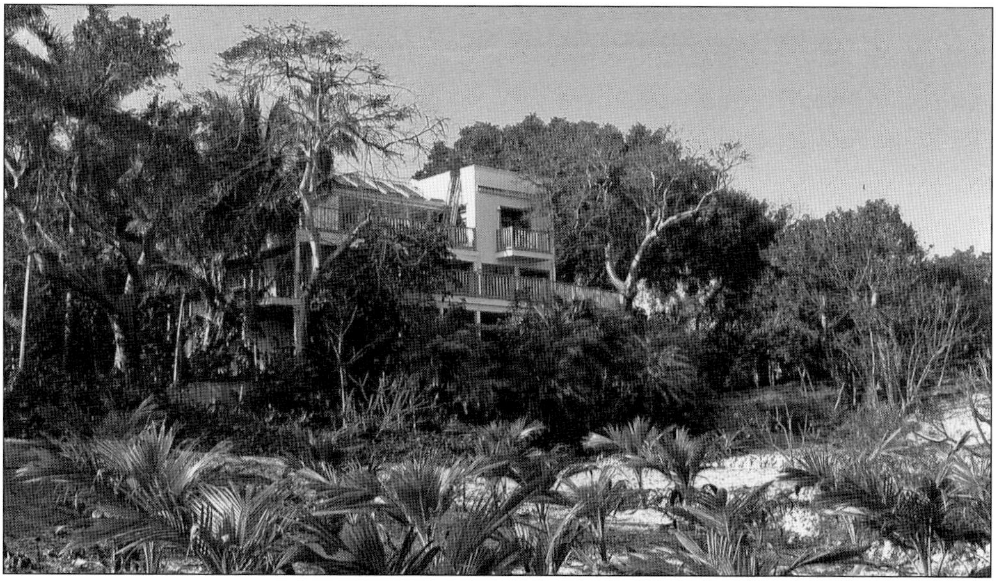

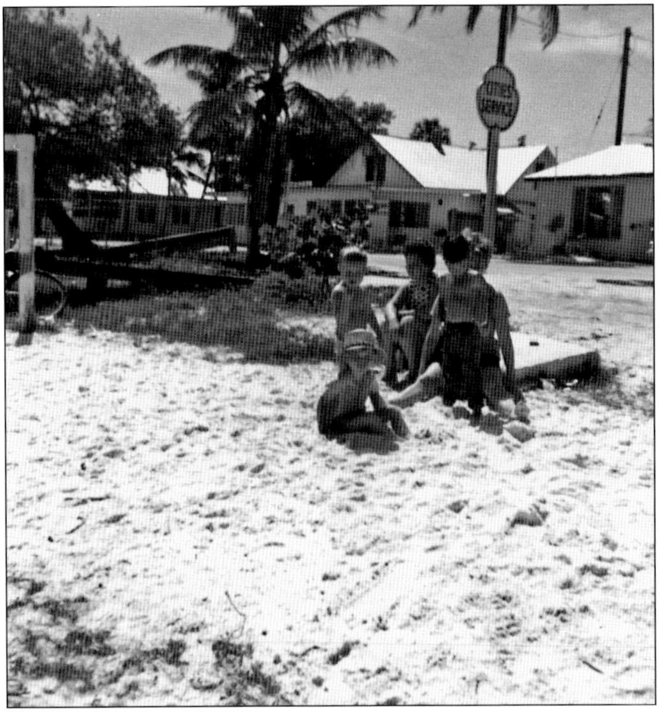

As seen in this image, Bokeelia had fine, white beach sand through the 1940s. Here, in 1965, an unidentified young family enjoys the sand and sun. In the background, the Cities Service gas station sign is visible. (Nancy Brooks.)

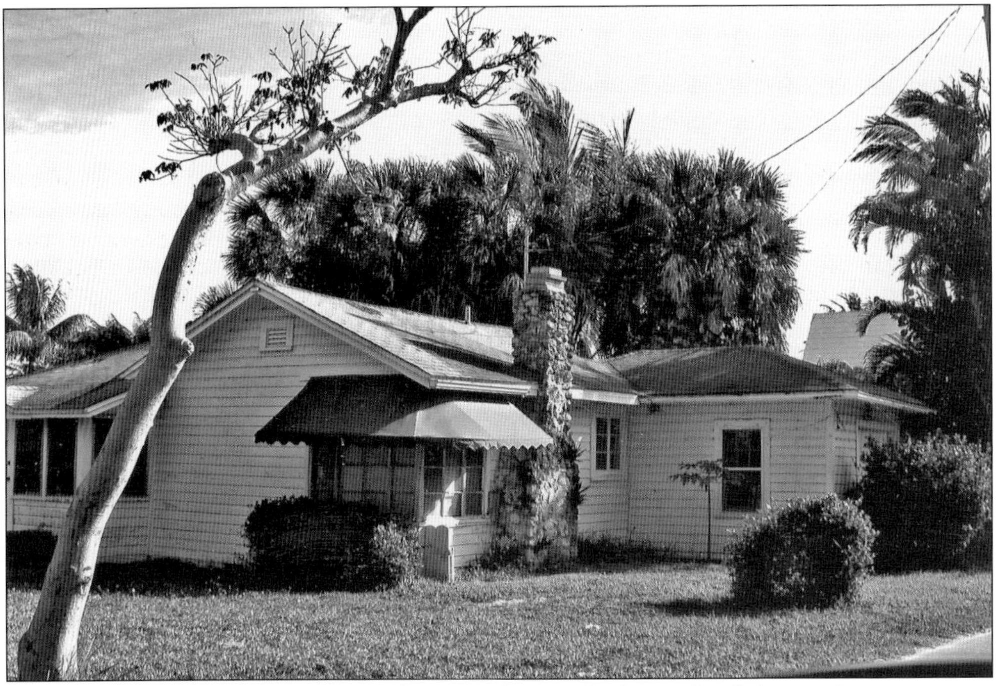

This stone-accented cottage on Bokeelia's waterfront is the Spicer family home. As an executive with General Electric, Spicer enjoyed the peace and quiet of laid-back Bokeelia in the 1940s. Friends with Norman Rockwell, the Spicer children served as Rockwell models for many of his folk-art paintings. Those who knew Spicer during his days on Pine Island, remember the little boats he made for the Bokeelia children out of palm fronds. (William McNagny.)

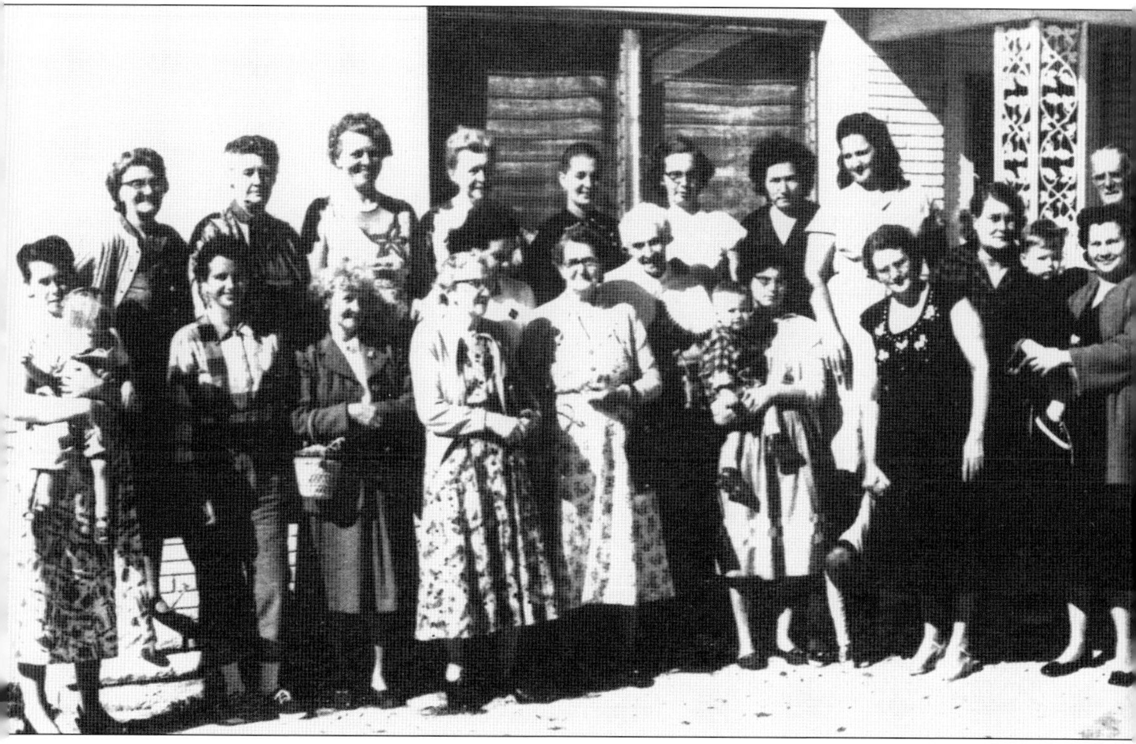

Under the presidency of Florence Hiltbrand, the Home Demonstration Club ladies enjoy a 1950s party in the Stillwell home in Bokeelia. Attendees were (from left to right) Eleanor and Linda Howard, Kay DellBitta, Florence Hiltebrand, Carol and Billy Joe Summerall, Ann and Larry Spearing, Betty Bryan, a Mrs. Macarthur, a Mrs. Simpson, a Mrs. Ross, Gracie Caputo, Louise Flowree, Marion Wells, Lois Summerall, and Norma Ballard, along with a Mr. and Mrs. Stillwell. The first club meeting on the island was held in May 1924, when a group of ladies met in the home of Minta Martin and enjoyed a demonstration on making hats. The implementation of later demonstrations, such as the canning of island-grown fruits and vegetables, brought home many blue ribbons from the county fair. The club continued to meet at various locations, including the Bokeelia School and the Civic Association Building at Pine Island Center. Due to lack of interest in the 1960s, it became inactive by 1968. With Arlene Gladstone as its president, the group reorganized as the Matlacha-Pine Island Extension Homemaker's Club in 1976. As one of the longest-running organizations on the island, the members are credited with meeting island needs through a variety of worthwhile projects. (Museum of the Islands.)

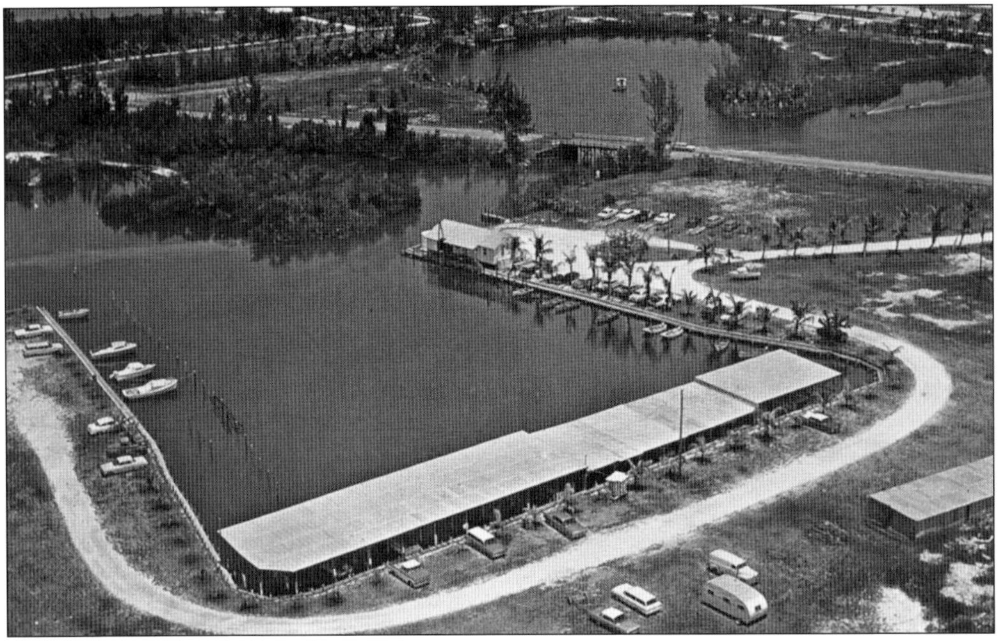

Owned by Frank and Kay DellaBitta, Frank's Fishing Camp was one of the first marinas on the island to cater to both commercial fishermen and sports-fishermen alike. Taken in the 1960s, before the large dry-storage buildings were on the property, this image shows the covered dockage and marina store (white building center). Stringfellow Road runs along the top of the image, with Jug Creek Bridge shown midway along the road. (Kay DellaBitta.)

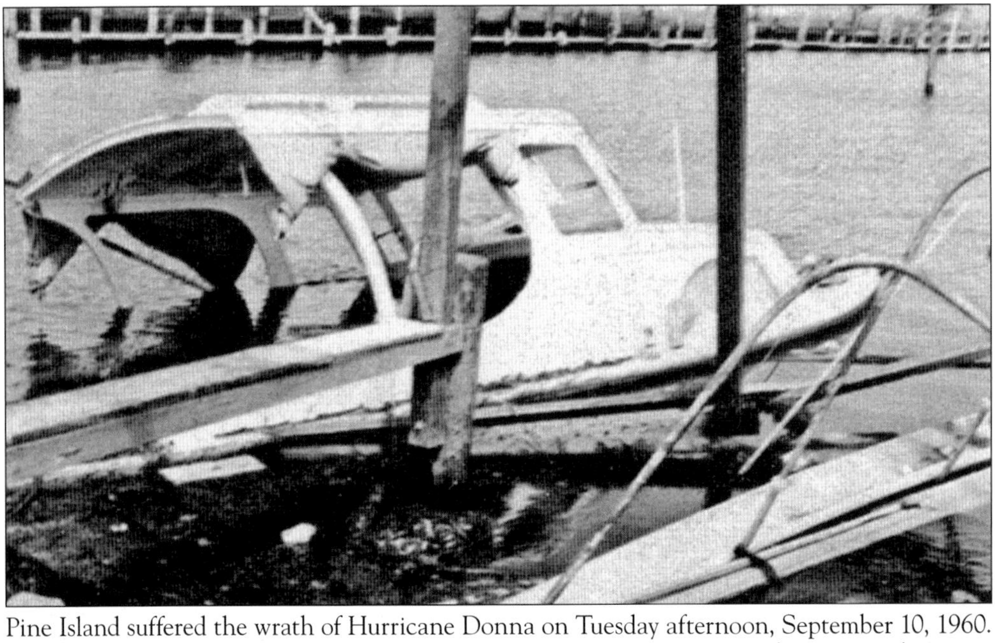

Pine Island suffered the wrath of Hurricane Donna on Tuesday afternoon, September 10, 1960. Winds gusted to more than 120 miles per hour, and tides ran up to 7 feet above normal. At one point, the Caloosahatchee River was drained nearly dry and then, with a rush, refilled. Stories are related about alligators, snakes, and rats as a menace for weeks after the storm. (Museum of the Islands.)

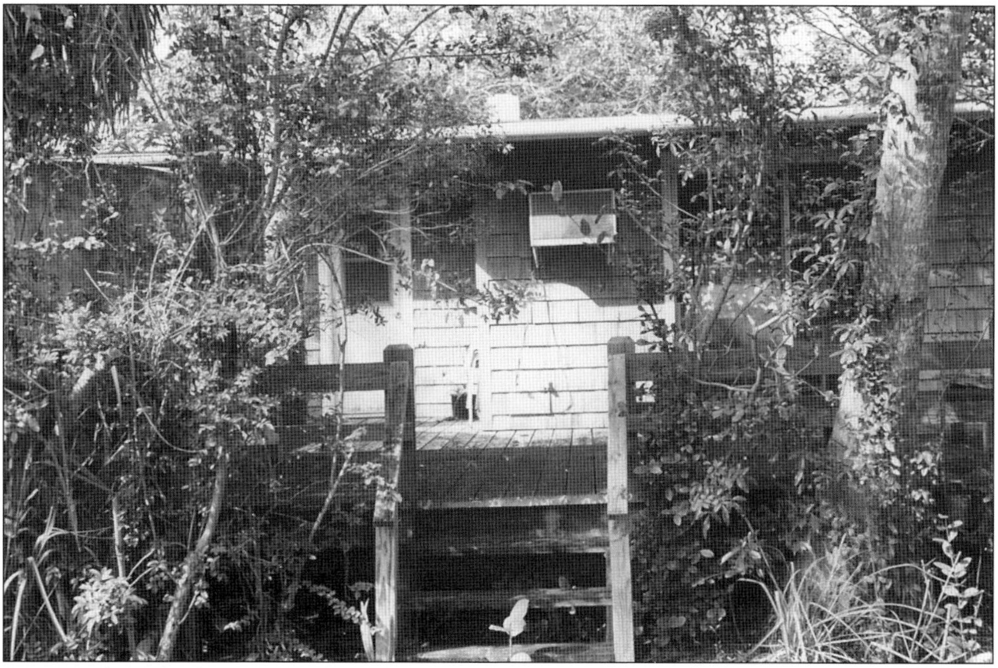

Upon finding this long-neglected building on Bokeelia's waterfront in the 1980s, Nancy Brooks came up with a plan: an upscale art gallery for Pine Island. Credited with being one of the first to bring art to the island, Brooks set about restoring this little shack into a highly acclaimed art gallery, leading the way for many other prestigious galleries to open on Pine Island. (Nancy Brooks.)

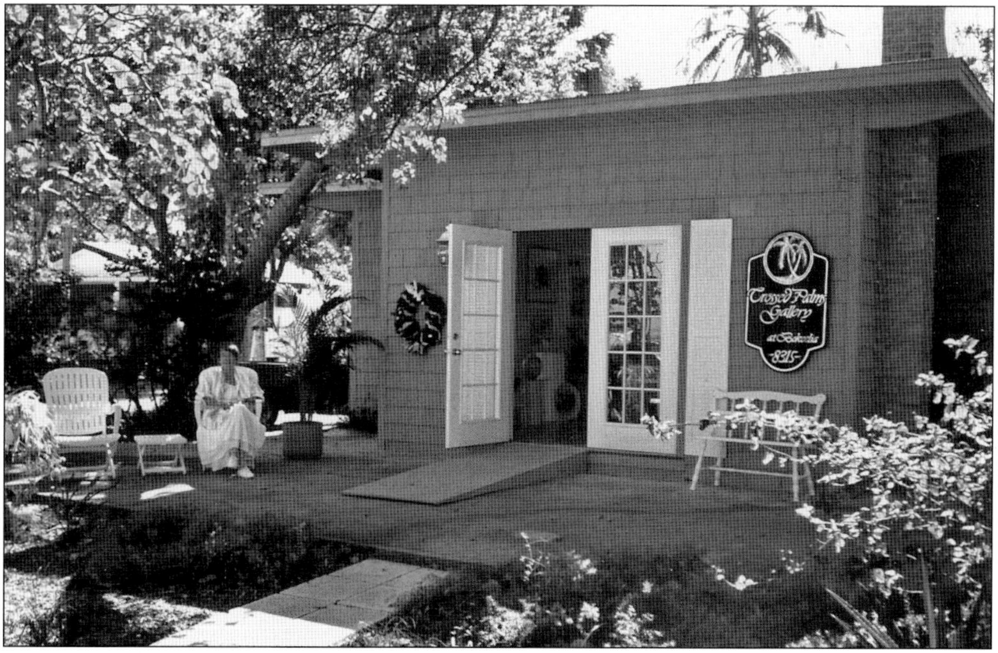

After a careful restoration with help from her husband, Bob, Nancy Brooks is seen here shortly after the opening of the Crossed Palms Gallery in 1990. With the works of renowned artists on display, this charming, cottage-like gallery is a delightful remnant of another era. (Nancy Brooks.)

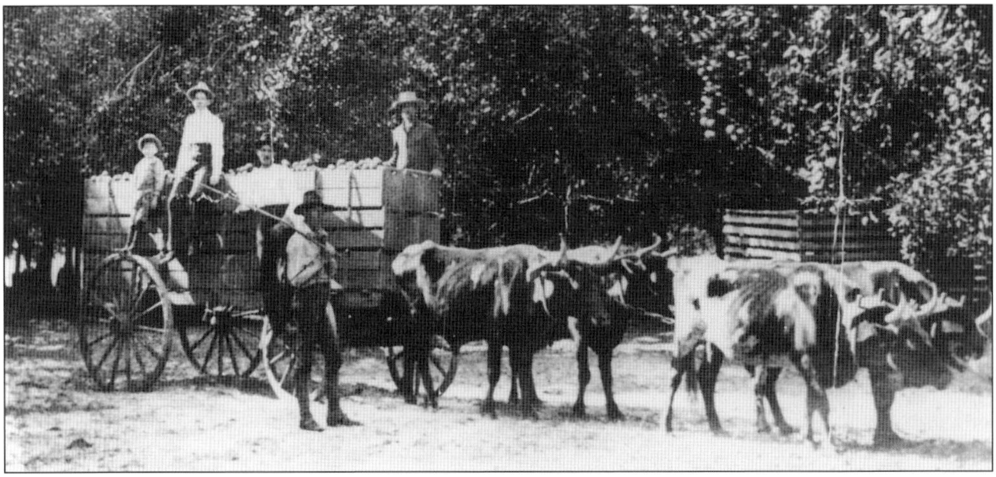

Citrus harvested from the groves of W. G. Masters and his business partner, Forbes, was hauled to the Masters Landing dock on wagons pulled by oxen, much like the one pictured here, at the Carlton farm near Wauchula. Masters Grove produce was loaded onto barges and was then towed to a Fort Myers packinghouse by a Kinzie Brothers steamer. Masters Grove, located in the Flamingo Bay area spreading from the east shoreline to the west, covered nearly 1,000 acres, of which 135 were planted in citrus. Eventually, the settlement grew large enough to have its own school building on the east side of the road, but it shared the teacher with the St. James City School. Following the death of Masters in the 1940s, the groves declined and were eventually abandoned. An electrical power station now rests on the site once known as Masters Landing. (Florida State Archives.)

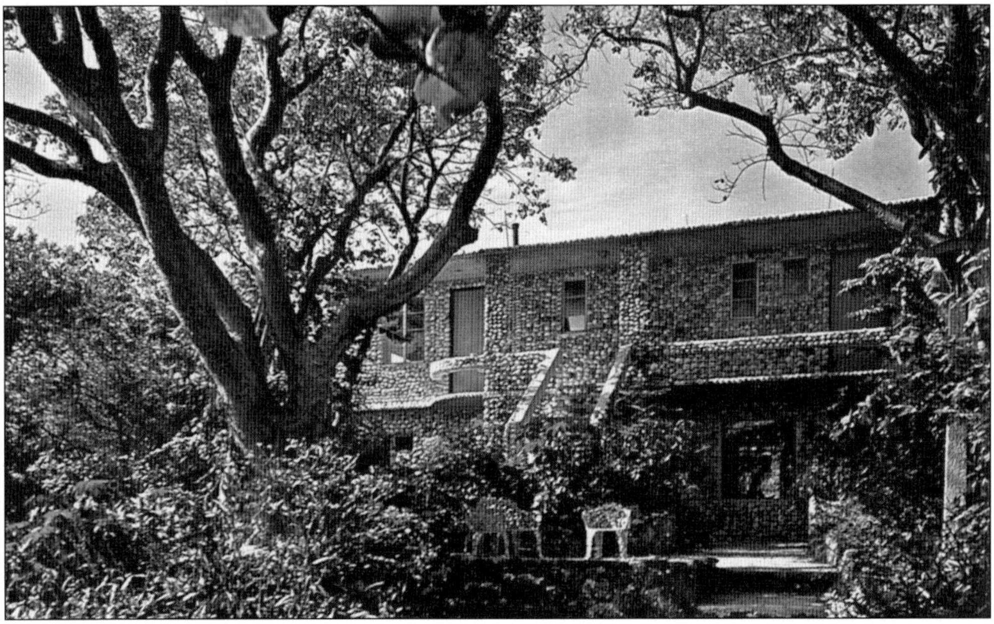

Numerous skeletal remains and Calusa artifacts were unearthed during the construction of the Sea Grape Lodge, built on Demere Key. In 1958, Phil DeGraff opened the quirky lodge amidst 400 varieties of plants and 44 varieties of tropical fruits. The novel buildings and walkways were carefully covered with a veneer of whelk shells. Due to DeGraff's flamboyant personality, the lodge became a popular destination for tourists during the 1960s. (Nancy Brooks.)

In the early 1960s, Pine Island Center was largely undeveloped, as pictured at right. Residents recall weekend square dances and freshwater from a deep well that did not smell of sulfur at the Roundhouse Restaurant. Built in the 1950s, the Parker family purchased the Roundhouse in 1960 and then added the little cottages to the property. This image was taken before the stop signs were installed. (Museum of the Islands.)

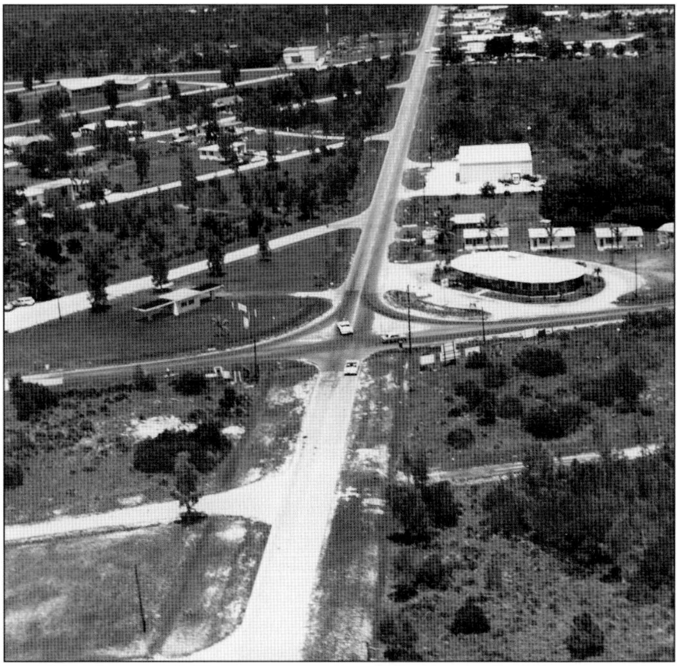

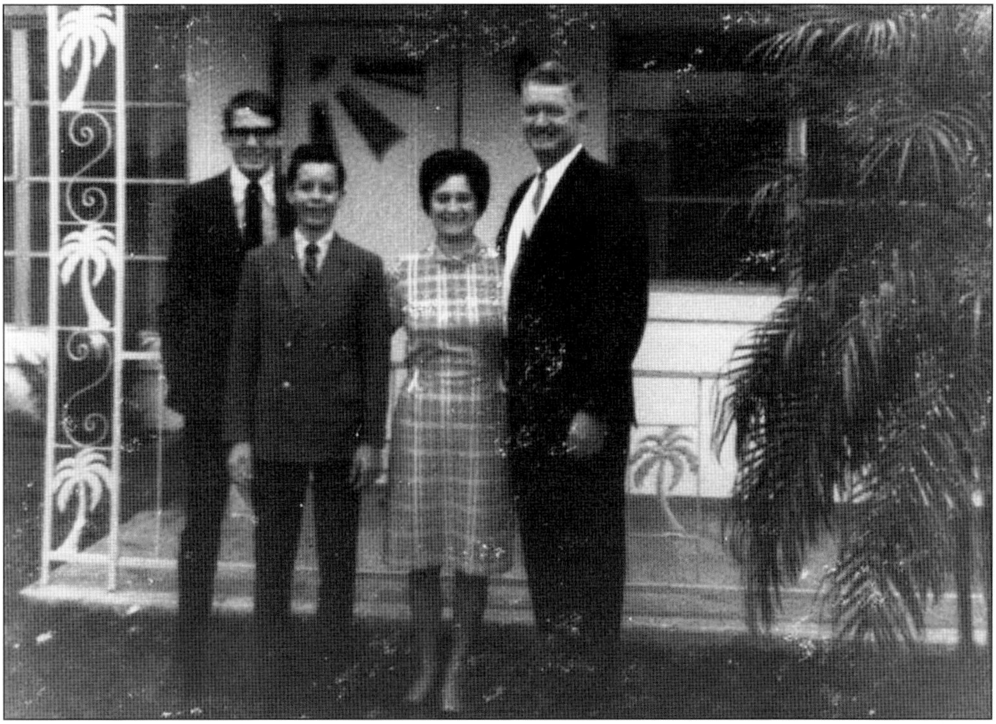

An almost hidden canal-front neighborhood located about four miles north of the Pine Island Center, Serenity Cove was developed by Bob Martin and Maurie Stevens in the 1960s. Because she thought the area was so calm and serene, Doris Stevens came up with the name Serenity Cove. Here Bob and Esther Martin with sons Bobby and Ben are in front of their home in Martin Cove in 1968. (Olin Odland.)

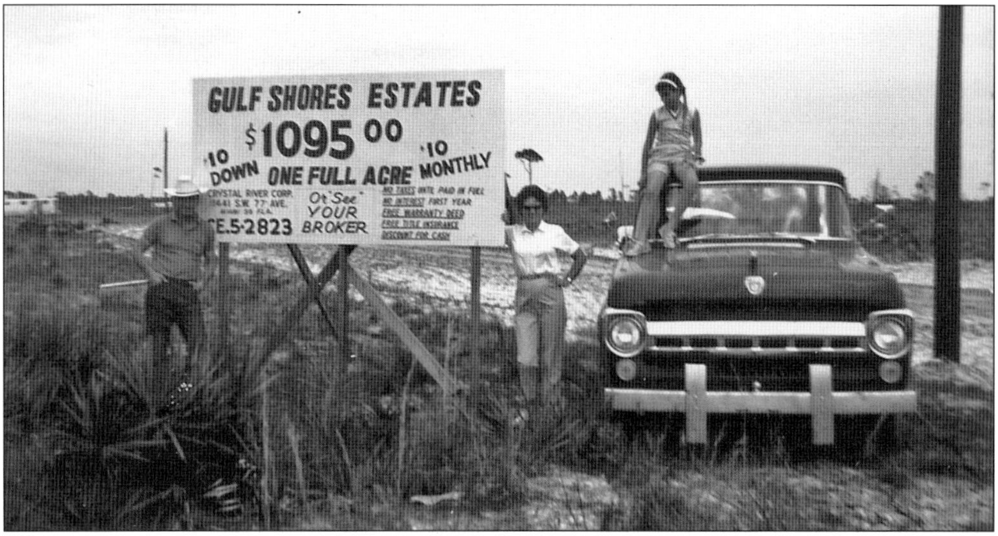

The Ben Traverse family, pictured here in 1962, was instrumental in the development of the 200-acre Charlotte Shores development. Like many Florida developments, a small down payment and, likewise, small monthly payments enticed many visitors into buying property for a permanent dwelling. (Judy Baxley.)

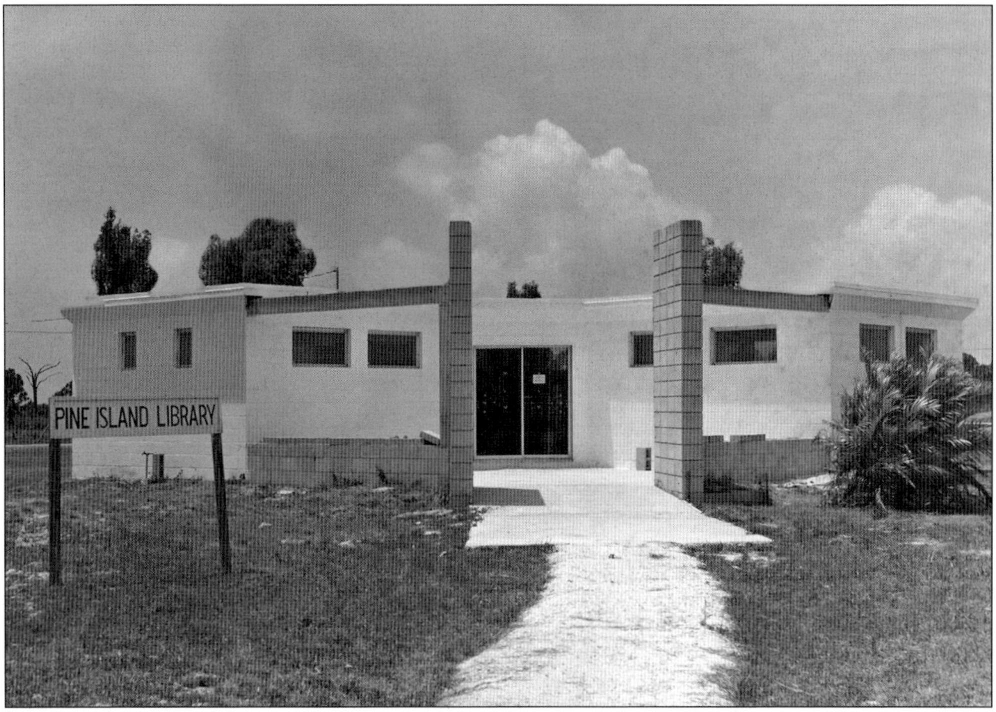

Preceding this building, housing Pine Island's first library, Mr. and Mrs. Roger Amory loaded books aboard their library boat at Boca Grande and then made rounds of nearby islands, including Pine Island, where they loaned books to island residents. Also predating the library, a Mrs. Eyster of Matlacha loaned books from her front porch. Islander Mary Wheeler is credited with initiating the campaign to build the library in 1966 at Pine Island Center. Today the building is home to the Museum of the Islands. (Museum of the Islands.)

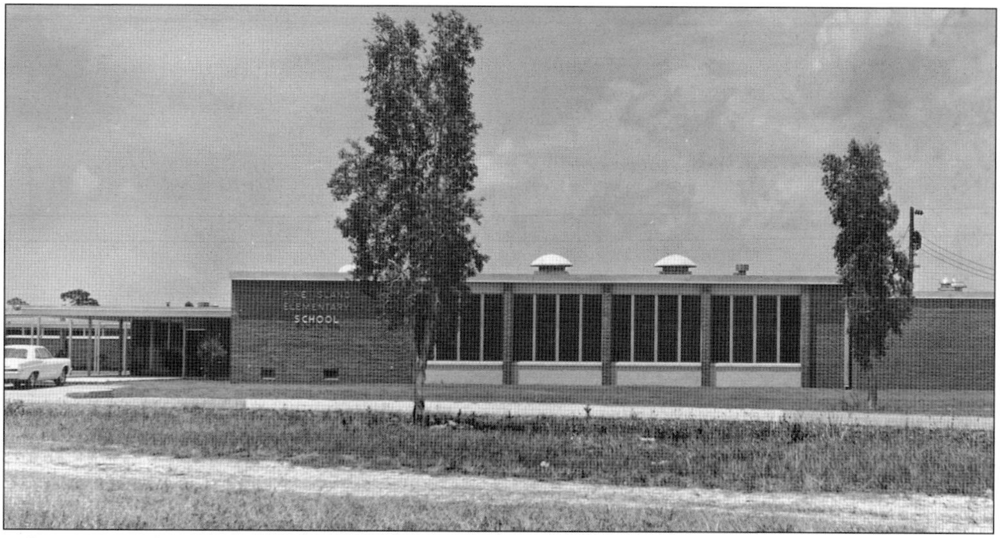

After years of busing the island children to J. Colin English Elementary School in North Fort Myers, the school district of Lee County built Pine Island's first school. Located at Pine Island Center, the school was built in 1960. Pine Islanders are proud of the school, a perennial "A" school per State of Florida standards. (Museum of the Islands.)

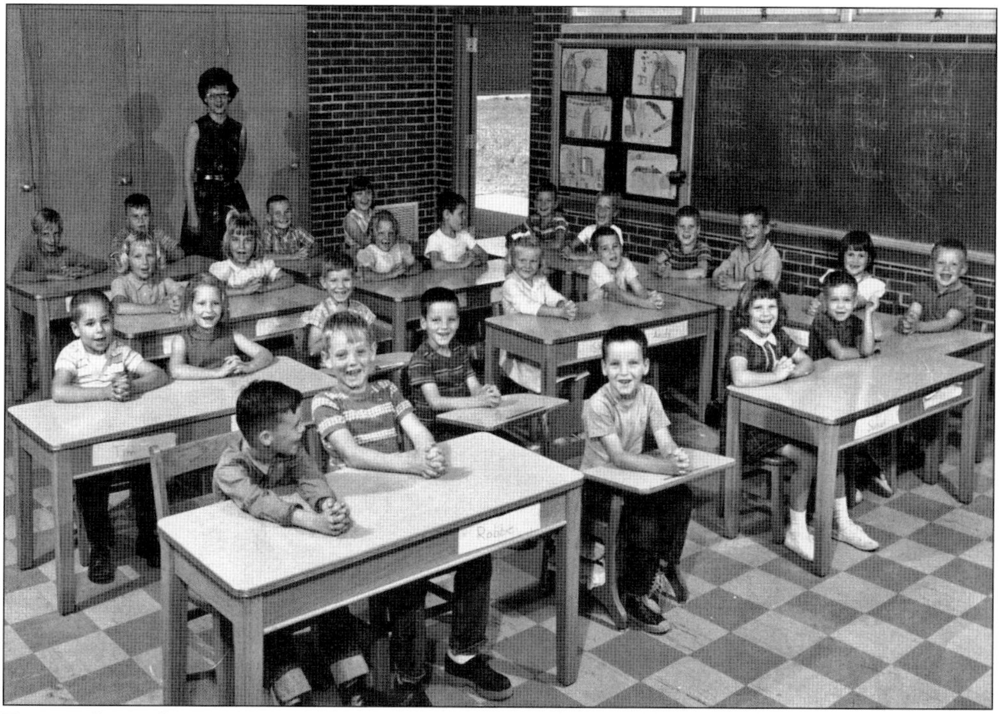

First-grade teacher Mrs. Gimber poses with her students of the 1962–1963 school year. Opened in 1960, the school was directed by principal Richard M. Ahern. Susan (Hunt) Laffitte sits in the first row, second from the right. Others in the class include Gary Padilla, Mark Poppell, Robbie Whidden, Barry Padilla, Sharon Nightingale, Adny Bryan, Nancy Waltz, Maria Mercer, Dawn Wollerman, Timmy Martin, Rodney Williams, Tony Green Rommie Taylor, and Margaret Skipper. (Susan Laffitte.)

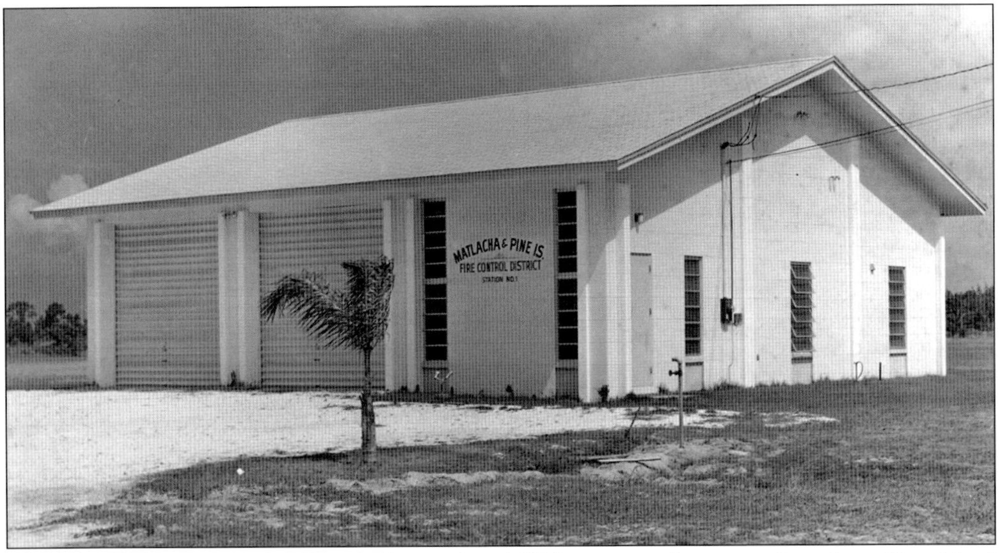

With the purchase of a 1924 La France fire truck in 1955 by a group of concerned residents, Pine Island began a volunteer fire department. Later hearses donated by a Mr. Engelhardt of Fort Myers were converted into ambulances. Ambulance subscriptions ran to $3 per year per family. Outgrowing the first station in Matlacha, a larger fire station was built at the Pine Island Center in 1966. Here Station No. 1 is shown as it appeared upon completion at Pine Island Center. (Museum of the Islands.)

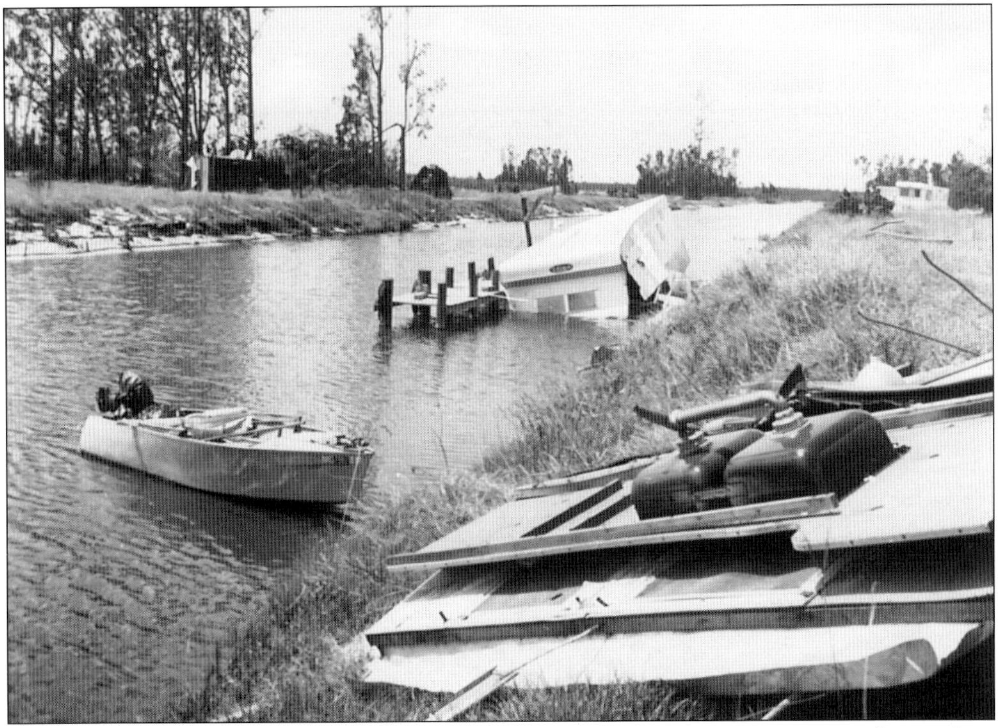

Located about five miles south of Pine Island Center, Flamingo Bay was in its infancy when Hurricane Donna struck in September 1960. With no permanent buildings in the community at the time of the storm, the travel trailers were tossed and sunk by the hurricane-force winds. (Museum of the Islands.)

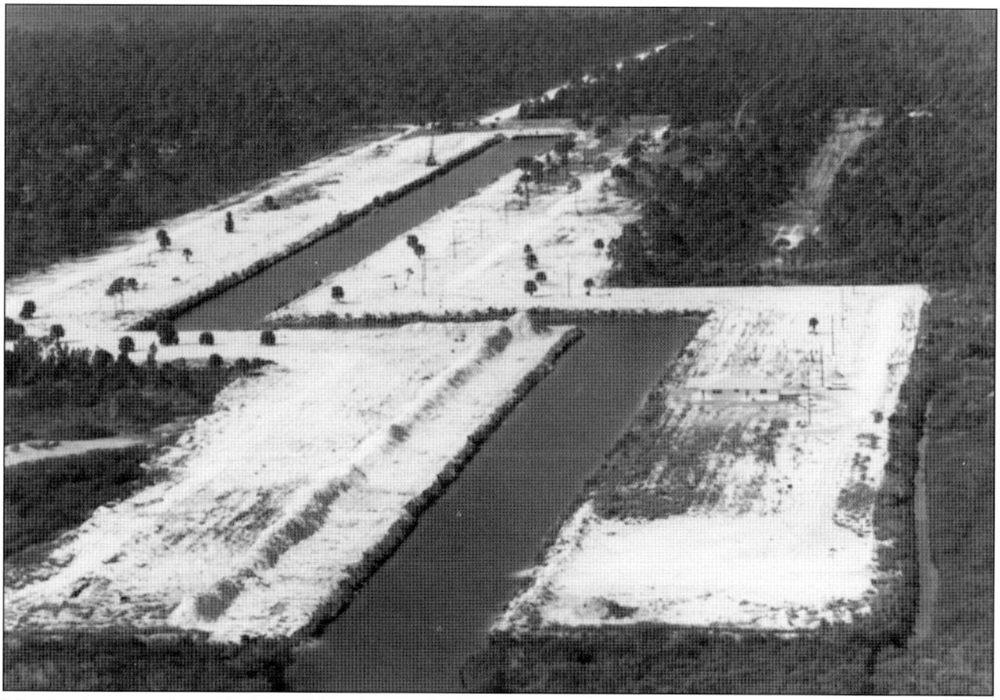

Newly dug canals and cleared land are all that existed in the early days of Manatee Bay. Three and one half miles north of St. James City, Manatee Bay became a fisherman's haven in the following years. (Judy Baxley.)

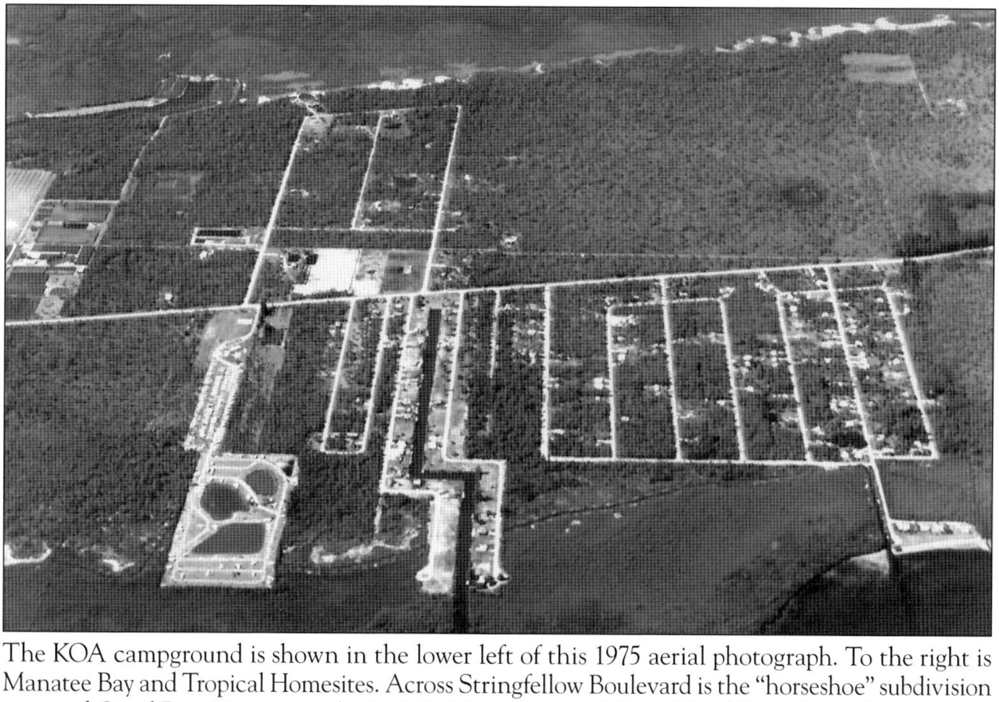

The KOA campground is shown in the lower left of this 1975 aerial photograph. To the right is Manatee Bay and Tropical Homesites. Across Stringfellow Boulevard is the "horseshoe" subdivision area and Quail Run Nursery to the far left. Mangroves and Pine Island Sound run along the top of the image. (Dorothy Muske.)

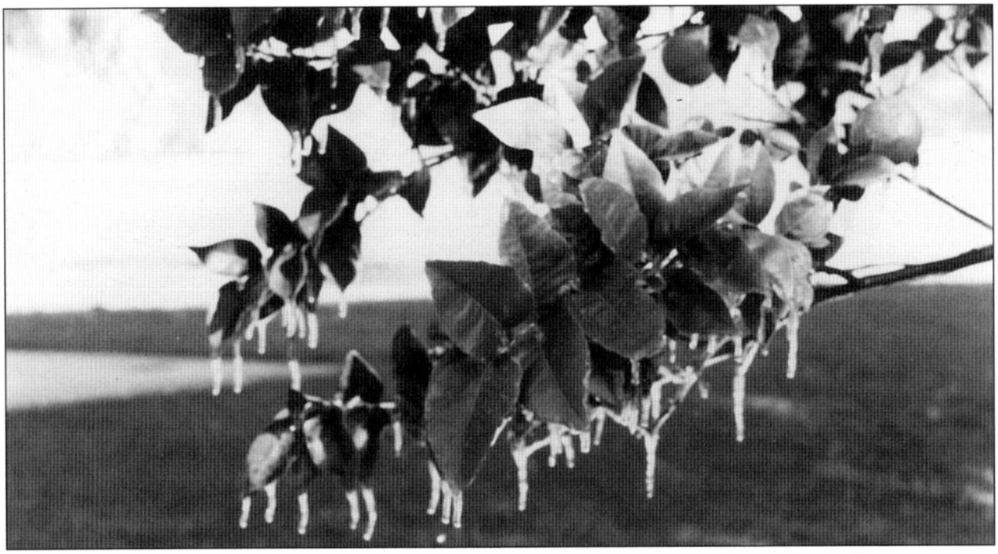

Recent weather patterns have brought mild winter temperatures to Pine Island. However, past winters have brought ice and even snowflakes to the island. Shown here, ice forms on a tree during the winter of 1976–1977. Residents of St. James City are on record for having seen snow so heavy it formed slush on the roads on December 24, 1976. (Judy Baxley.)

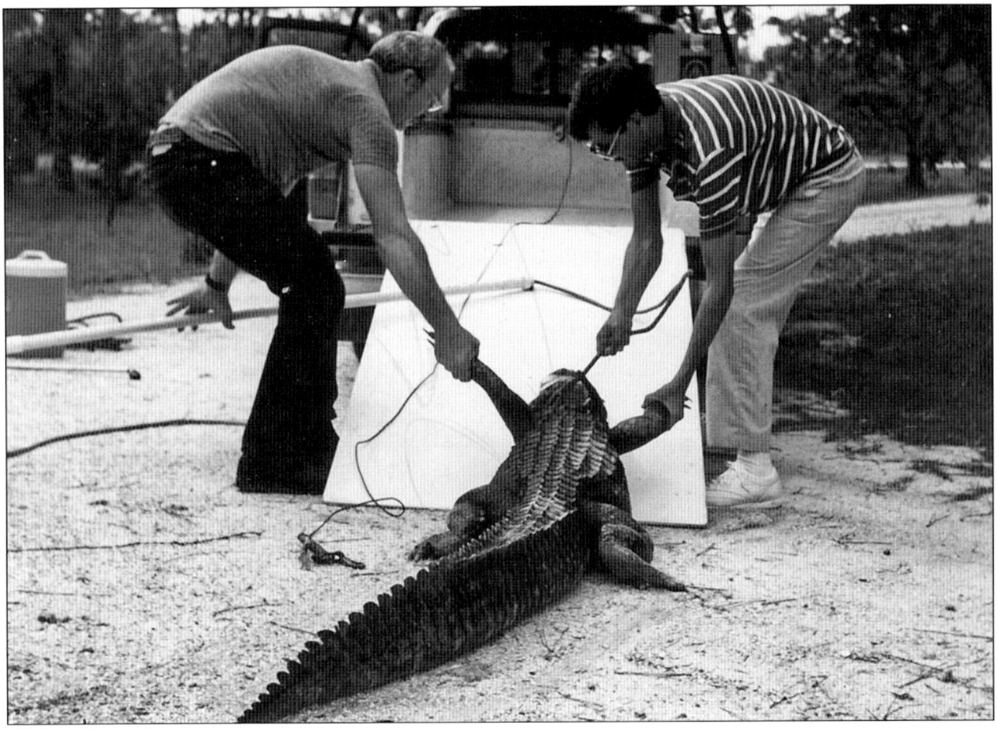

Trapping and removing a nuisance alligator from the Ben Traverse property on Pine Island in the 1970s are Lee County's legendary alligator trapper John French, left, and an unidentified assistant. Responsible for trapping thousands of alligators that threatened residents of the area, French died of a heart attack while securing his last catch at the age of 63. Statewide, out of a population of about two million alligators, trappers like French relocate about 8,000 per year. (Judy Baxley.)

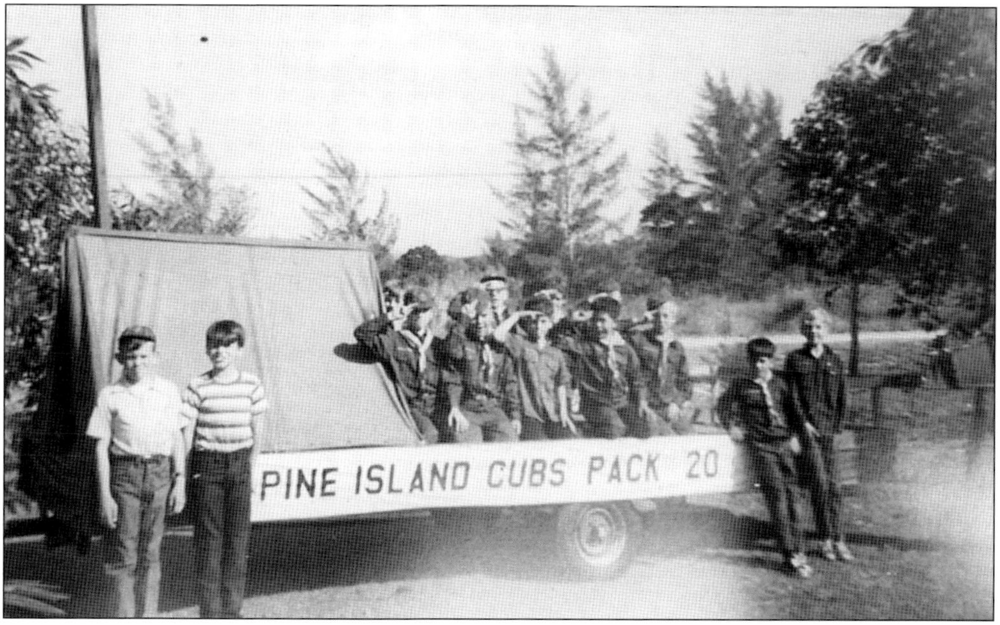

Scouting is one of Pine Island's longest active youth programs. Pictured here, for a 1970s local parade, are unidentified boys of the Pine Island Boy Scouts of America troop. (Museum of the Islands.)

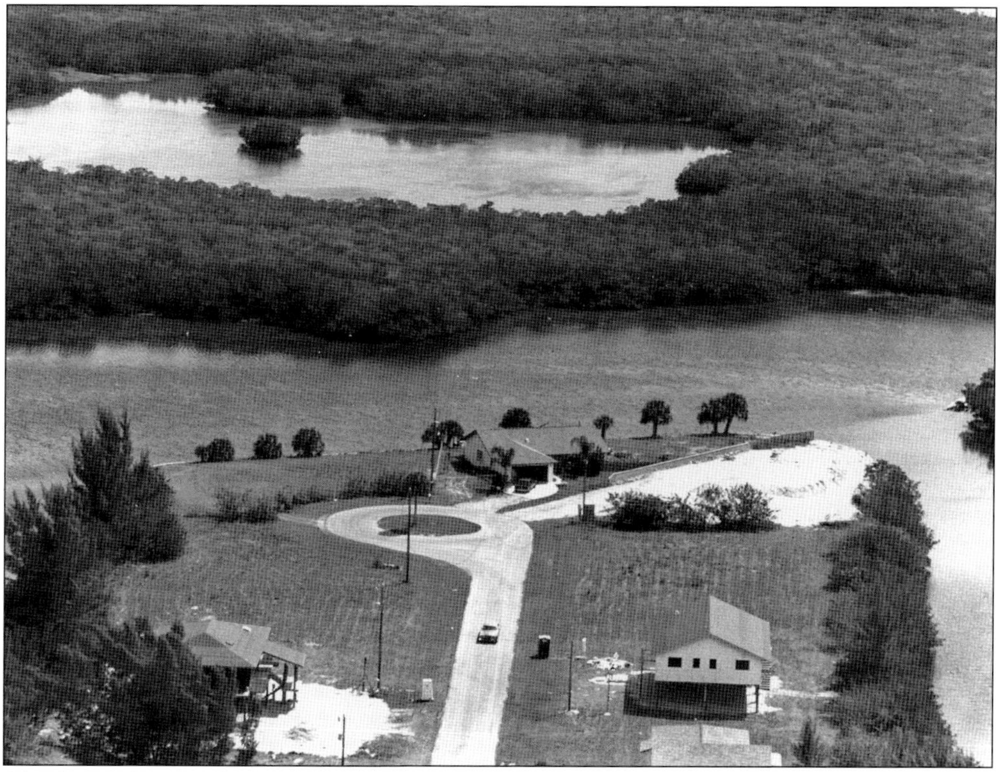

Charlotte Shores, a housing development located north of Pine Island Center, is a secluded waterfront neighborhood. In 1988, as pictured here, lots had been sold, and several stilt home had been built. (Judy Baxley.)

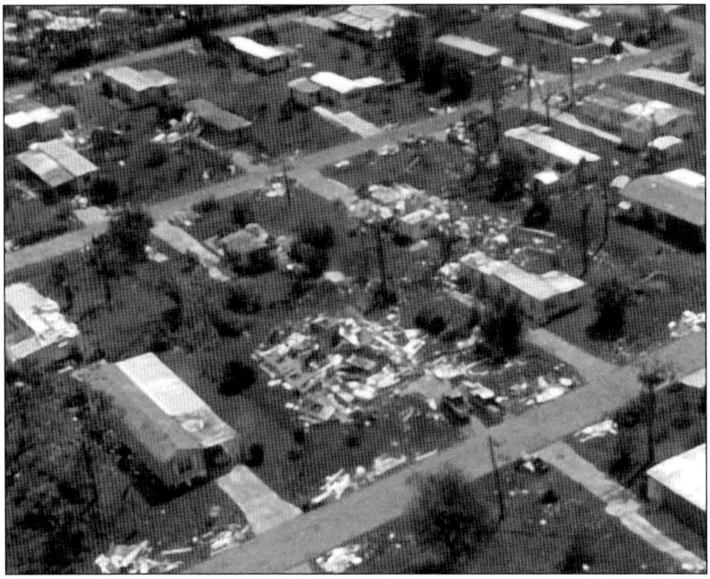

"Our worst fears have come true," said Florida governor Jeb Bush of the 2004 hurricane season. Four major hurricanes made landfall in Florida: Charley, Frances, Ivan, and Jeanne. Here Hurricane Charley exploded mobile homes in the Pink Citrus Park, located three miles south of Bokeelia. (Genev Koonce.)

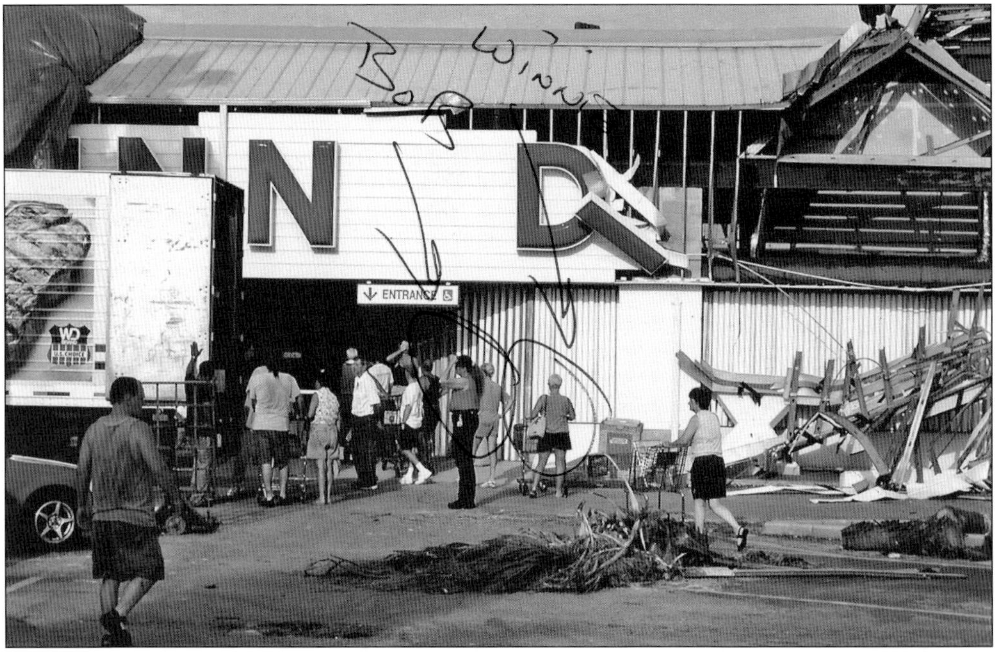

Pine Island's only grocery store, a Winn-Dixie, came to the rescue for island residents following Hurricane Charley. With much of the roof missing and no electricity, the store remained open. In addition, it brought in truckloads of free ice and water for those in need. Here residents line up in sweltering August temperatures for the much-needed supplies. (Deb Wedeking.)

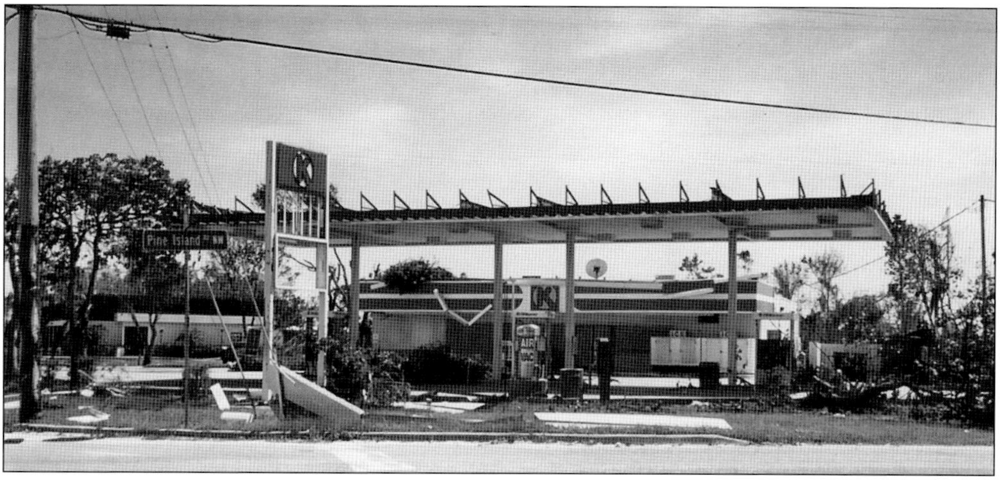

Located at the four-way stop, Pine Island's main gas station and mini mart, the Circle K, received extensive damage from Hurricane Charley. Residents had to rely on off-island fuel for several days following the storm. (Judy Baxley.)

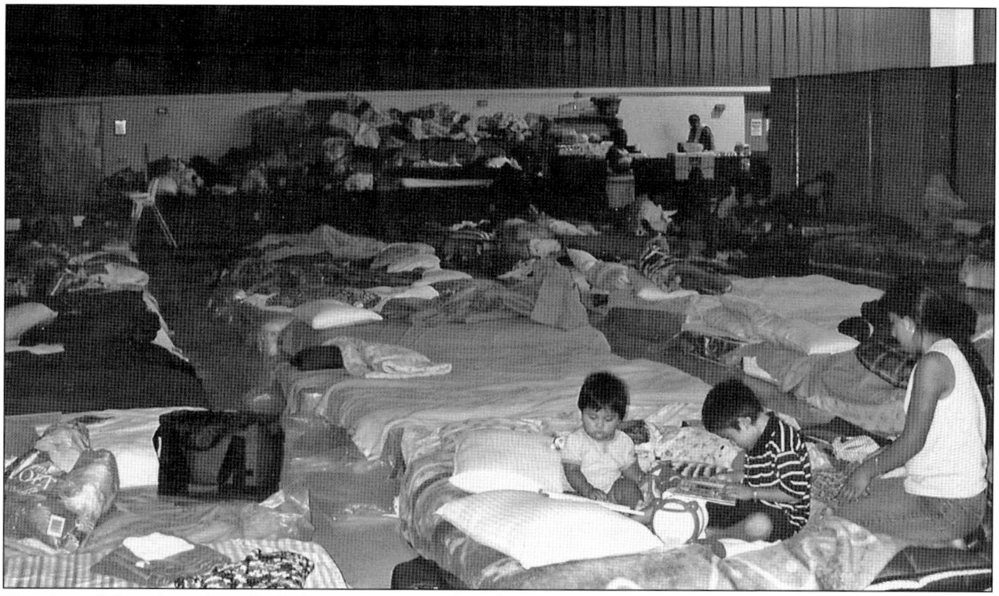

Displaced families found shelter at Our Lady of the Miraculous Medal Catholic Church in the aftermath of Hurricane Charley in 2004. Immediately following the storm, churches on the island offered their facilities to meet resident needs. In addition to the Catholic Church, singles and the elderly were cared for at St. John's Episcopal Church, the Federal Emergency Management Agency (FEMA) and service organizations set up at Fishers of Men Lutheran Church, and volunteers were centered at Pine Island United Methodist Church. (Courtesy of Deb Wedeking.)

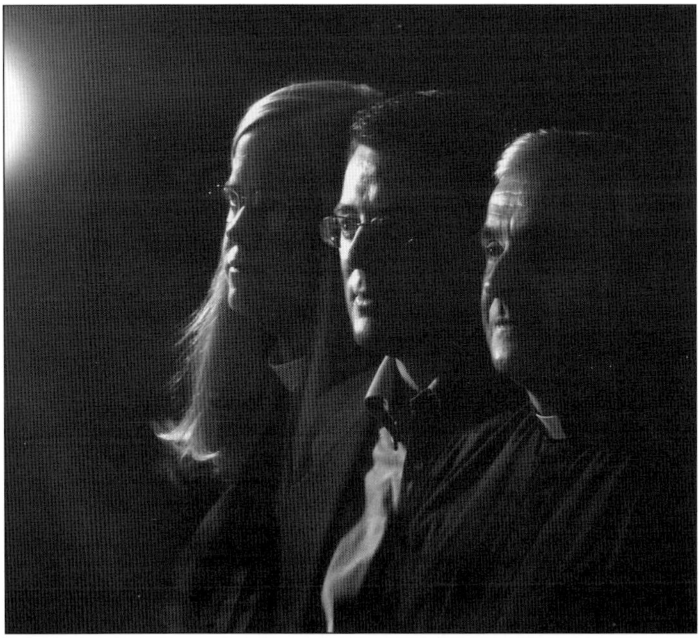

These island pastors united as a team dedicated to the recovery of storm-ravaged Pine Island following Hurricane Charley. Honored as the 2004 News-Press Persons of the Year they are (from left to right) Ann Mclemore (St. John's Episcopal Church), Scott Harris (Pine Island United Methodist Church), Thomas Pohto (Our Lady of the Miraculous Medal), and (not pictured) Roger Lemke (Fishers of Men Lutheran Church). (Ann Mclemore.)

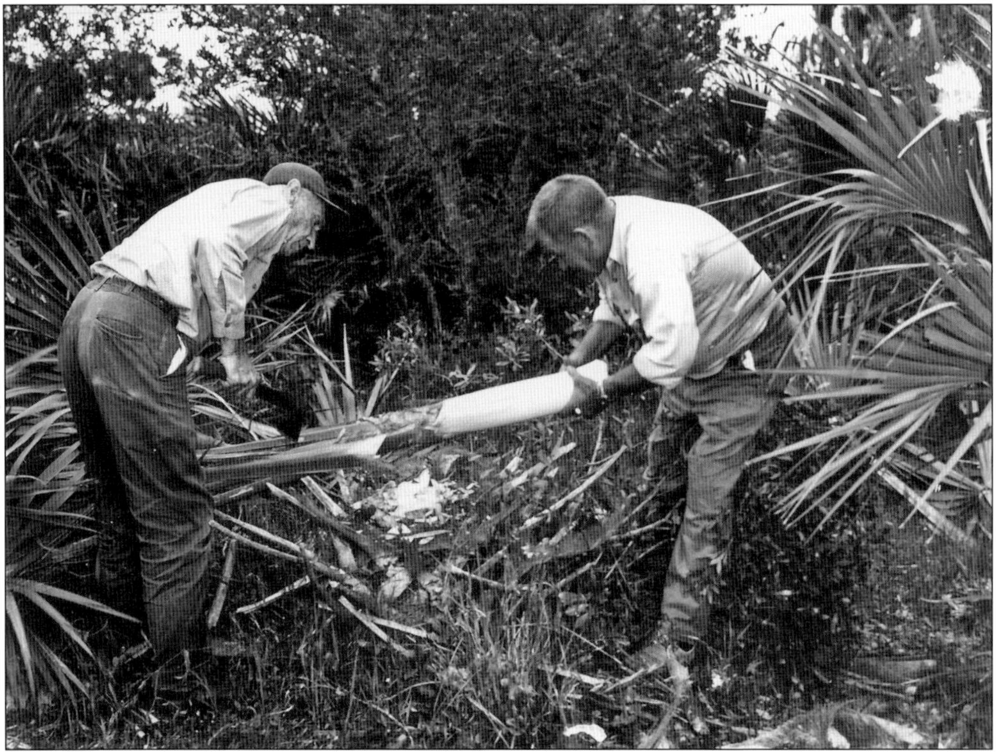

Native sabal palms provided the early settlers with what is now called Swamp Cabbage. Here two unidentified men have stripped the outer boots from the trunk and fronds from the head of a sabal (cabbage) palm. Peeling away the outer layers revealed the tender heart of the palm. Along with some fatback and onion, the diced heart of palm simmered for several hours before being served. (Florida State Archives.)

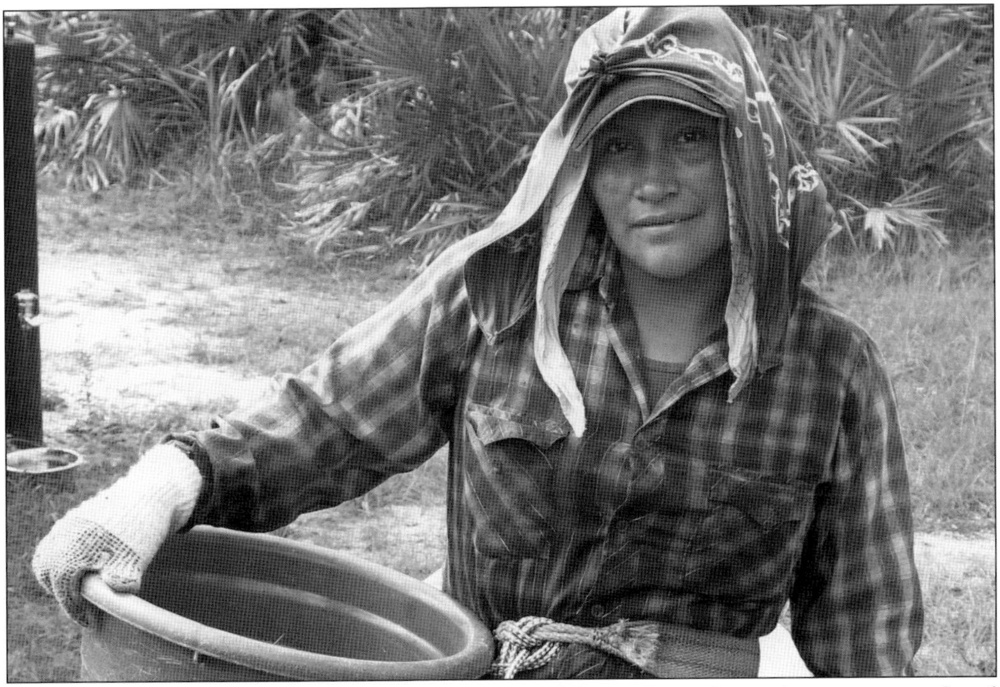

Collected during the rainy season months of August and September, palmetto berries are transferred from Pine Island to Immokalee, where the fruit brings under $1 per pound. Ground into powder, it is sold for a variety of folk remedies. Several hundred acres of previously native palmetto land has been cleared in recent years, making it difficult for the harvesters to continue the tradition. Here an unidentified berry picker takes a break during the harvesting. (Photograph by the author.)

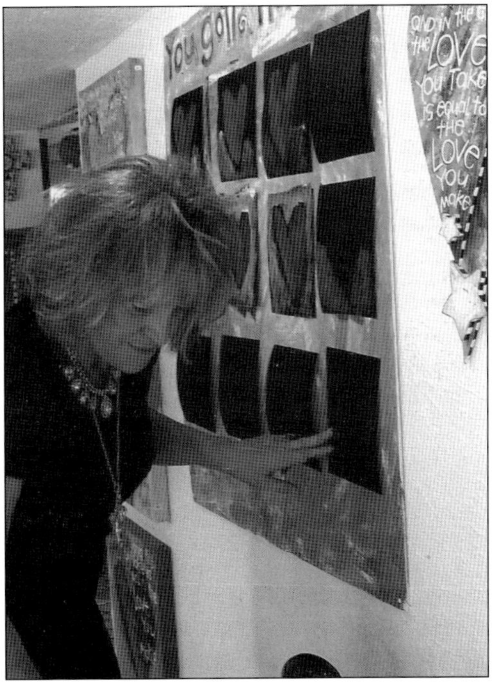

In recent years, Matlacha has become an artistic center, drawing both artists and collectors to the colorfully restored cottages and galleries. Leoma Lovegrove, an artist and the owner of the Lovegrove Gallery, has been instrumental in encouraging both tourism and art appreciation in the Pine Island area. Writers such as Robert Macomber of the Peter Wake maritime novel series and Randy Wayne White of the Doc Ford mystery series both make Pine Island home. Not only have the artists and writers made the island home, they have also become a part of the community, giving of themselves to many worthy causes. Here Leoma Lovegrove paints hearts for an American Heart Association benefit. (Photograph by the author.)

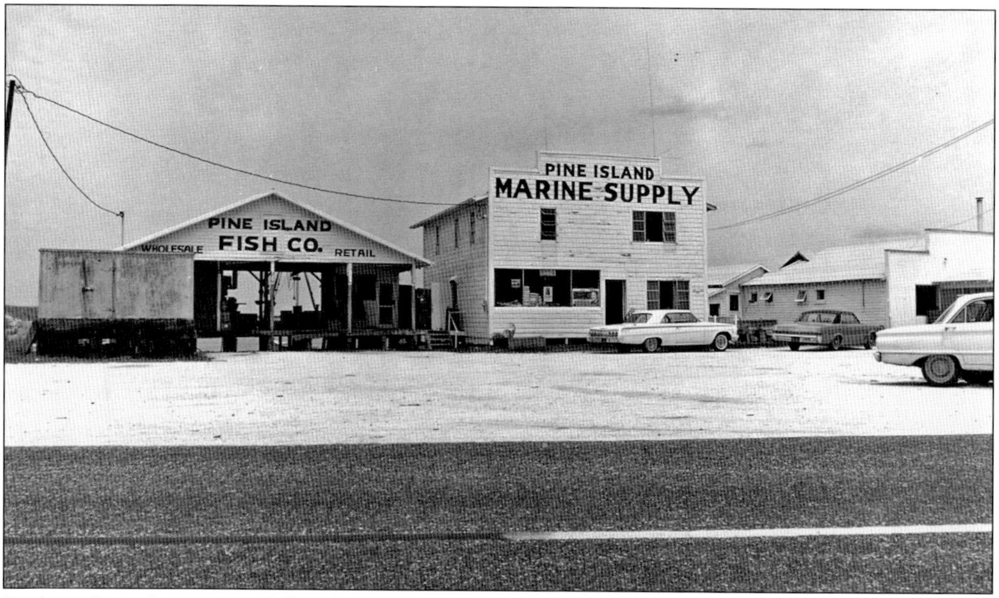

Built and run by Jesse Padilla, this icehouse and freezer provided commercial fishermen with a dock for unloading their catches and a convenient loading area for trucks hauling seafood off the island. Located next to Piner's Seafood and the Padilla family Marine Hardware, the icehouse/freezer marked an end to the stilt fish houses and runboats of earlier days. (Padilla Family.)

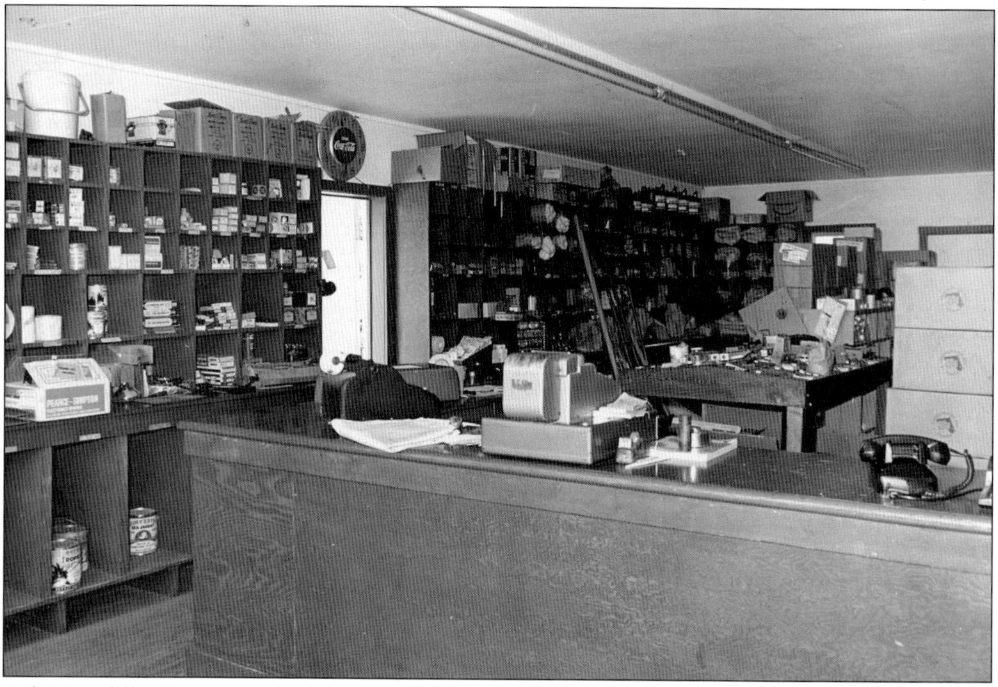

Velma Padilla ran the family-owned Marine Hardware in Matlacha in the 1940s. Located by their icehouse and Piner's Seafood, the marine supply store was the first business specializing in products needed by Pine Island residents. The Padilla and Piner families were the first Pine Islanders to get phone service; one family's phone number was 5000 and the other's was 5001. (Padilla Family.)

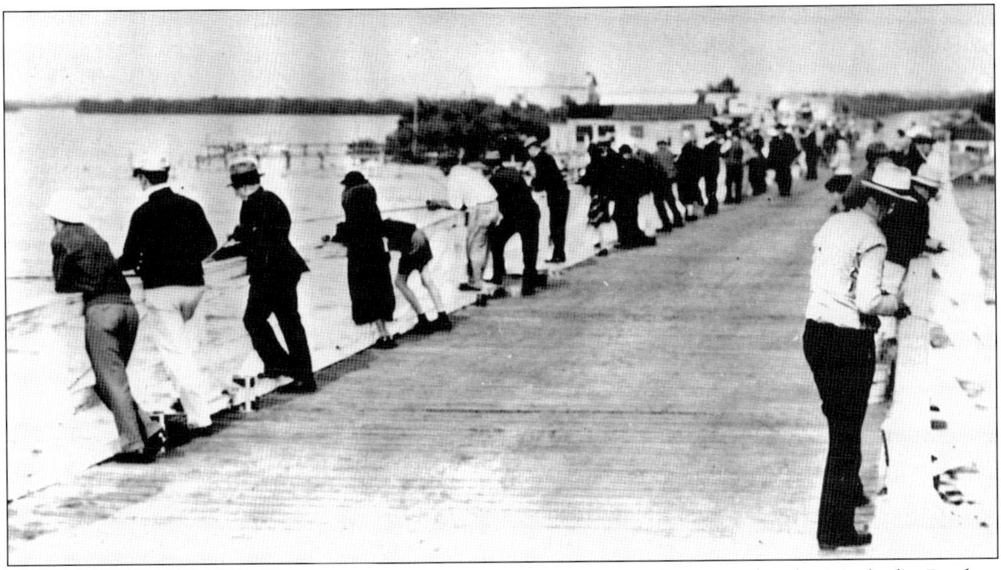

Fishermen soon discovered an abundance of snook around the pilings under the Matlacha Bridge. Georgiana Plewe said, "In winter, people would stand shoulder to shoulder to swirl poles off Pine Island Bridge to catch snook, using just leaders and plugs—no bait! And they would catch them by the bucketful!" Here in the 1940s, men and women wearing hats and fur-trimmed coats are giving it a try. (Georgiana Plewe.)

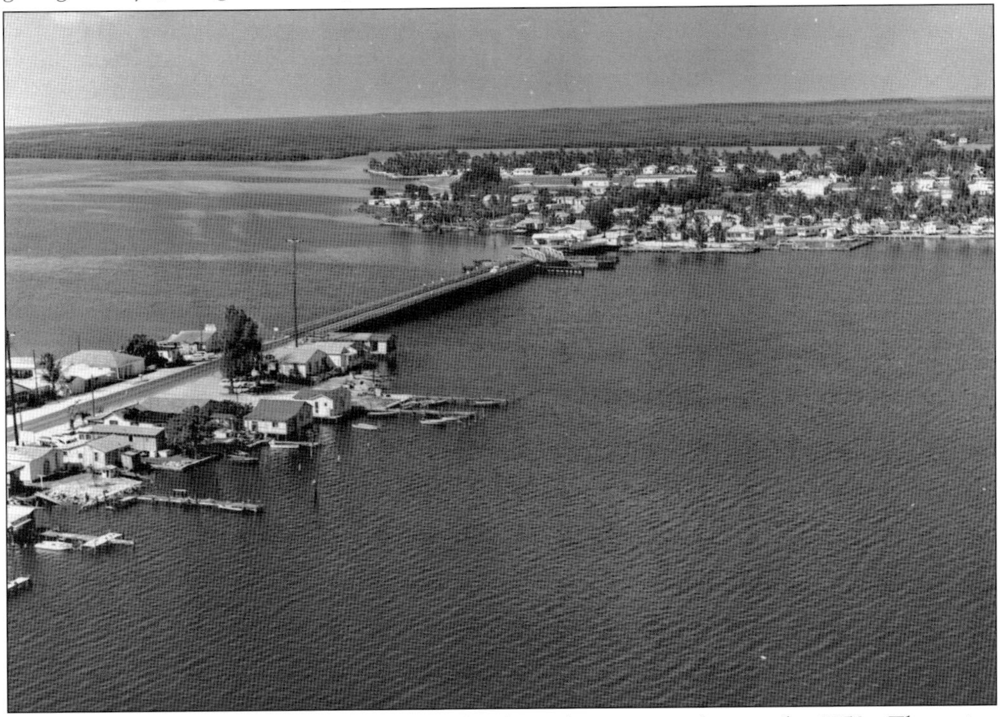

The Matlacha "swing bridge" can be seen clearly in this image, taken in the 1950s. The swing section is on the far side, with white sides at an angle, allowing for boat traffic to pass through. Due to increased traffic and aging timbers, this bridge was replaced with a concrete drawbridge in 1968. (Fort Myers Museum of History.)

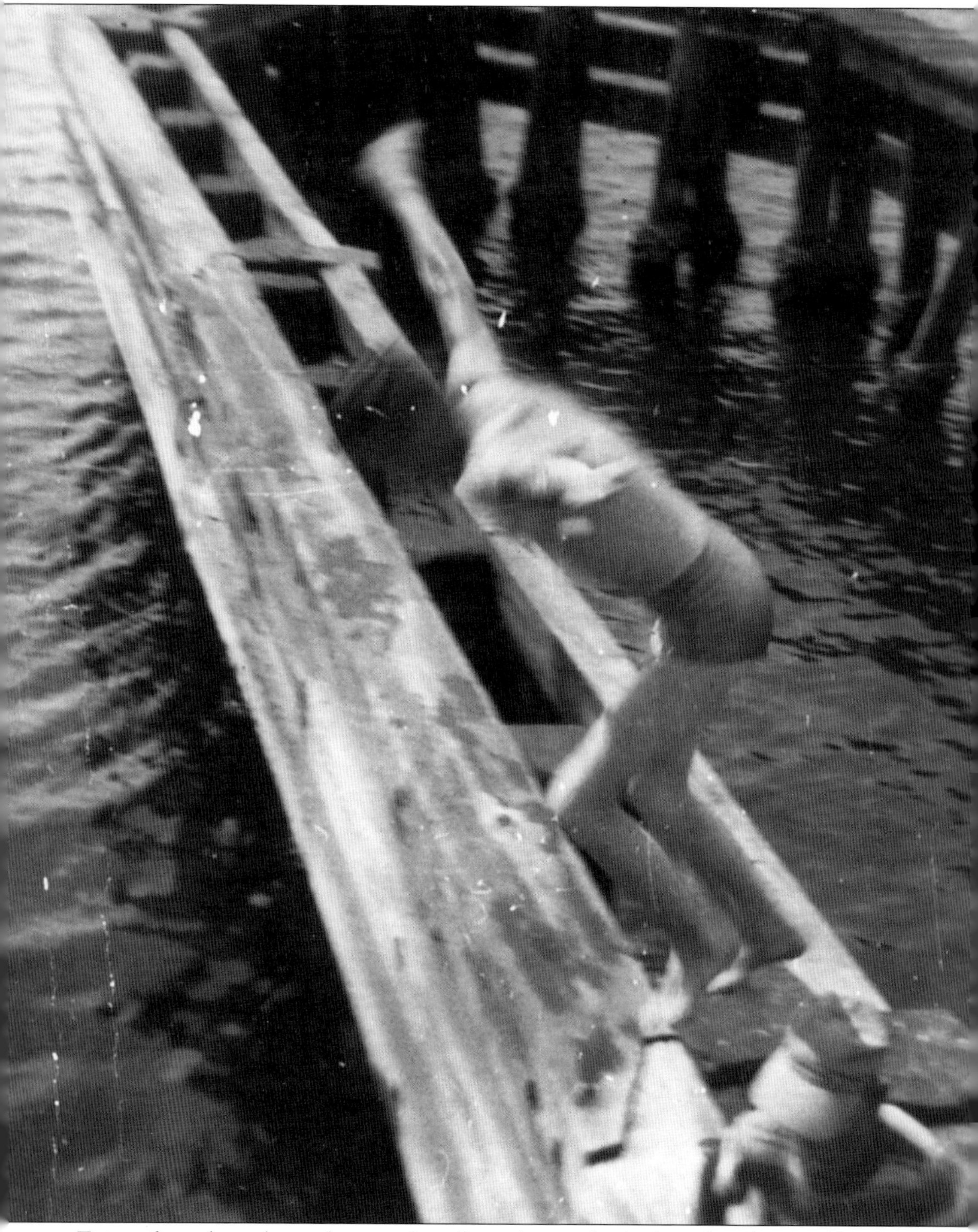

Tiring of mundane play, such as simply walking the wooden bridge side rails, Ronald Bragg of the Little West Virginia community off Pine Island Road, takes a dive from the Matlacha Bridge in the 1950s. Although several adult men still boast of diving off the bridge, women of the time deny having done so. (Padilla Family.)

Georgiana (left) and Gloria Plewe in a goat-drawn cart look like they are enjoying their childhood. Recalling another childhood memory, Georgiana said, "Every year at Christmas, Clyde Geary would put up a great big tree back in the empty lot off the highway and hand out gift bags for all of the community. The daughters, Velma and Jane, participated, and Velma eventually married Bruce Scott Jr., Lee County commissioner." (Georgiana Polk.)

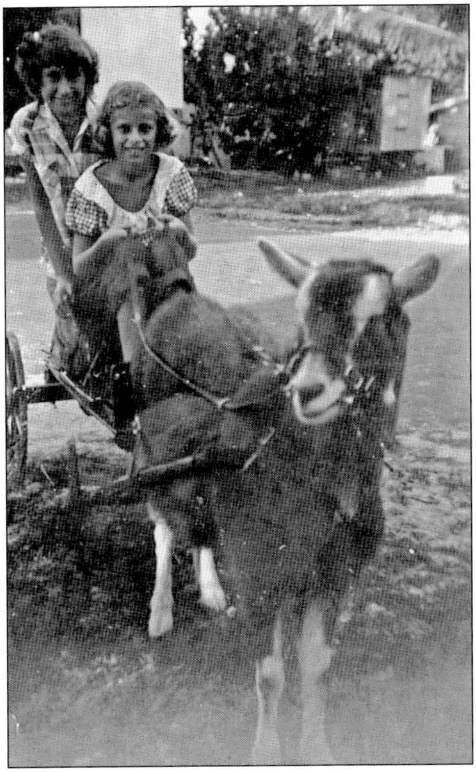

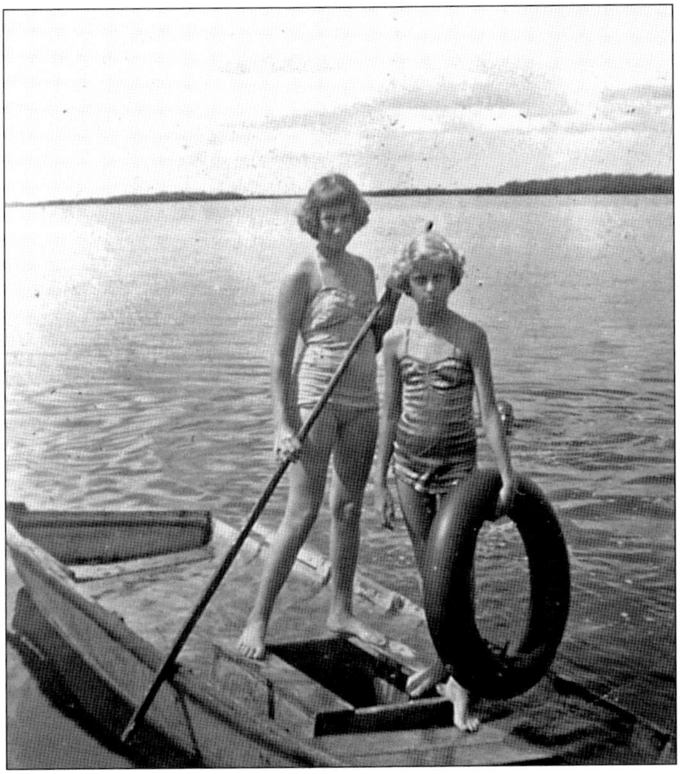

Georgiana Plewe, aged 12, and her sister Gloria, aged 10, found the water to be a cooling spot on a hot summer day in 1946. Georgiana said, "My daddy found the property in 1934 for $1. He cleared the property and built a small house on it. You didn't have contractors or permits back then. We had two doctors in town, and when us kids got a splinter or was cut on oyster shells, we went to see these two doctors for Band-Aids. They used a lot of mercuricone back then." (Georgiana Polk.)

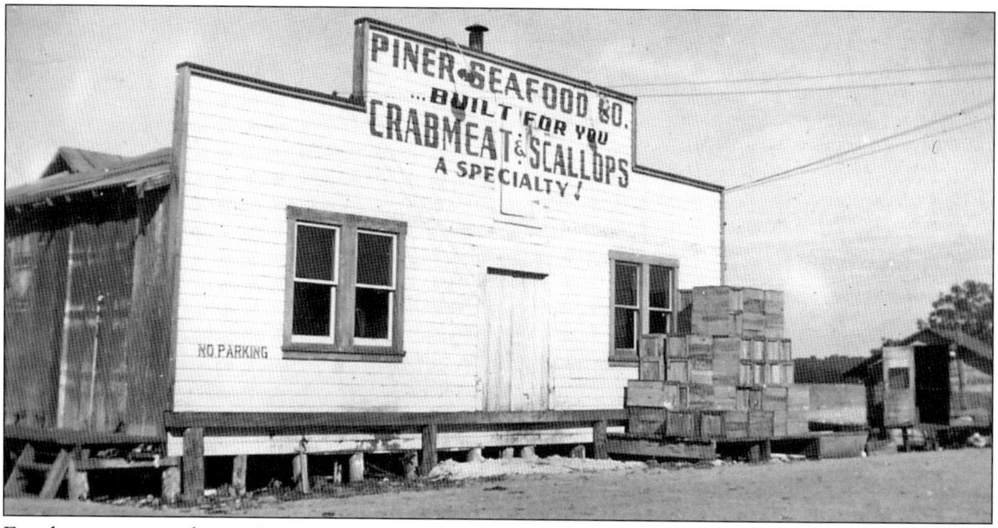

Employing more than 150 Pine Island and Fort Myers workers, Piner's Seafood Company was Pine Island's biggest business in the 1940s and 1950s. Crabbers sold their catches at the dock out back, and then the crabs were cooked and cleaned of their meat. When the company started purchasing and cleaning scallops, Louis Piner purchased 200 acres of mangrove land at the end of Maria Drive so he had a place to dump the shells. Huge scallop shell piles are still visible there during low tide. He dug a canal and a fish house there, and called it Piner's Point. Later it was sold to the Pine Island Fishermen's Co-op. Pictured here (above) is the front of Piner's Seafood Company in 1944. (Corella Stahl.)

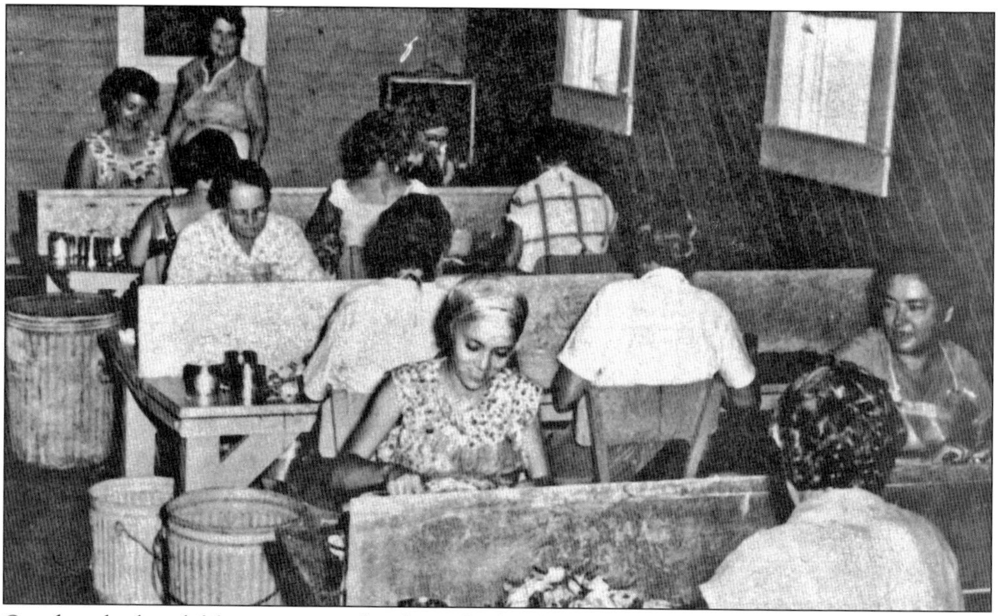

One hundred and fifty women and girls worked at long, stainless steel tables picking the meat off boiled crabs at Piner's Seafood Company. Working for pennies per hour, girls as young as 11 had their time logs added to an adult's time log, in order to avoid problems with the authorities. According to Virginia Padilla Morton, the young girl pictured above, "Even worse than the memories of raw, cut fingers are the squeals and cries of crabs as they hit the boiling water in the mammoth kettles." (Museum of the Islands.)

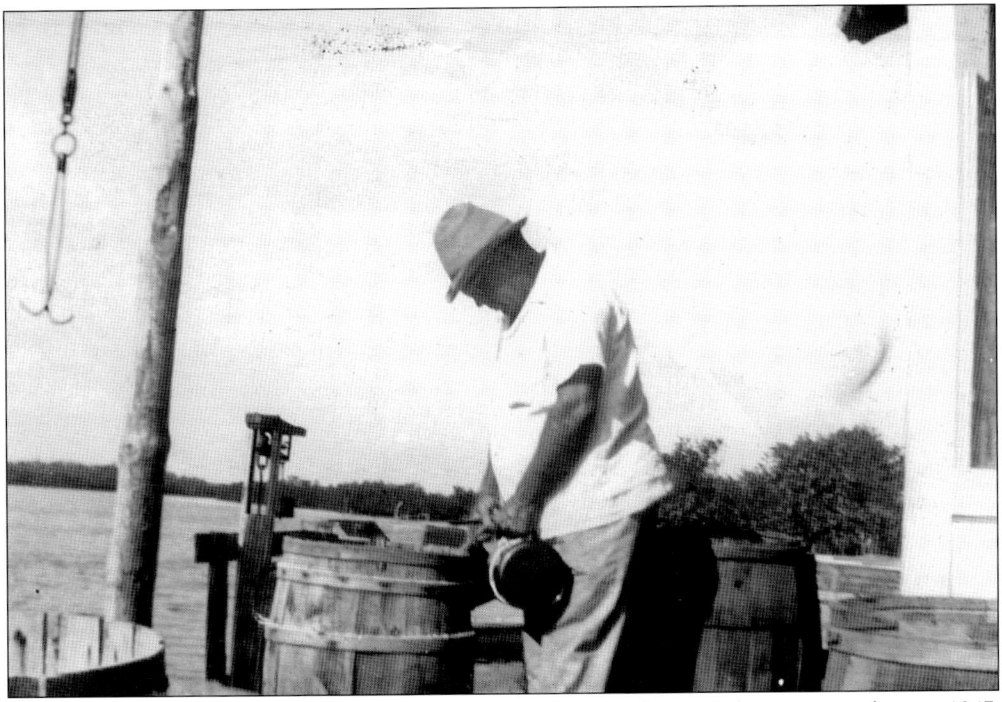

Owner of Piner's Seafood Company, Lewis Piner baits crab lines in this image, taken in 1947. Rather than use crab traps, Piner would use a technique much like trout lines, where he would attach bait at intervals along a rope line. The crabs would grab the bait, and the crabber would simply pull in the rope with the crabs hanging on. (Corella Stahl.)

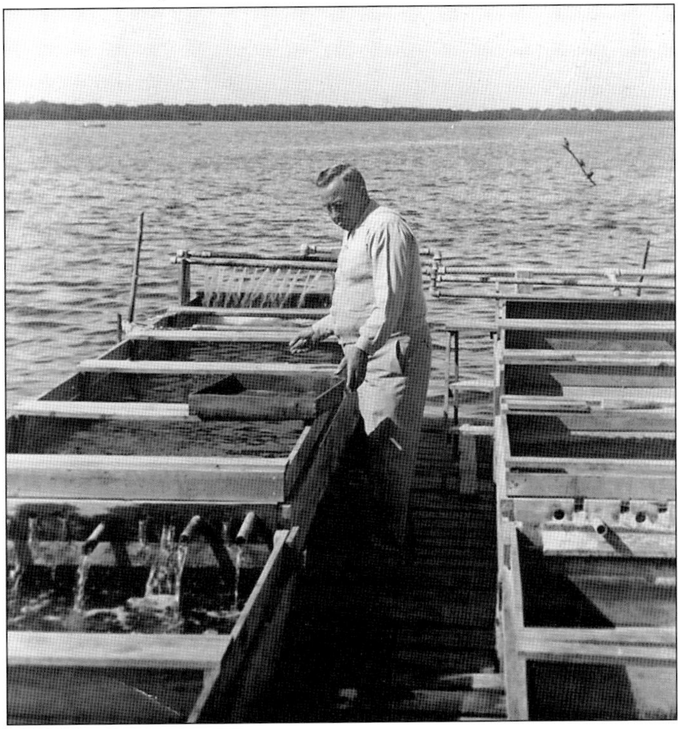

Awaiting the exact moment of molting, Lewis Piner inspects his soft-shell crab tanks in 1954. Daughter Corella recalled, "Daddy predicted the Sanibel Bridge would destroy the seafood industry. Before the causeway [in 1962], we would process an average of 3,000 pounds of crab and 500 bushels of scallops per day, running 24 hours. In 1963, after the dredging, the crabs and scallops were almost gone, and they never came back." (Corella Stahl.)

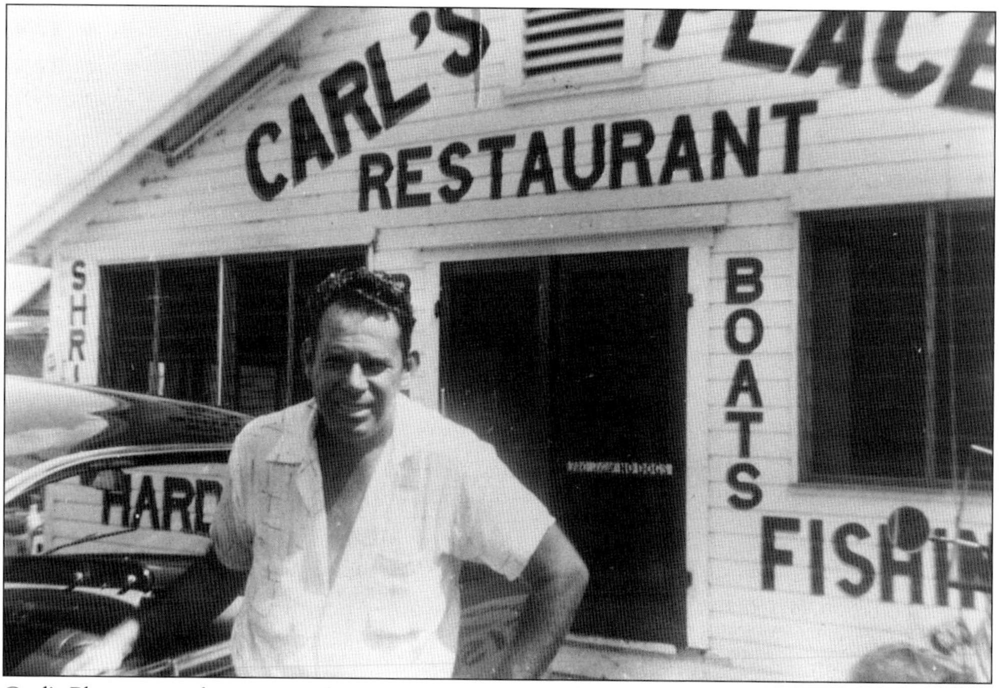

Carl's Place was a favorite Matlacha hangout in the 1940s. Offering good food and a jukebox filled with the latest songs, Carl's Place was the place to be. Virginia Padilla said, "Oh, there were about seven of us [teens] that Carl would let come in and dance to all the Hank Williams's songs on the jukebox." Pictured here is Ernie Skillahan, who lived next door to Carl's Place. (Padilla Family.)

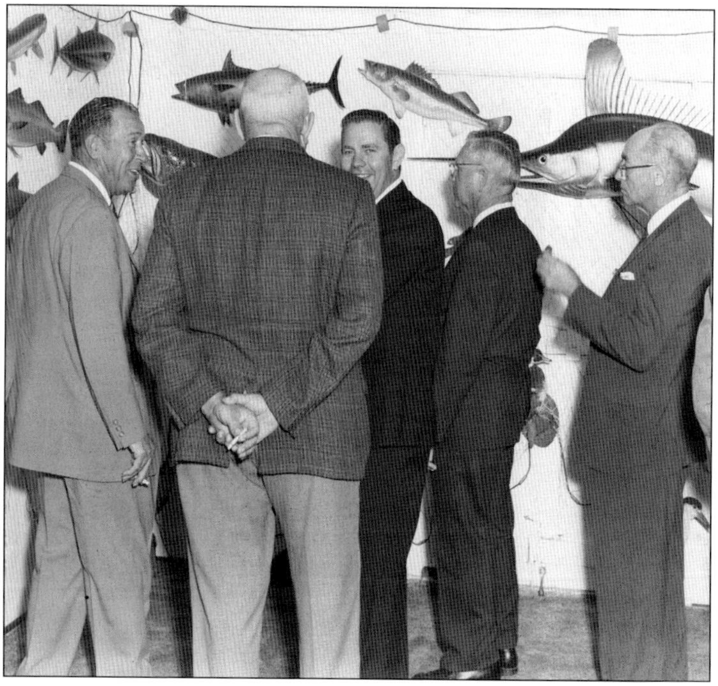

Three island businessmen built what is now the Matlacha Oyster House and opened the Fishing Hall of Fame in the 1930s. Here they displayed taxidermy fish. Bruce Scott Sr. (facing front), along with Jesse Padilla and Clyde Geary, opened it as a social place for the local residents, but they also anticipated it would bring other fishermen to the area. The taxidermy fish hanging on the Oyster House walls today are original fish from the 1930s. (Museum of the Islands.)

Velma Padilla recalls the arrival of Susie, the baby pictured here. "We had a flat tire on Pine Island Road when it was just a dirt lane of a road. The men folk went to fix the tire, and my mother-in-law and I started walking. We walked a good long ways, and nobody passed us. Finally, a car came up, and this gentleman was in it, and he asked us if we'd like to have ride. He carried us right up to the door, and I had Susie the next morning." Here Velma, with daughters Virginia and Susie, are pictured in 1940. (Padilla Family.)

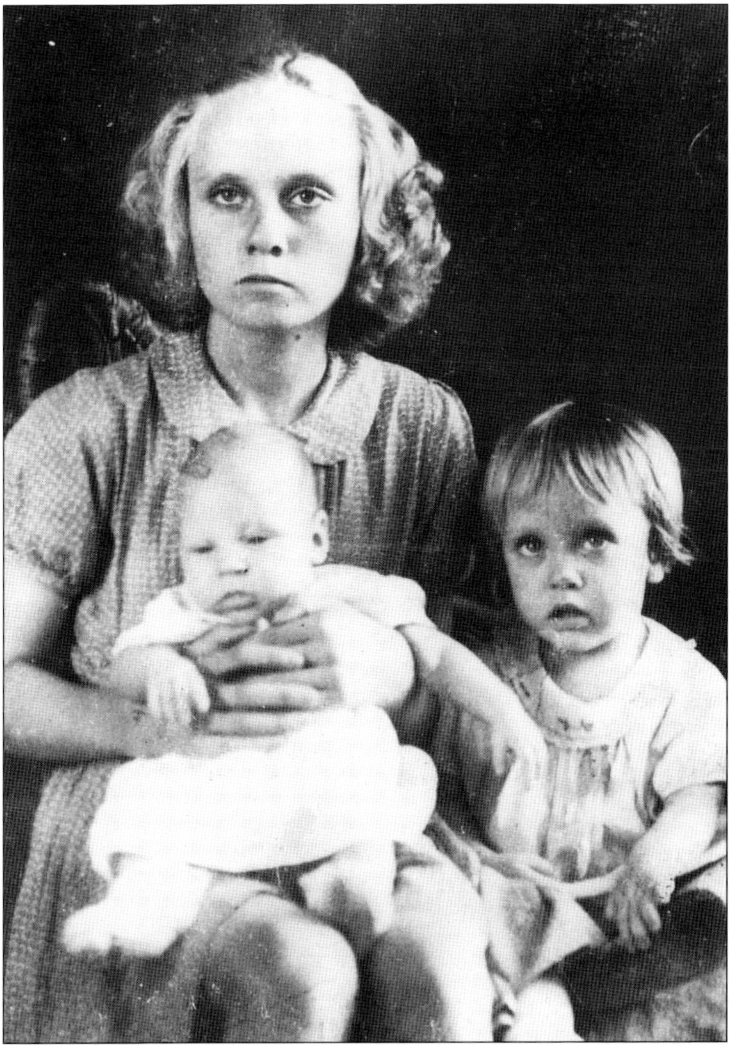

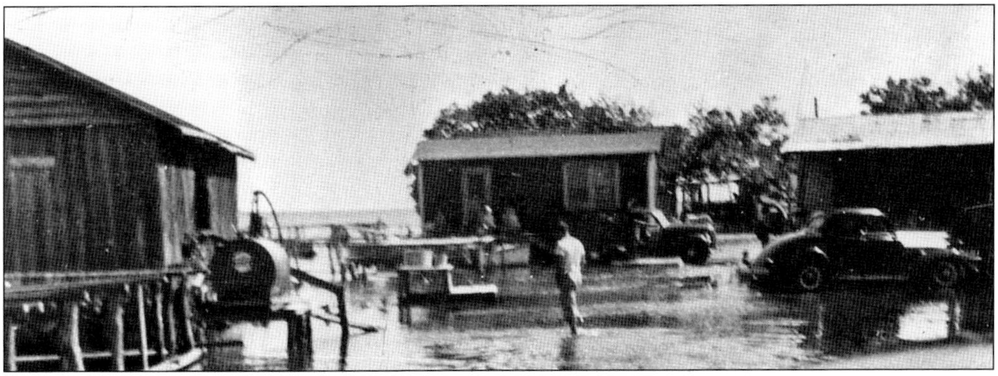

Located on the south side of Pine Island Road in Matlacha, across from the Marine Hardware and fish house, was the Jesse Padilla home. Family members occupied several cottages between the highway and the water of Pine Island Sound. At high tide, the water would come up in the "yard," as pictured here in the 1940s. (Padilla Family.)

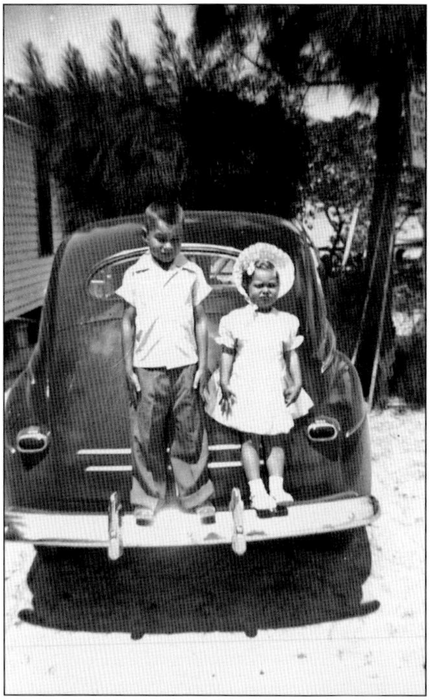

All five-year-old Sharon Morton talked about was how excited she was about starting school. Yet, before the school year began, she died of leukemia, a relatively unknown disease in the early 1950s. Pictured here with brother Joey, Sharon was loved and doted upon by the community of Matlacha; one citizen gave her a pony, in hopes it would ease the pain associated with her impending death. (Virginia Morton.)

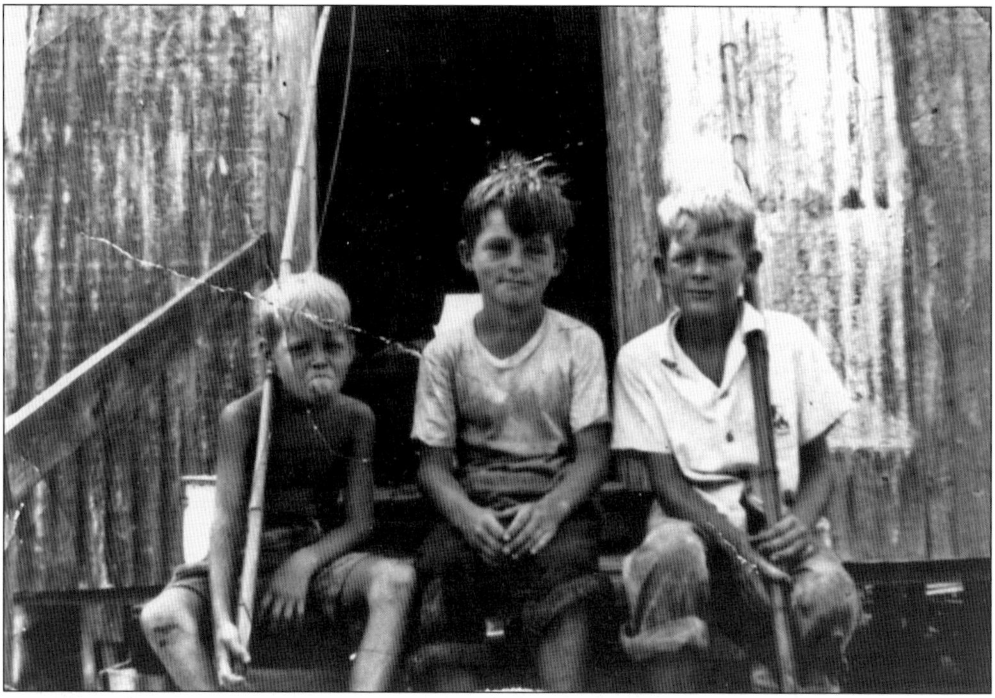

Georgiana Plewe said, "Playtime was being gone all day, building tree houses, walking the old wooden bridge railing, and making hopscotch drawings on the road, as there were so few cars. Riding bikes with Timmy Wade, we sold the *Grit* paper." Virginia Padilla tells of visiting the "Swamp Angel," a woman who loved children, but lived alone in a mangrove tree house. Here three unidentified boys anticipate fishing with their cane poles. (Padilla Family.)

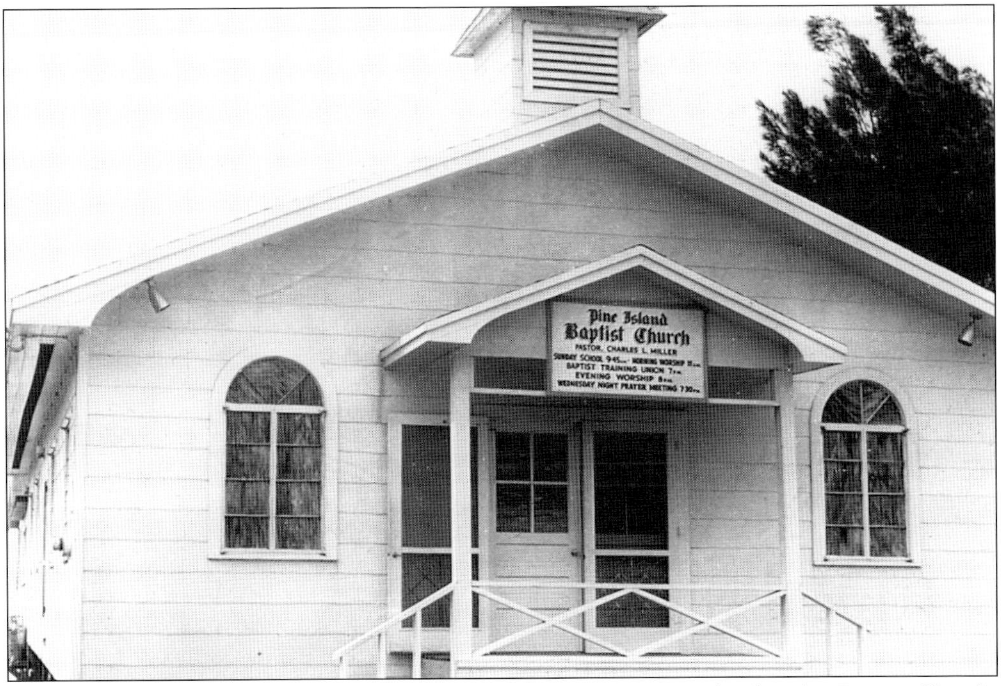

Built in the 1930s on the "fill," Matlacha's first church was the Pine Island Bridge Baptist Church. Windows above the platform area provided views of Matlacha Sound to the congregation. Many confess it was difficult to concentrate on the message when net fisherfolk drifted within their view. Another distraction came from the whistling of the wind between the wallboards. (Susie Robinson.)

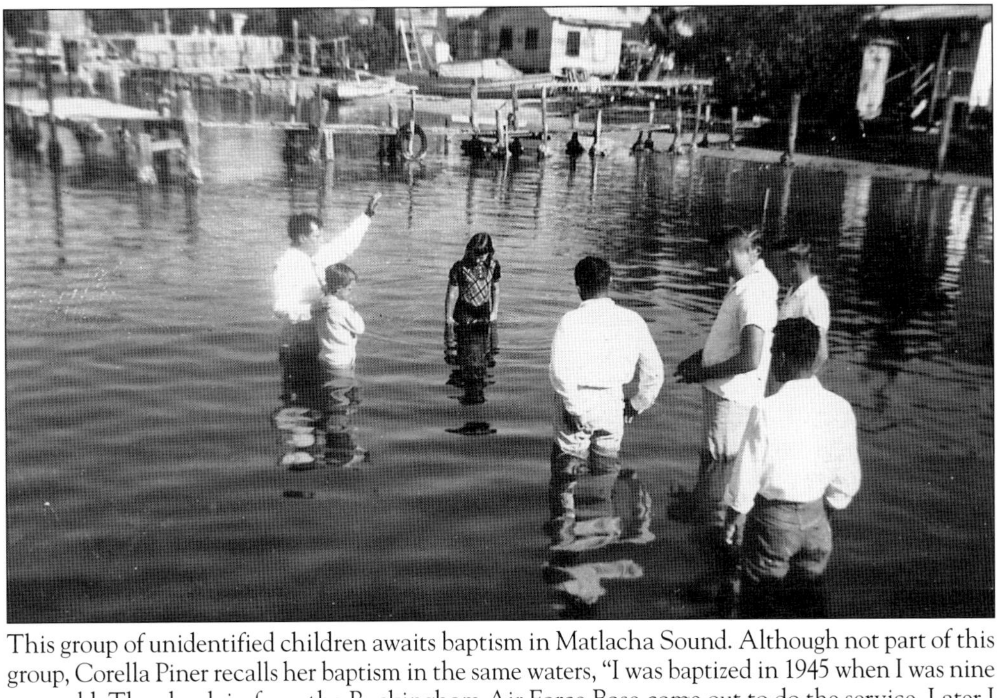
This group of unidentified children awaits baptism in Matlacha Sound. Although not part of this group, Corella Piner recalls her baptism in the same waters, "I was baptized in 1945 when I was nine years old. The chaplain from the Buckingham Air Force Base came out to do the service. Later I was the church pianist, and I was the only one with the key to the church." (Virginia Morton.)

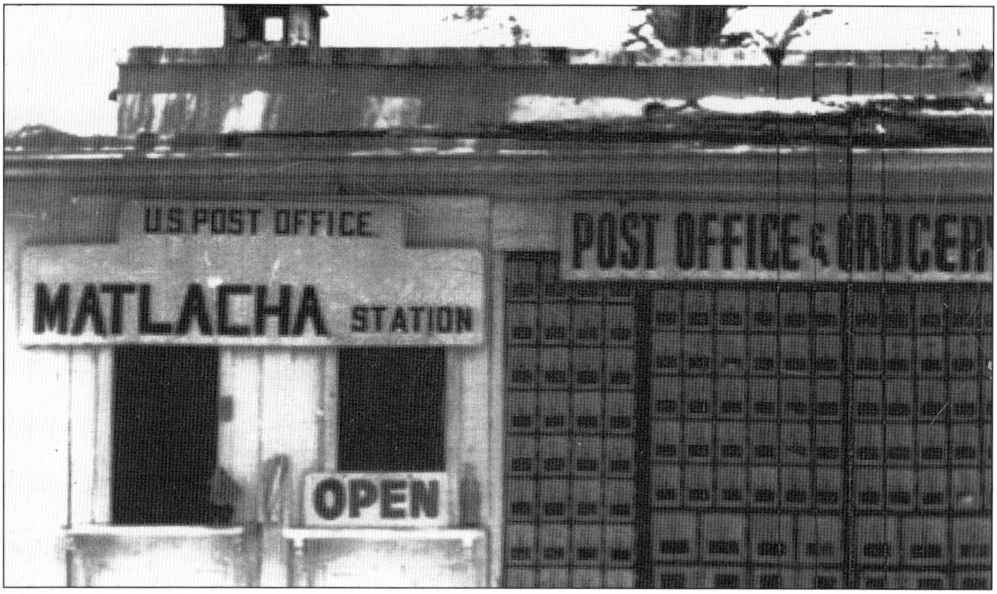

The mailboxes of the Matlacha Post Office were on the outside wall, as pictured here in 1956. All mail had the same address, at least through the 1960s: Star Route C, Fort Myers, Florida. When zip codes were assigned, the 33901 Fort Myers number was also given to Pine Island. A Mr. Dorcus, the postmaster, also provided transportation to Matlacha residents when he made the mail runs to town. (Susie Robinson.)

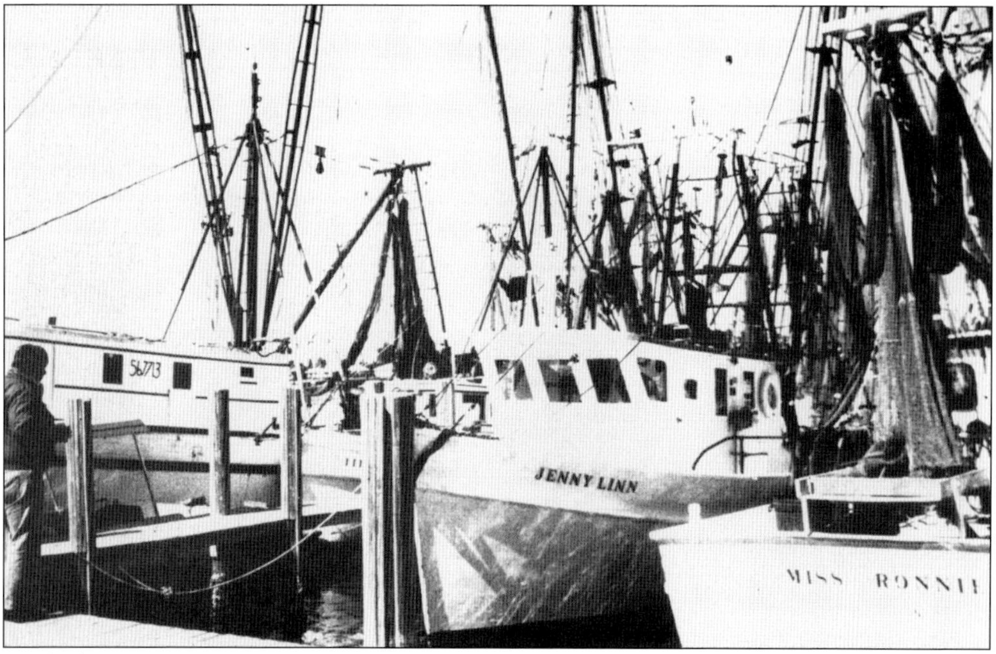

Docked in Matlacha since the 1950s, the picturesque shrimp boats have become one of Matlacha's major industries. Usually going out at night, the shrimpers gather bait and "eating" shrimp into their nets, and return by morning. Bait shrimp are sold to the various marinas and bait shops, while the eating shrimp go to restaurants and seafood shops, or are sold to individuals right off the boat. (Museum of the Islands.)

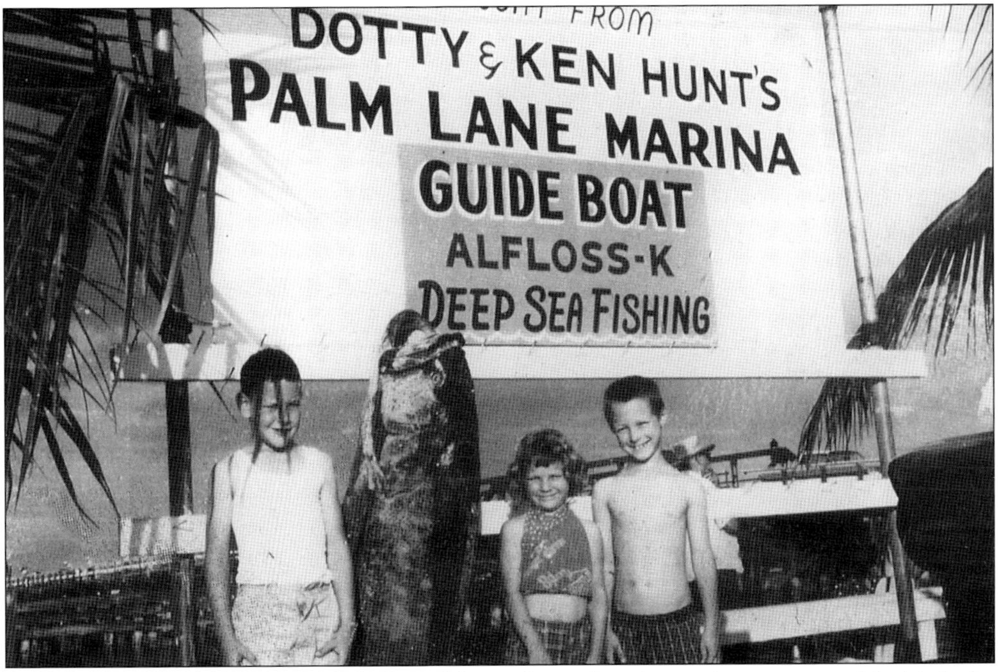

Standing in front of their parent's Palm Lane Marina, located on the northwest corner of the Matlacha Bridge, are Kevin and Susan Hunt with friend, Rocky Lamp. The Goliath fish weighed in at 120 pounds and was caught on Avery's Albatross on February 25, 1962. Dobby's Bait and Tackle is now located where this picture was taken. The "Fishingest Bridge in the World" is in the background. (Susan Laffitte.)

From a 1960 brochure that reads, "Pine Island offers you a Treasure of Pleasure in Florida's Newest Frontier," this map shows Pine Island and its surroundings. The brochure went on to say, "Imagine the pleasures of a wonderful vacation or permanent residence in this Pine Island Paradise. The modest cost will amaze you!" Ironically, the city of Cape Coral is located to the east and is not labeled. (Susan Laffitte.)

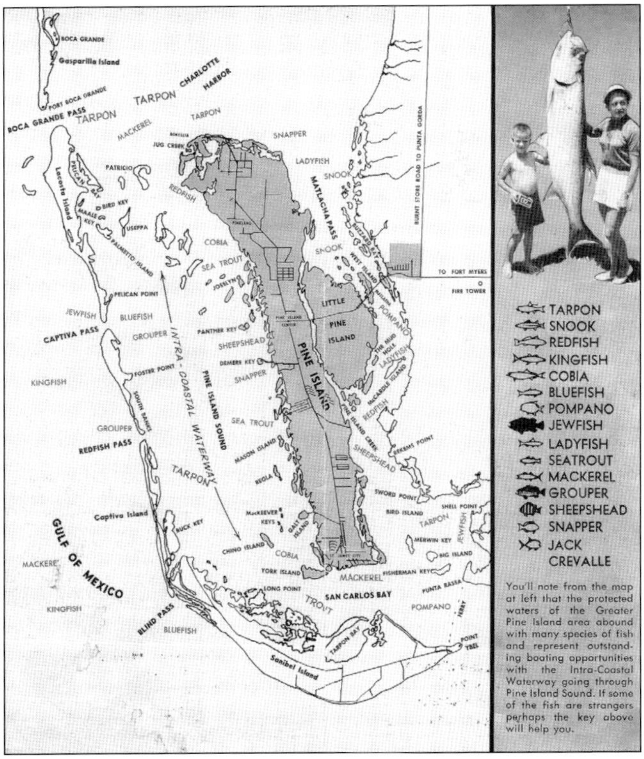

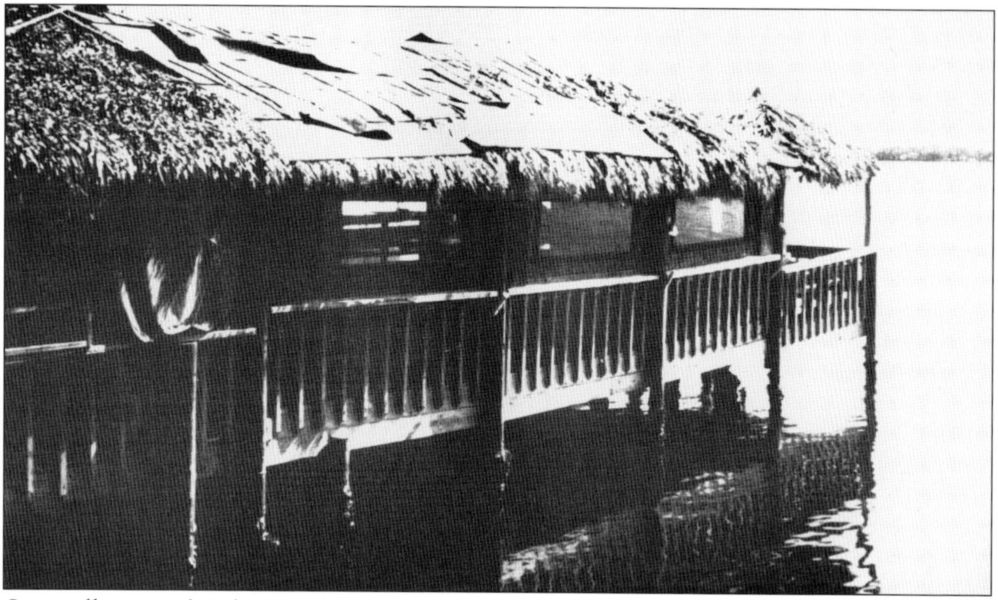

Originally just a frond-covered pier with a bar on it, the Bridgewater Inn shows roof damage following a storm in the 1960s. The bar, it is told, had many a brawl spilling out into the road. Children of the area would line up on the Matlacha Bridge rails to watch the chaos unfold. Located nearby, what is now Bert's Bar was the Sweet Shop where residents could purchase not only candy, but the best grilled hamburger west of Fort Myers. (Museum of the Islands.)

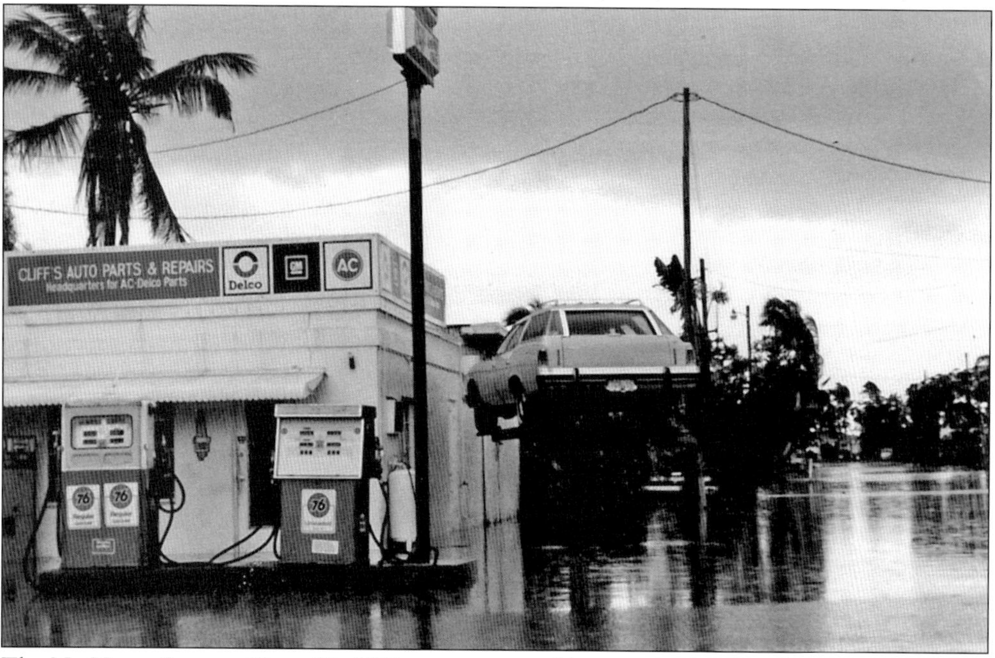

The No Name Storm of June 18, 1982, was so named because it developed so quickly weather forecasters did not have time to give the tropical-strength storm a name before its Southwest Florida landfall. Cliff Simer Jr, of Cliff's Auto Parts and Repairs (pictured here), recalls, "The water got so high I remember swimming in it on Pine Island Road and seeing mullet swimming inside our shop." (Museum of the Islands.)

Four

FISHERFOLK

Neither sore hands nor no-seeums could deter his love for the water.

—*Fort Myers News-Press*, Sam Cook

Following the path of the Calusa Indian culture, Pine Island fisherfolk sought their livelihood from the sea. As early as 1765, Cuban fisherfolk had set up fishing ranchos in the Charlotte Harbor area. Their fishing gear relied on nets and the supplies needed for salting or smoking the fish. Traveling regularly to Cuba, they traded fish, as well as fruits, vegetables, and hides. It was not until after the English rule of Florida from 1763 to 1783 that the fishing ranchos became established year-round communities. Beginning in 1814, the fisherfolk faced a series of wars, both directly and indirectly affecting their livelihood. The Spanish-American War, Second Seminole War, and the Civil War interrupted the fishing culture of Southwest Florida. Yet after the Civil War, the fishing ranchos were reestablished, and by 1879, there were four fishing villages operating in Charlotte Harbor.

A descendant of one well-known fisherfolk family, Frank Padilla Sr. wrote of living off the sea and land in a fish rancho as a child in the late 1800s. In addition to fish, he said, "We never ran out of food . . .there were five of us kids, and we waded around the island looking for clams, oysters, or whatever we thought we could eat. We found a hermit crab one day and found they were good to eat. We would build a fire and boil them in a can and eat the delicious tender meat. We also dug for gophers, and mama would roast them. They tasted like beef."

In the 1970s and 1980s, commercial fishermen were sometimes accused of fishing for a new species of fish found in local waters called "square grouper." Drug enforcement agents patrolled the waters looking for fishermen picking up floating square-shaped bails of marijuana that were dropped off of drug-runner boats under the cover of night.

Until the 1995 net ban implementation, commercial fishing remained an integral part in the local economy. Four fish houses—Bokeelia, Matlacha, Pineland, and St. James City—were all kept busy as the fisherfolk lifestyle was passed from generation to generation. Today few can afford to live as commercial fishermen. Some have turned to clam farms, crab traps, or the role of charter captain for livelihood from the sea. It remains unclear how much longer they can count on the bounty of Pine Island's waters for their sustenance. In the meantime, the fisherfolk's traditional way of life is quickly disappearing.

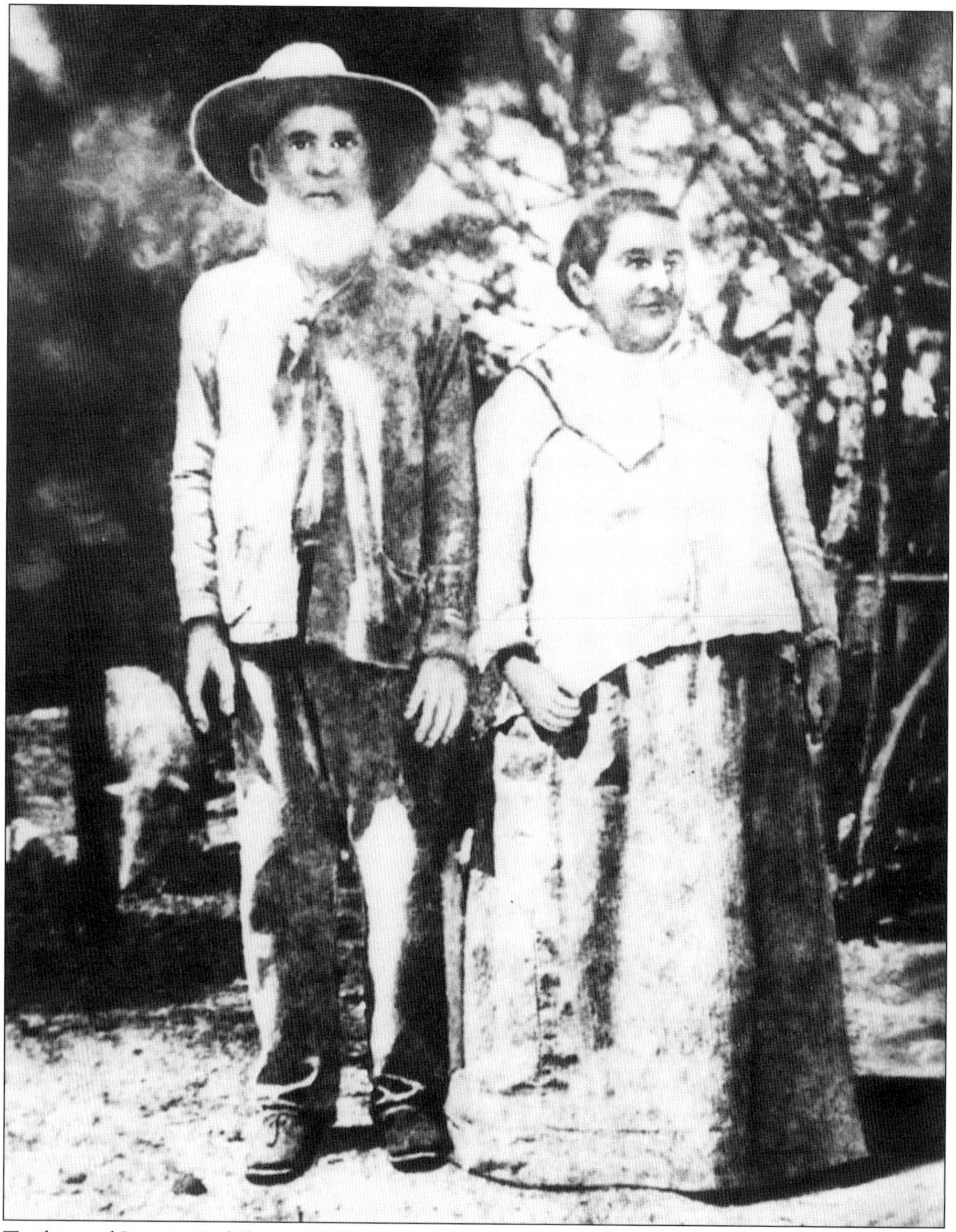

Toribio and Juanita Padilla established the first fish ranch in the area in the 1870s. At the ranch, Toribio Padilla's family caught and processed fish, which they shipped to Cuba. At the outbreak of the Spanish-American War, his fleet was burned and scuttled. He replaced the boats and returned to fishing, selling his catches to Cuban importers, known as Cuban smacks. (Padilla Family.)

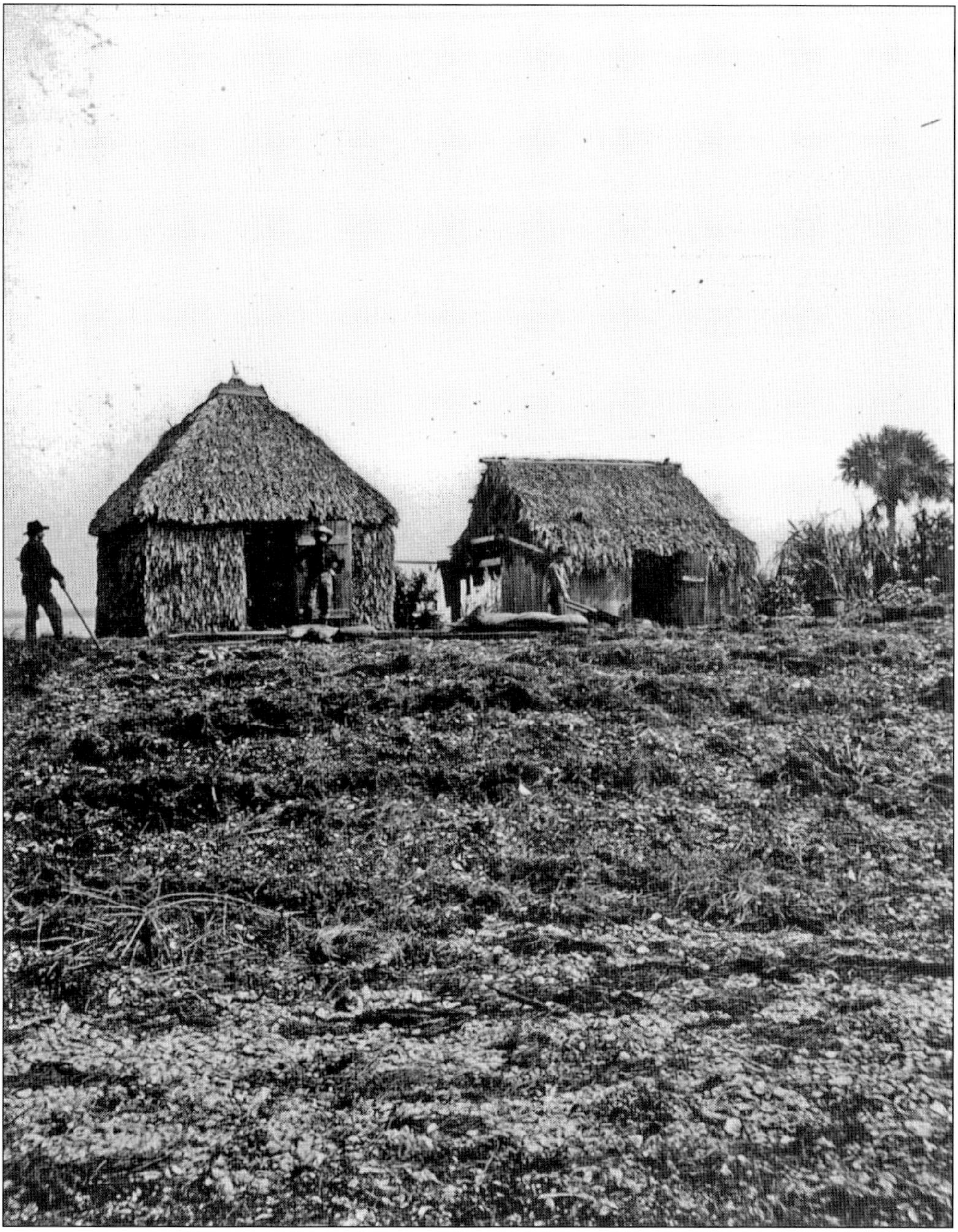

Constructed of a frame covered with palm fronds, this early fisherfolk cabin is typical of the homes found on fishing rancheros. Born in 1924, Frank Padilla Jr. said, "Dad finished our house, and we moved out of our cabbage-fan hut. We children took [the hut] over as a playhouse. We would climb up the middle pole and get on the cabbage-fan roof and slide down." (Florida State Archives.)

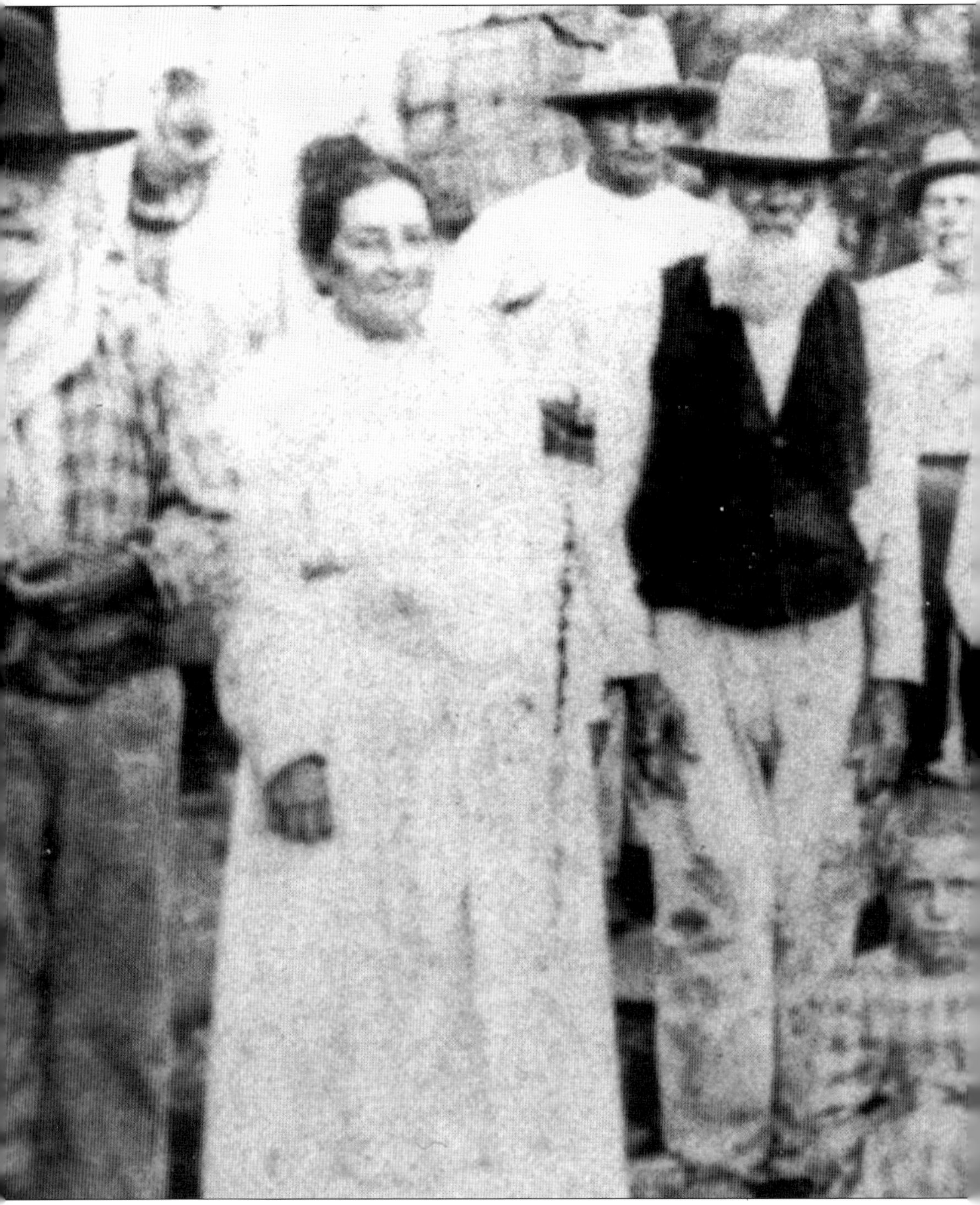

One of Pine Island Sound's most tenacious commercial fishing families, the Toribio Padilla family is shown in this 1901 photograph. Pictured center, with a beard, white hat, and dark vest, is "Captain Pappy" Toribio Padilla (head ranchero). Left of Padilla is his wife, "Juanita" Laini Padilla. Coming from the Canary Islands by way of Cuba, Padilla founded the Cayo Costa Fishery in the 1870s. Life for Padilla and his family was hard as they lived by nature's cycles of weather,

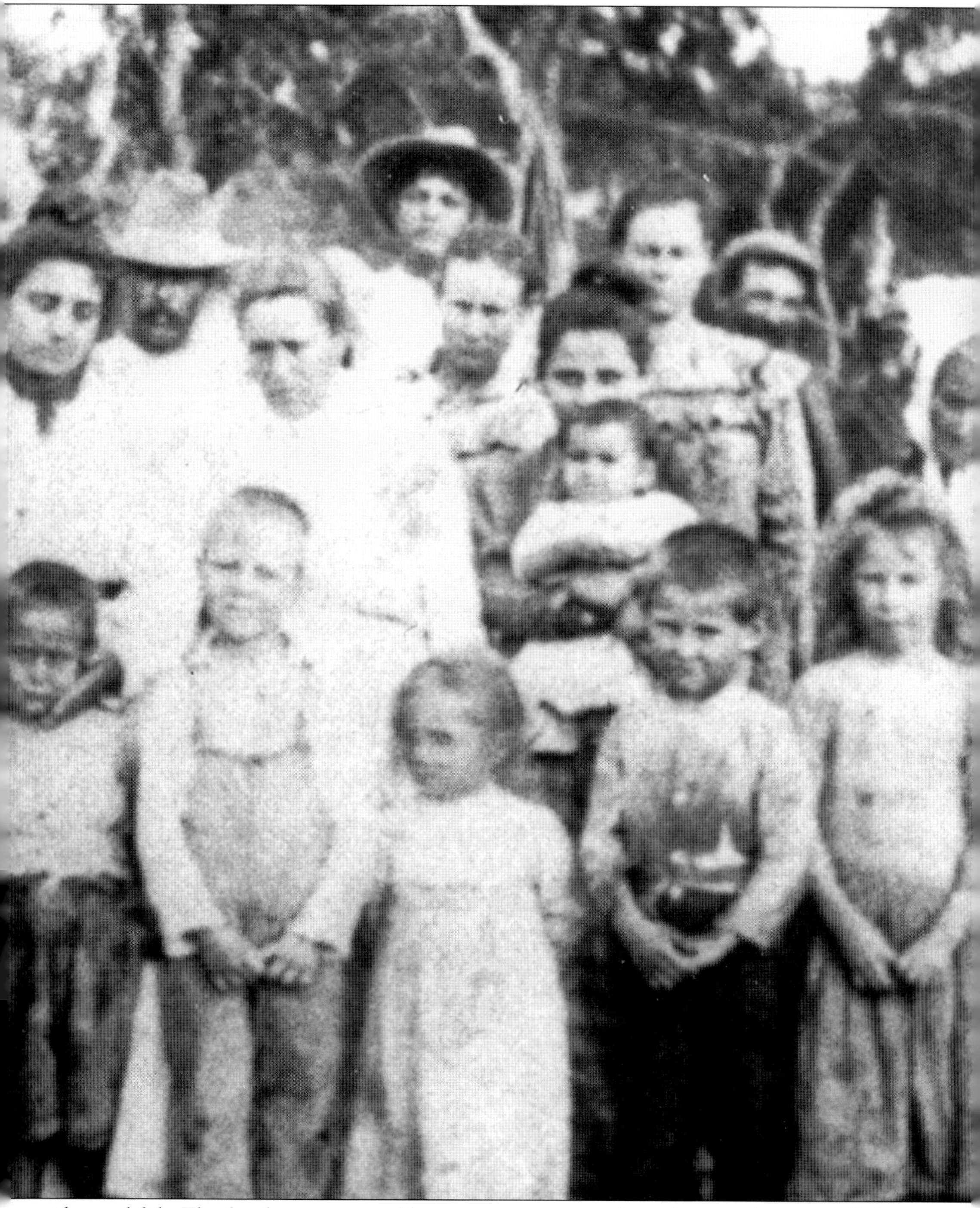

tides, and fish. The family was removed by government agents from their ranchero in 1901 for smuggling aguardiente (rum) from Cuba. A few years later, Padilla returned to the island, while other family members relocated on Pine Island and its environs. Frank Padilla Sr. is the blond boy in the front row wearing overalls and a white shirt. (Padilla Family.)

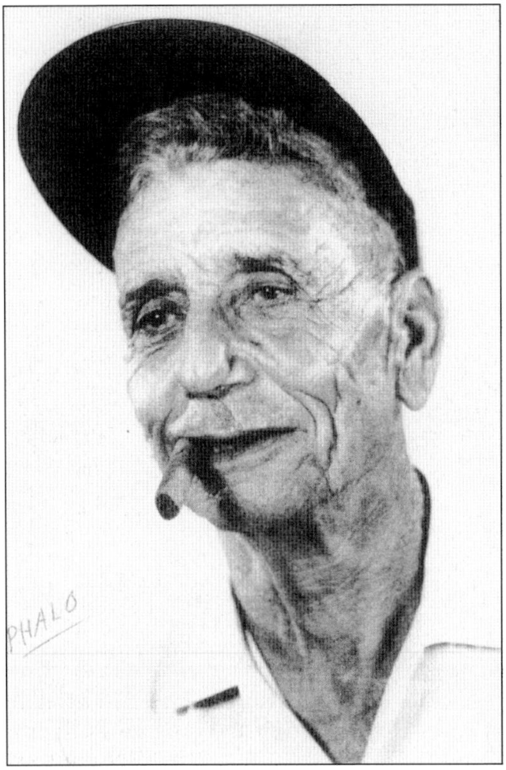

Phalo Padilla, son of Toribio and Juanita Padilla, was part of a long family tradition of fishing and trading in the Pine Island area in the early 1900s. Phalo's nephew, Frank Sr., remembers, "We waded around the island looking for something to eat. We found hermit crabs good to eat. We would build a fire and boil them in a can and eat the tender meat." (Padilla Family.)

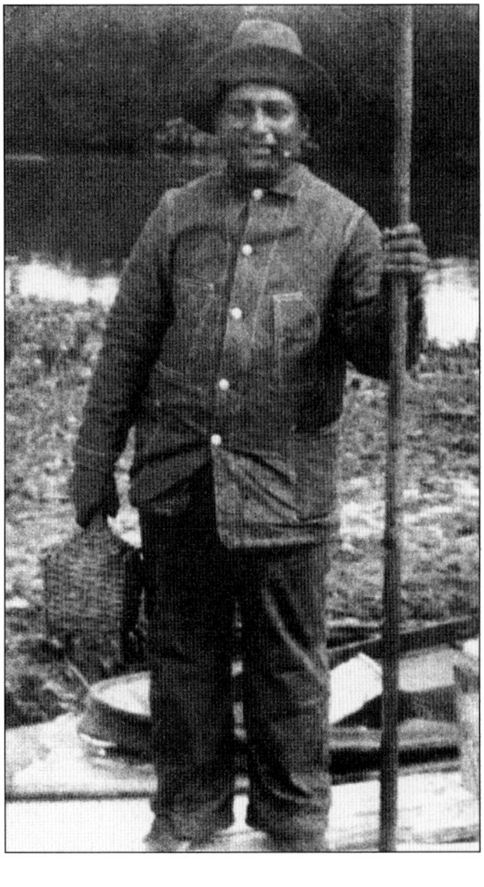

Taken in 1900, this faded image is of an unidentified Pine Island fisherman who caught mullet, trout, pompano, and various other fish, depending on the season of the year. Living on a fish ranch, the pole he holds in his left hand was used to move his boat through the shallow water between Punta Blanca, Cayo Costa, and Pine Island, while in his right hand he holds a woven wicker jug. (Padilla Family.)

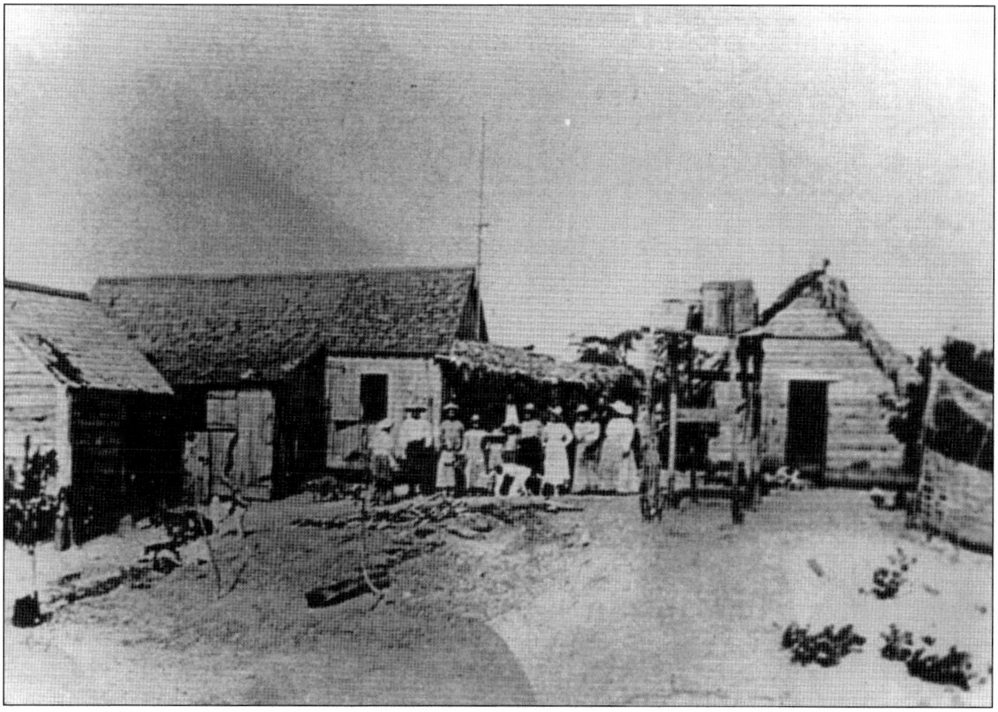

Frank Padilla Sr. told of living at the family fish ranch in the late 1800s and early 1900s. "They would get sugar and olive oil from trading with the Cuban Smacks. I don't remember them using money. They just traded back and forth." Pictured here, in addition to the family, are chickens and hogs. The Padilla descendents credit Toribio Padilla with bringing the hogs to Cayo Costa, some of which still roam the island today. (Padilla Family.)

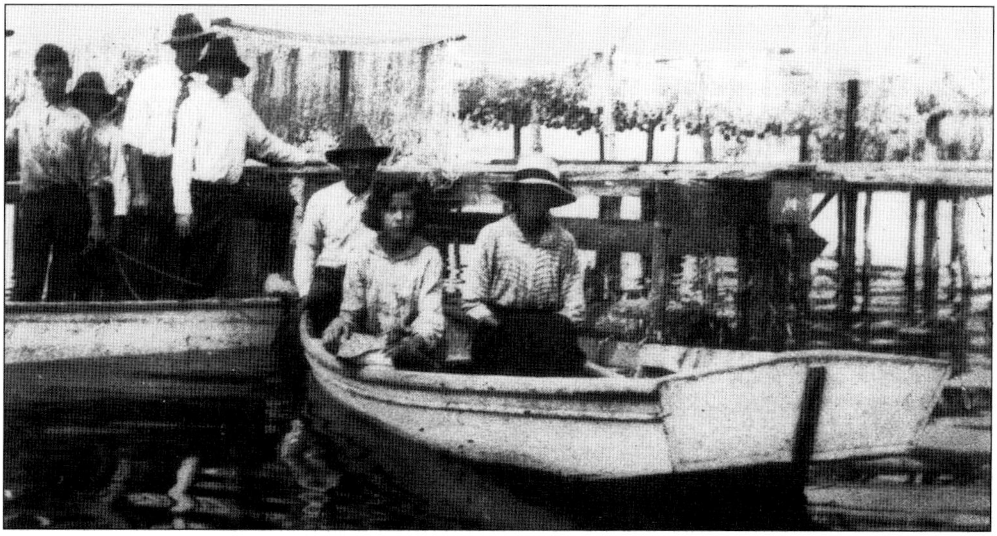

This charming photograph is of John Padilla, his wife, Dollie, and their daughter on an outing in the early 1920s. Coleman family members are in the boat at left. Net spreads can be seen on the docks, having been rinsed in limewater and hung out to dry on the racks. (Dr. William Marquardt.)

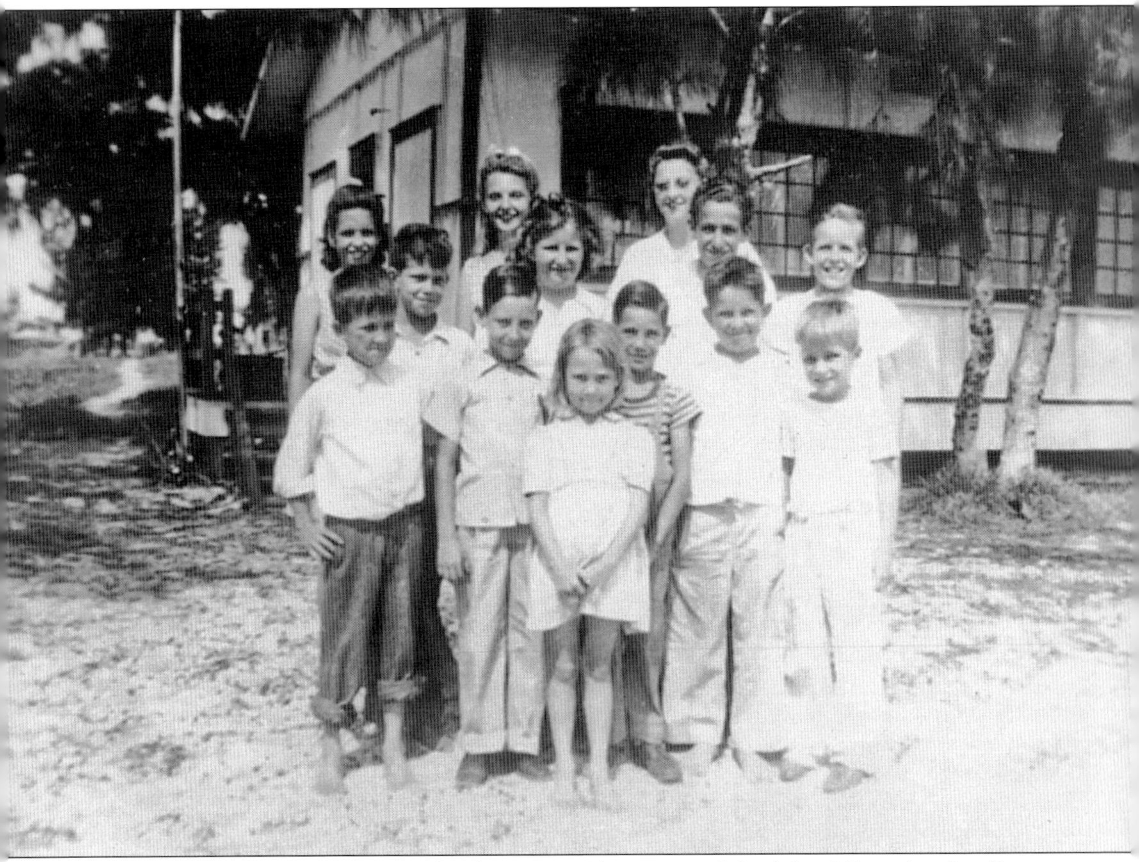

Beginning in the early 1900s, a school on Punta Blanca served the fisherfolk settlers. Joe Darna ran the school boat, picking up children from the various islands. Taken during the 1943–1944 school years, teacher Mrs. Christian is shown with some of the last children to attend the one-room school. Pictured are (first row) Guy Darna, Conrade Padilla, Ruby Coleman, Dick Darna, Pat Coleman, and Tiny Darna; (seond row) Rufus Darna, Frances Levens, Raymond Rodriqus, and Earl Leven; (third row) Frances Barnes, Freddie Lee Joiner, and Mrs. Christian, the teacher. (Virginia Morton.)

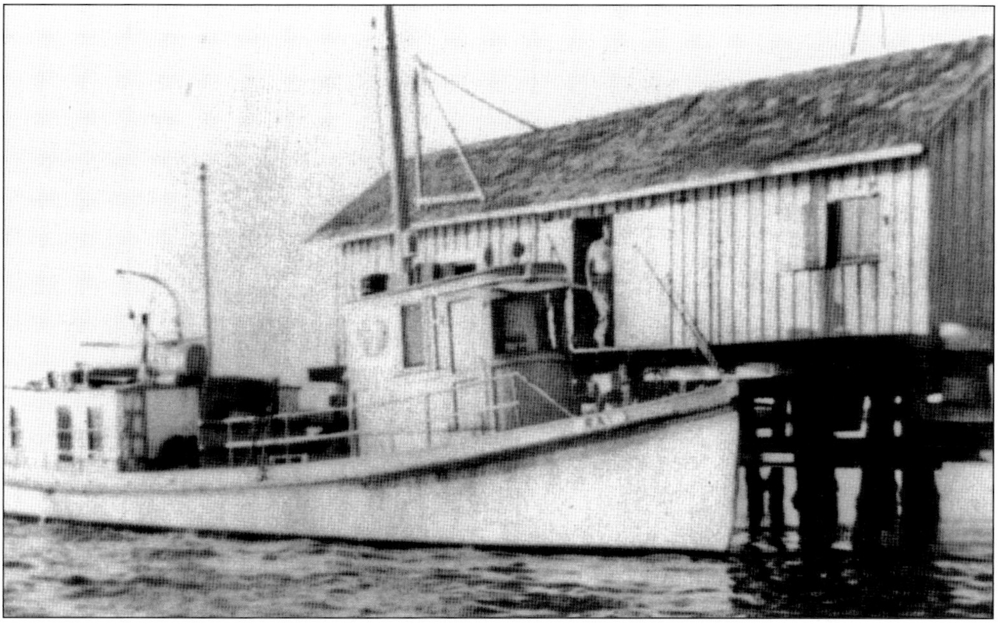

Delivering ice and supplies, and picking up catches of local fish for market shipment were the runboats out of the Punta Gorda Fish Company. The boats skimmed the waters of Charlotte Harbor and Pine Island Sound, providing a lifeline for commercial fishermen during the early 1900s. They were replaced by trucks when the Matlacha Bridge was completed in 1927, linking all of Pine Island with the mainland. (Museum of the Islands.)

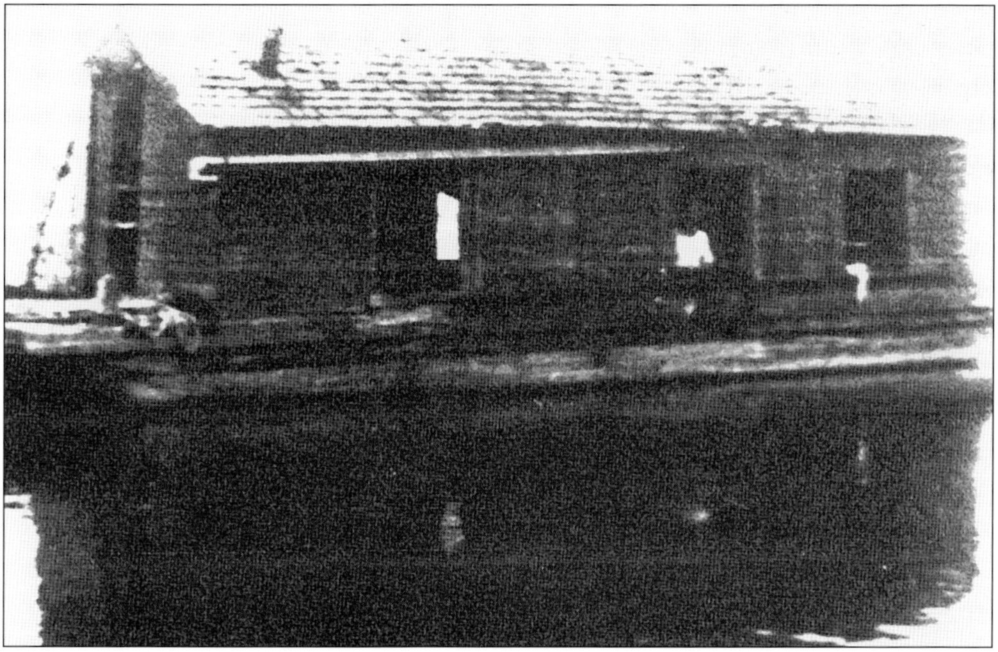

The forerunner of today's houseboat, the "lightern" was a palm-thatched or wood-framed building sitting atop a boat deck. Long poles were used by the fisherfolk to move the houseboat through shallow water as they followed the schools of fish. This Padilla lightern was eventually permanently moored in Matlacha along the "fill" in the mid-1920s. (Padilla Family.)

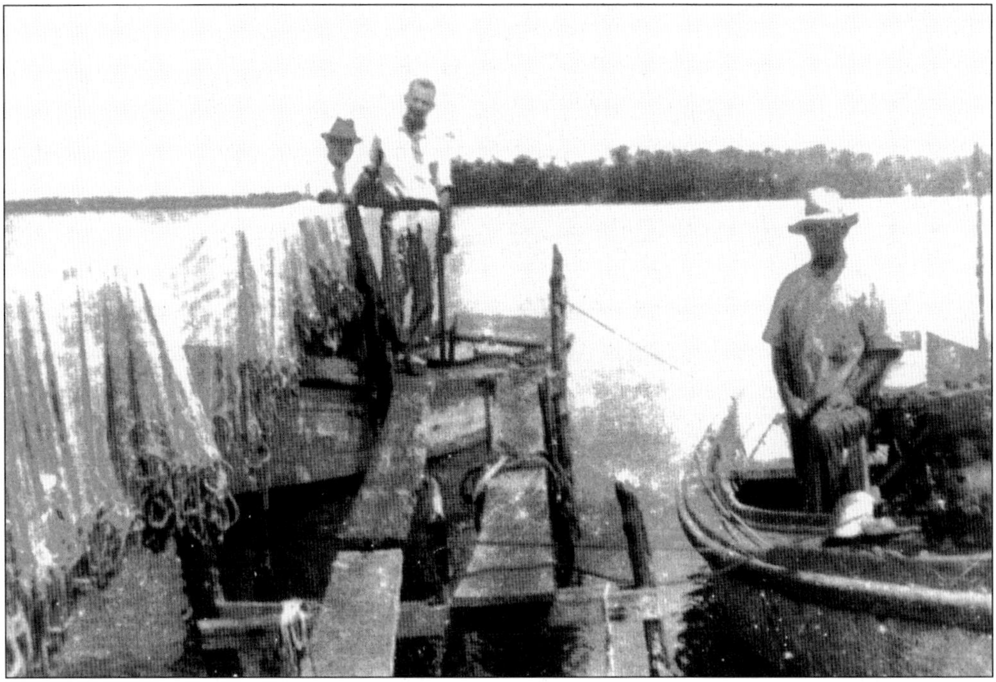

These unidentified fishermen stand on a dock in Matlacha in the 1940s. Surprisingly, the men in the boat at left appear to have on white shirts and ties, while one also wears a dress hat. The nets at left are spread for drying on the racks after being limed. (Padilla Family.)

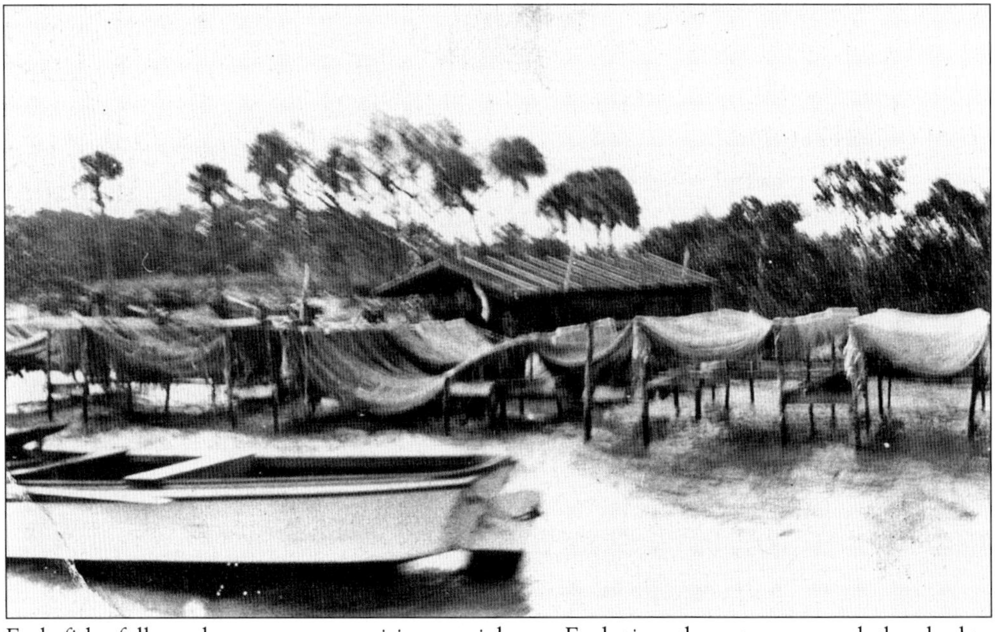

Early fisherfolk used cotton nets requiring special care. Each time the nets were used, they had to be washed and rinsed in limewater to prevent rot. To allow the nets to dry, they were spread over and between racks. Thus, the fisherfolk referred to the racks of drying nets as net spreads. The net spreads pictured above were at the Padilla Fish Ranch on nearby Cayo Costa Island in the early 1900s. (Padilla Family.)

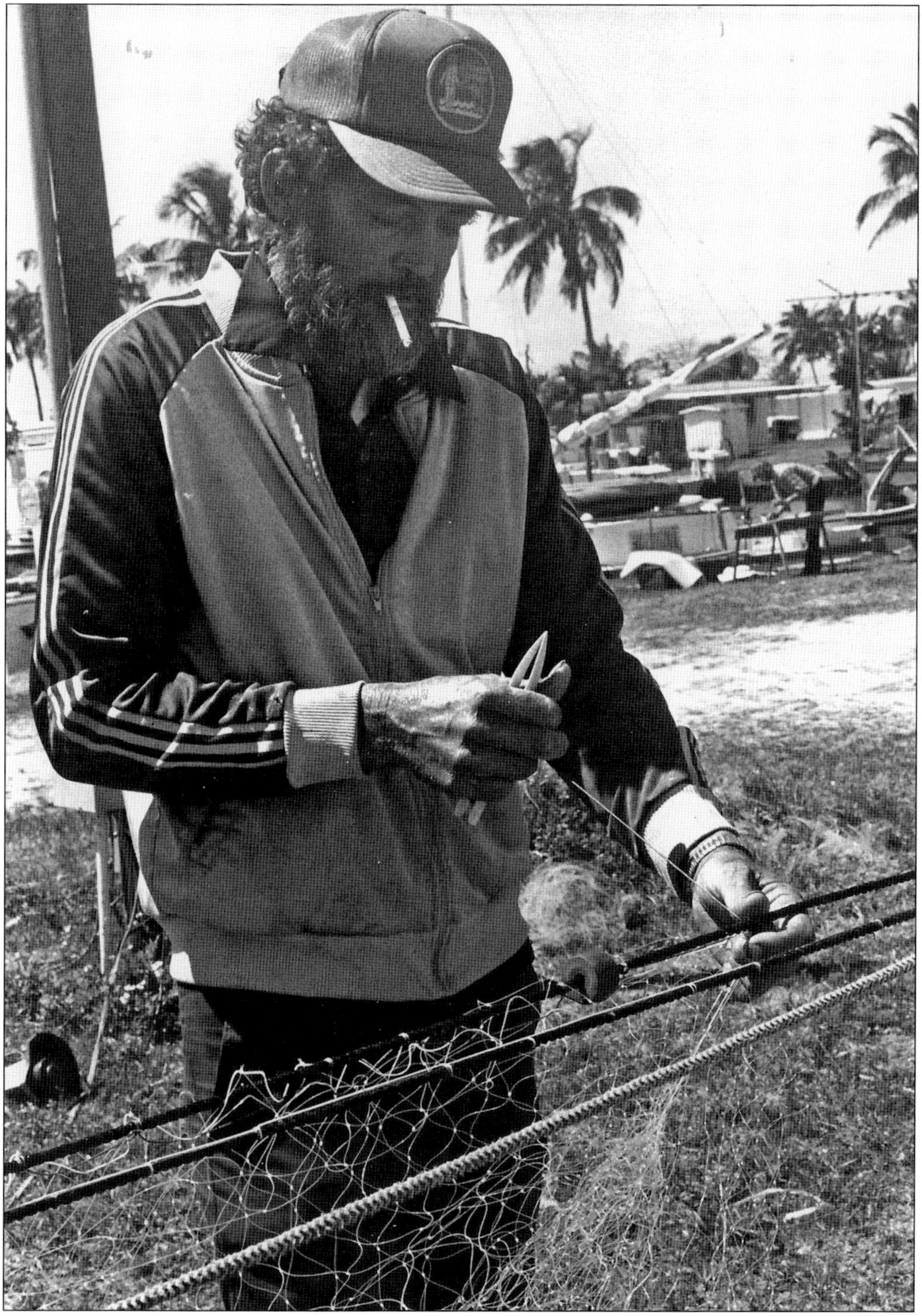

The earliest Pine Island fishing nets were made by hand with cotton and had to be limed after each day's use. Later nets were made of flax and most recently monofilament. Here Lavon Gawn mends a handmade monofilament gill net in the 1980s. Beginning in 1995, gill nets were banned from use in Florida's waters. (Florida State Archives.)

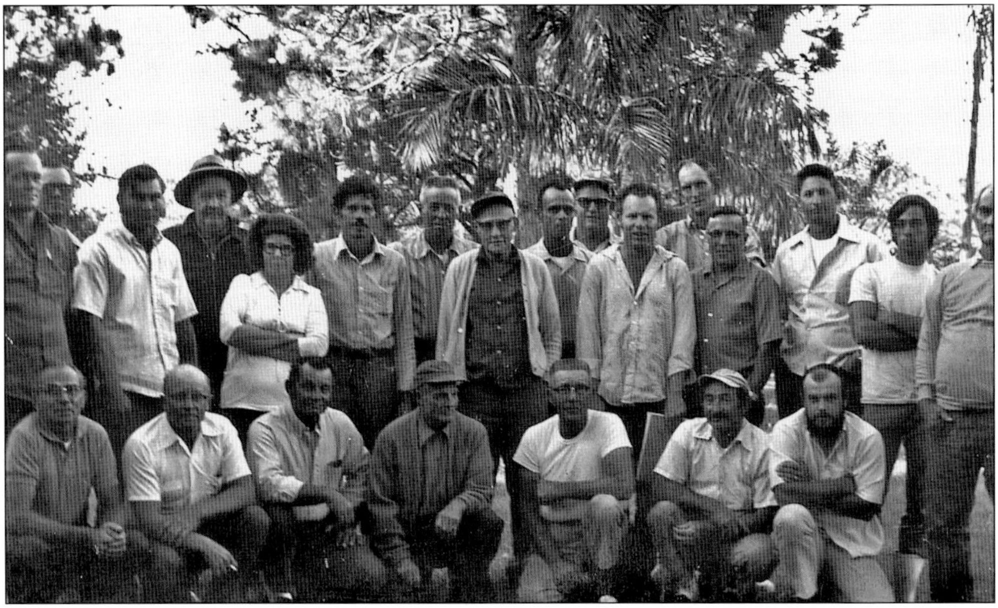

Commercial fishermen of Pine Island meet to discuss the formation of a fishermen's co-op on February 4, 1973. Many multigenerational commercial-fishing families were represented at the meeting. Such meetings led to the formal organization of the Pine Island Fishermen's Co-op in 1977. (Breese Glennon.)

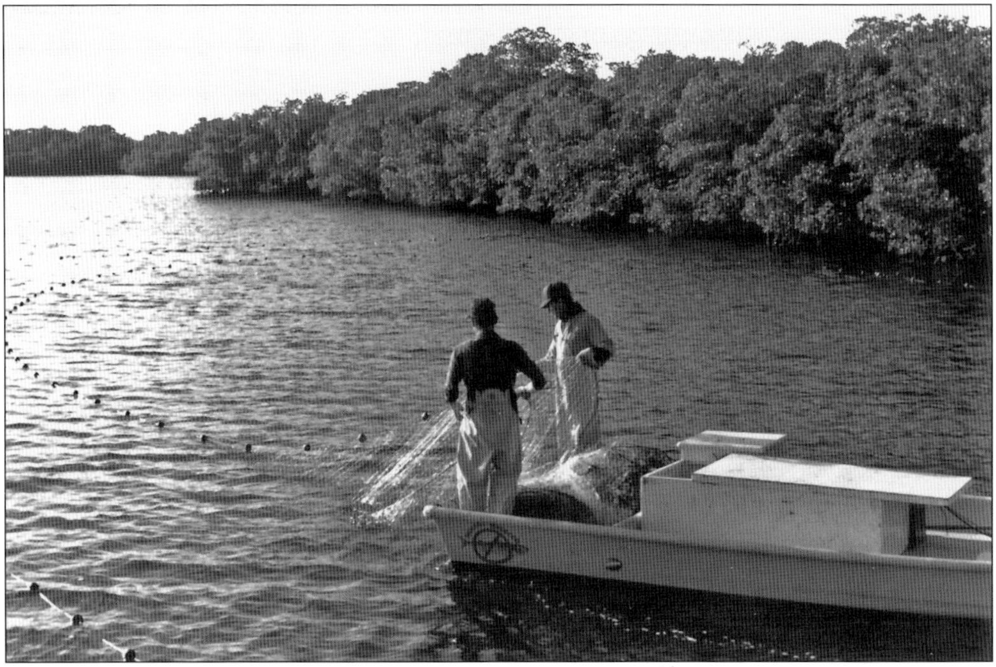

After Capt. Mike Dooley yelled, "Let 'er go," Shane Dooley released the weighted net into the water, allowing the net to pull out into the water as the boat continued on its course. Striking the mullet, Mike and Shane Dooley work as a fishing team in this pre-1994 photo. The Dooleys remain part of several multigenerational commercial-fishing families on the island. (Rhonda Dooley.)

Unloading their mullet catches are commercial fishermen Kim Gerz and Craig Stevens at the fishermen's co-op fish house in the early 1990s. The mullet-filled baskets are hoisted to the dock where they are weighed. Of note are the white boots worn by the fisherman on the dock above. Known by islanders as "Pine Island Reeboks," most commercial fishermen wear the white rubber boots while fishing. (Photograph by the author.)

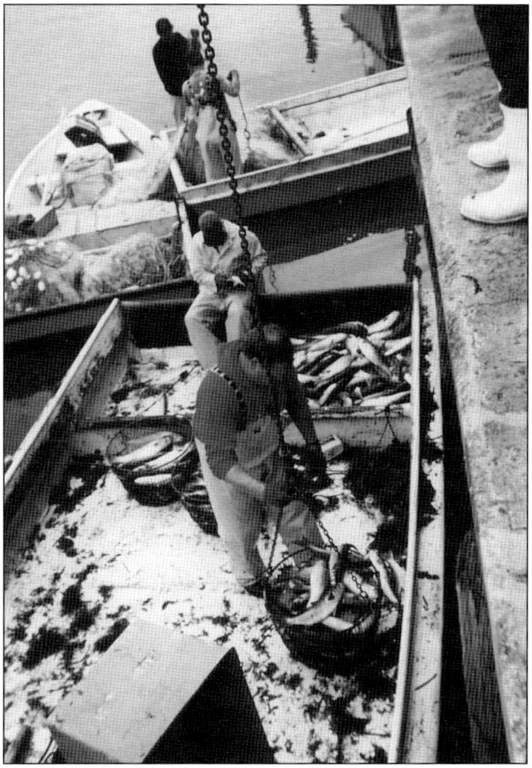

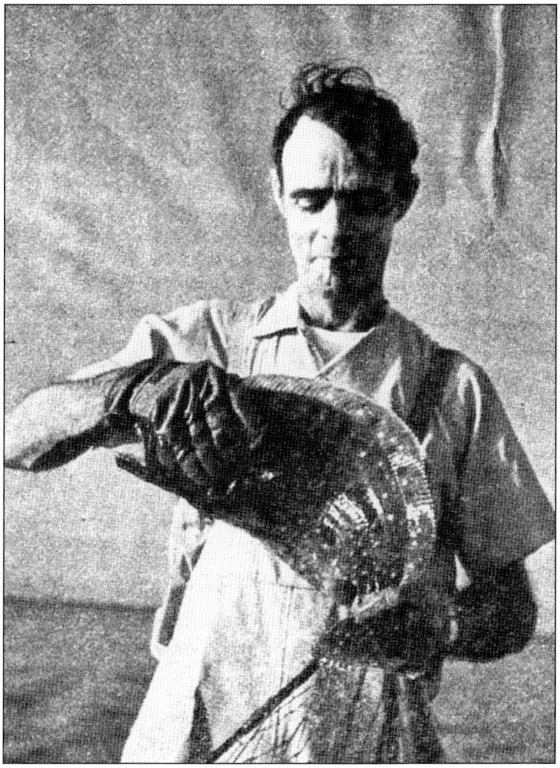

Perhaps Coy Kersey's comment in a 1973 interview best sums up a major difference between commercial and sport fishermen: "Commercial fishermen always remember where snook are in great numbers because they have to *avoid* those spots unless they are willing to have their nets ripped by the snooks' sharp gill covers." Kersey was a commercial fisherman and managed the fisherman's co-op off and on for more than 50 years. (Randy Kersey.)

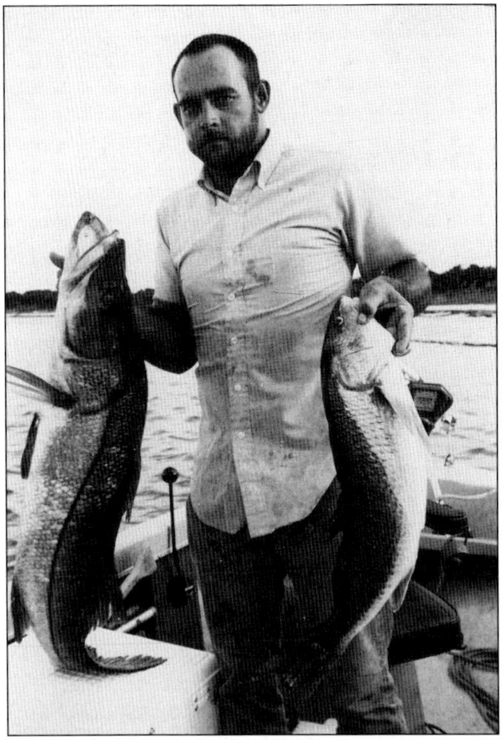

Randy Kersey, son of a Pine Island commercial fisherman, remembers his father's words of advice when, as a teen, he went to his dad for some cash one day. His dad took him out back to the water and pointed, saying: "You need some money? Well, there's the bank." He learned at a young age that fishing paid the bills. Kersey poses with game fish in 1973. (Randy Kersey.)

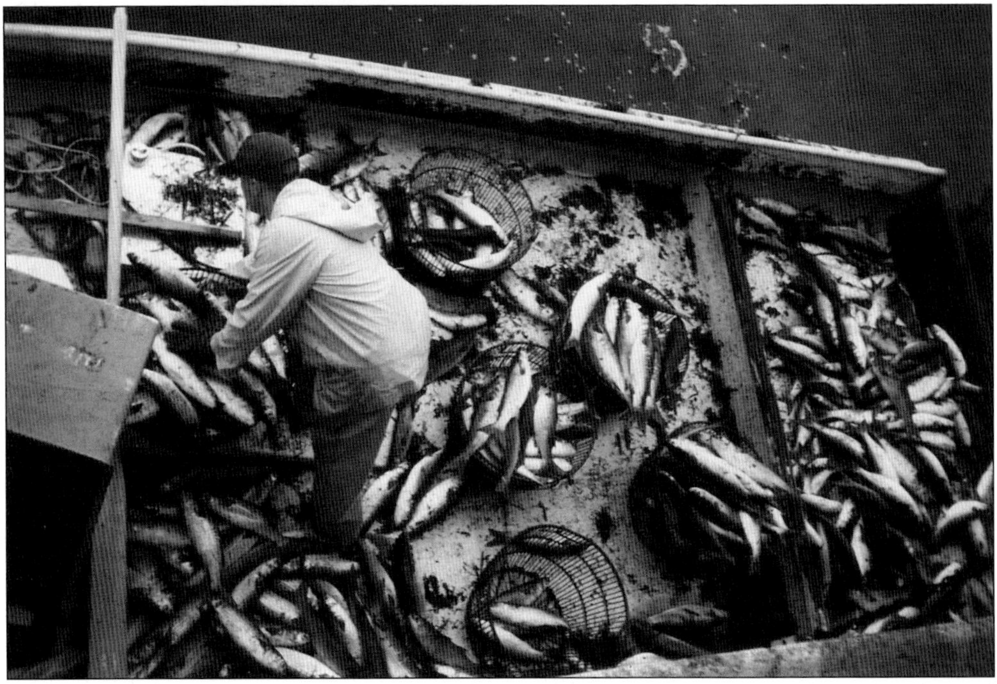

Prior to the 1995 net ban, island teens crewed commercial fishing boats in lieu of traditional part-time jobs. Although it did not supply a steady income, some nights on the water could bring in a couple hundred dollars for the crew member. Here in 1994, Craig Stevens sorts and loads a catch of mullet at the co-op dock for weighing and selling. (Photograph by the author.)

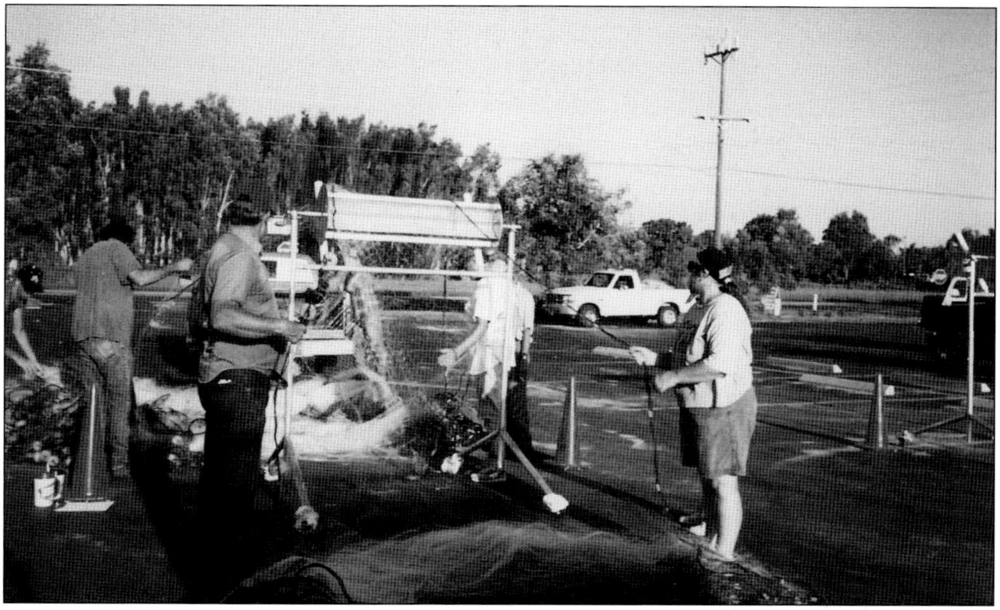

In November 1994, 72 percent of Florida voters chose to enact a constitutional amendment that banned net fishing, effectively ending a way of life for some 300 commercial fishermen on Pine Island. The ban outlawed the use of both gill and entangling nets in state waters and went into effect in July 1995. Anticipating possible unlawful outbursts of protest during the state's net buy-back, a Florida law enforcement officer stands guard as fishermen pull their nets to be measured. The nets were then stuffed into bags to be transported for destruction, effectively eliminating them from commercial fishing use. It was an emotional time for Pine Island's fishermen, and many people are still reluctant to talk about it. (Rhonda Dooley.)

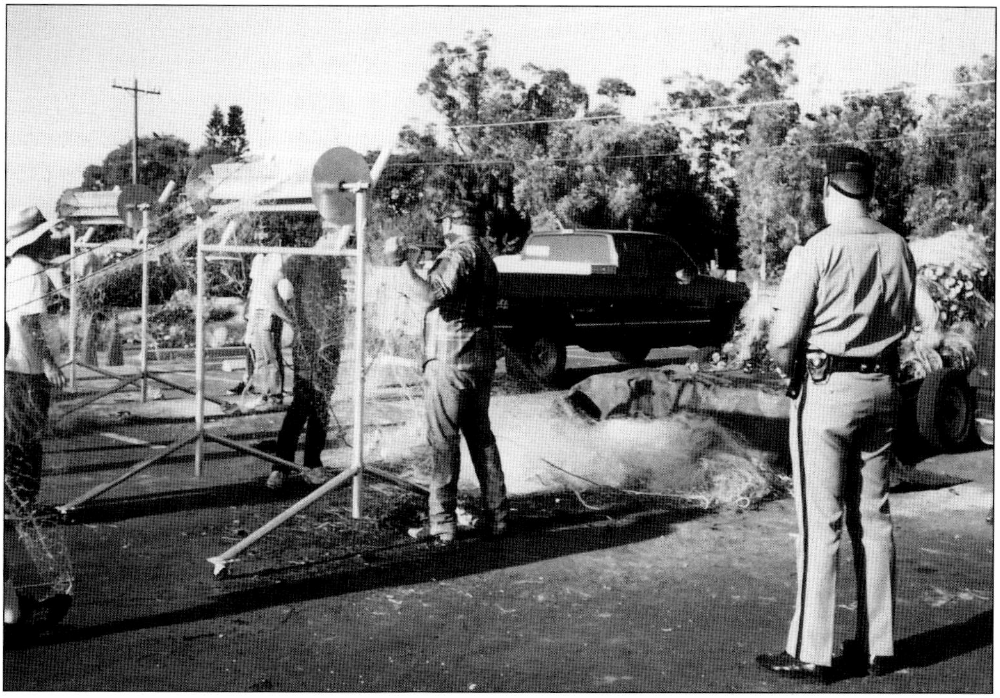

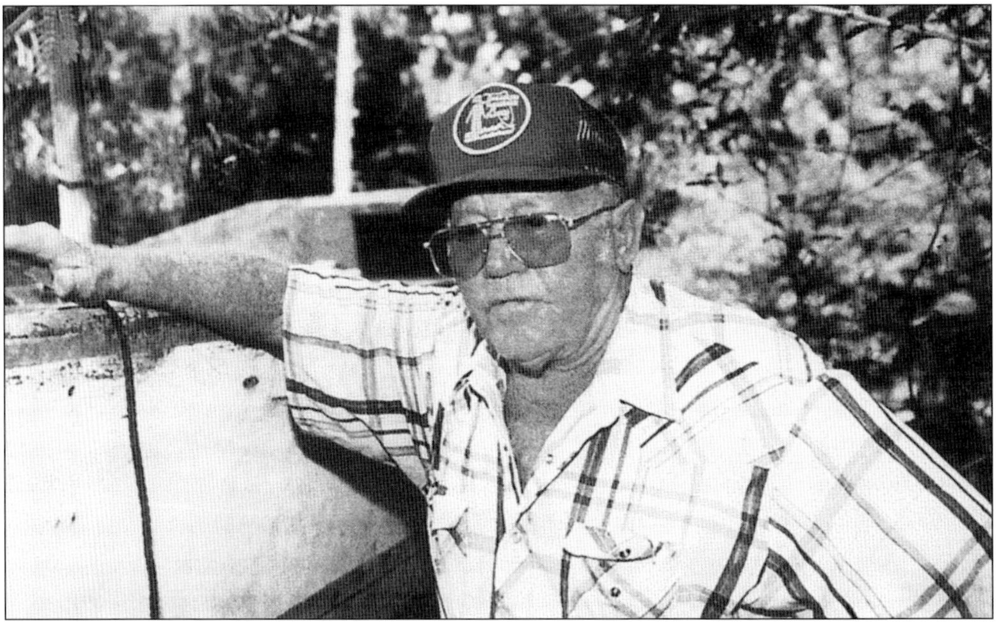

Commercial fisherman Tootsie Barnes said before his death in June 2000, "I'd get up and get out on the water long before dawn and lay 250 yards of net by hand. The work was hard . . . but there was always so much to see—the different birds, manatees, sunrises, sunsets." Following the net ban, he said, "I've been pretty depressed. It's like somebody locking you up in a prison—fishin's all I ever done." (Rhonda Dooley.)

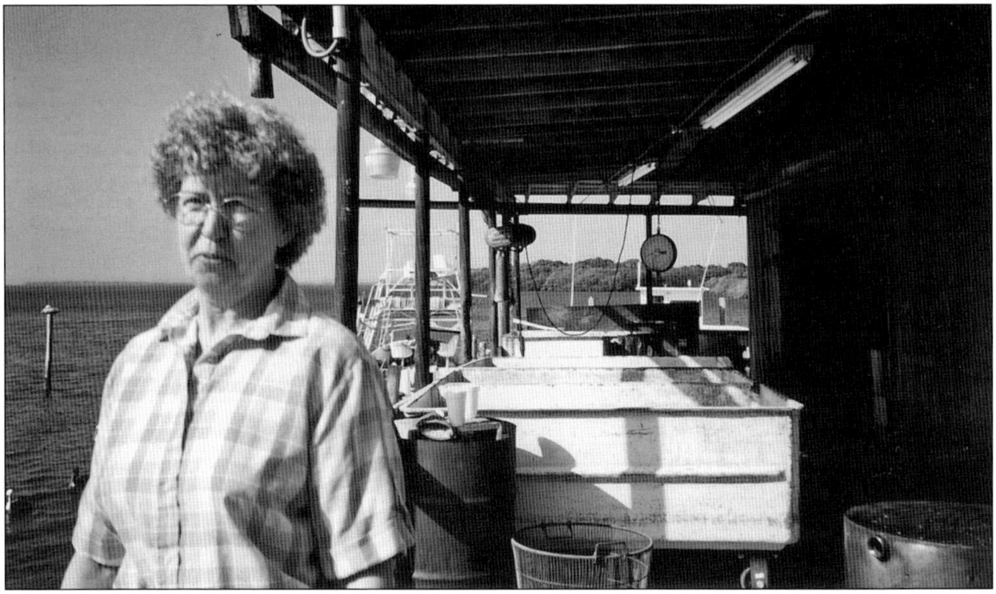

Island resident Shirley Nielson moved to Pine Island in 1958, 11 years after her future husband, Johnny, became an islander. Playing a major role in the building and running of the Pine Island Fishermen's Co-op, Shirley is shown here on the co-op's deck area in 2000, seven years before the co-op closed. Her husband Johnny enjoyed bragging about a commercial-fishing run in 1985 where, along with Steve Kersey, he caught over 3,000 pounds of mullet in what is called a "Black Bunch of Mullet" off Redfish Pass. (Breese Glennon.)

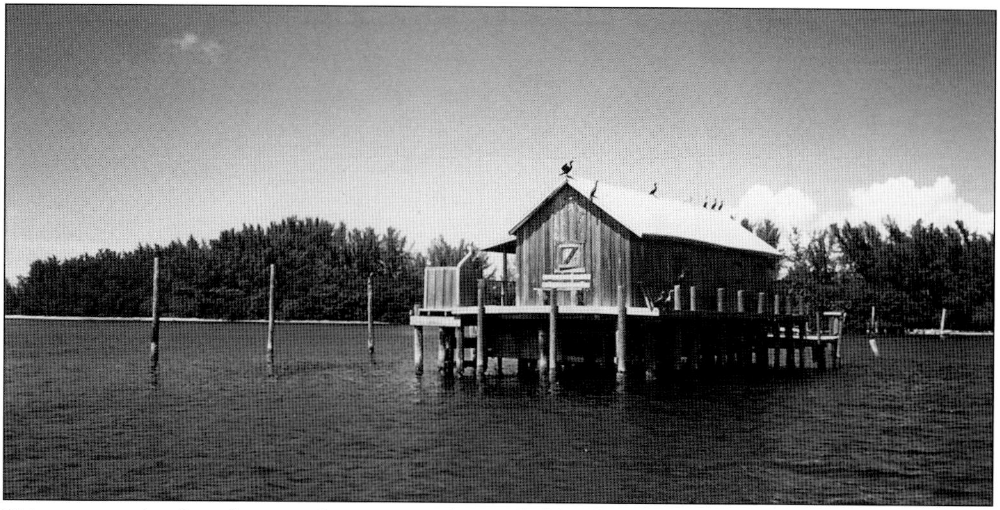

Tying up to the foundation pilings, ascending a ladder from waterline to deck area, and then finding the comforts of home within its walls, early commercial fishermen found peace with nature in their stilt fish houses. The structures also proved to be a place of safety for fishermen caught in unanticipated storms, as fish house owners never turned away a fellow fisherman in need of shelter. (Fort Myers Museum of History.)

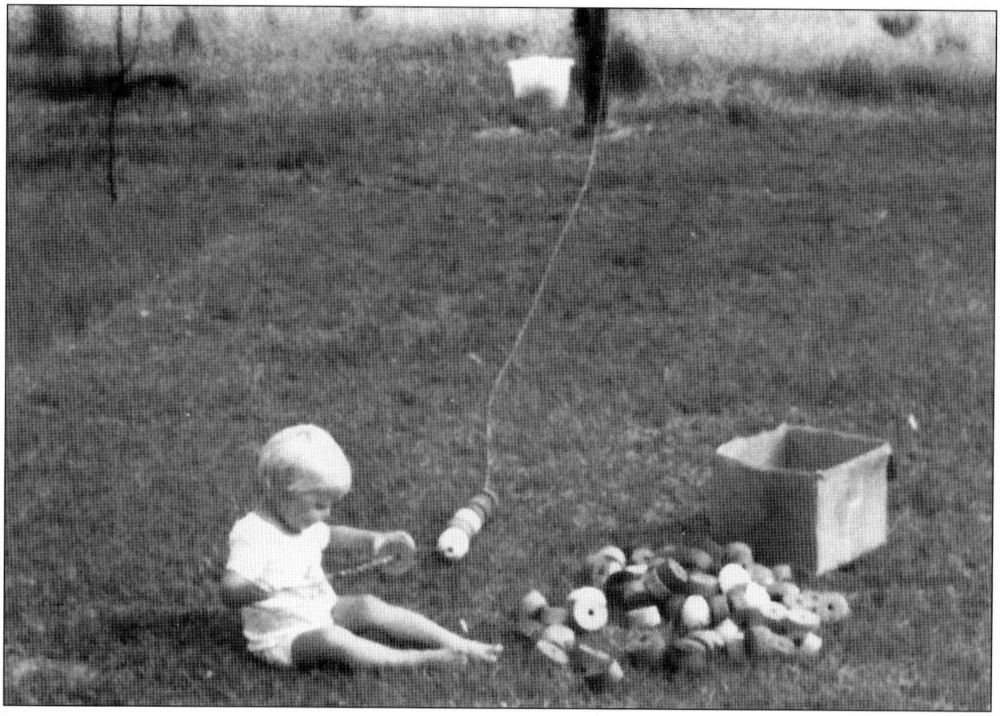

Never too young to learn the commercial fishermans' skills, the toddler Shane Dooley strings floats on a rope in the early 1980s. One of the few multigenerational commercial-fishing families left on the island, Shane is now a third generation commercial fisherman in the Dooley family. Mother, Rhonda Dooley, remarked of her fishermen family members, "I think it [fishing] is something they really have to do. They're compelled to be there, and you're not going to take it out of them." (Rhonda Dooley.)

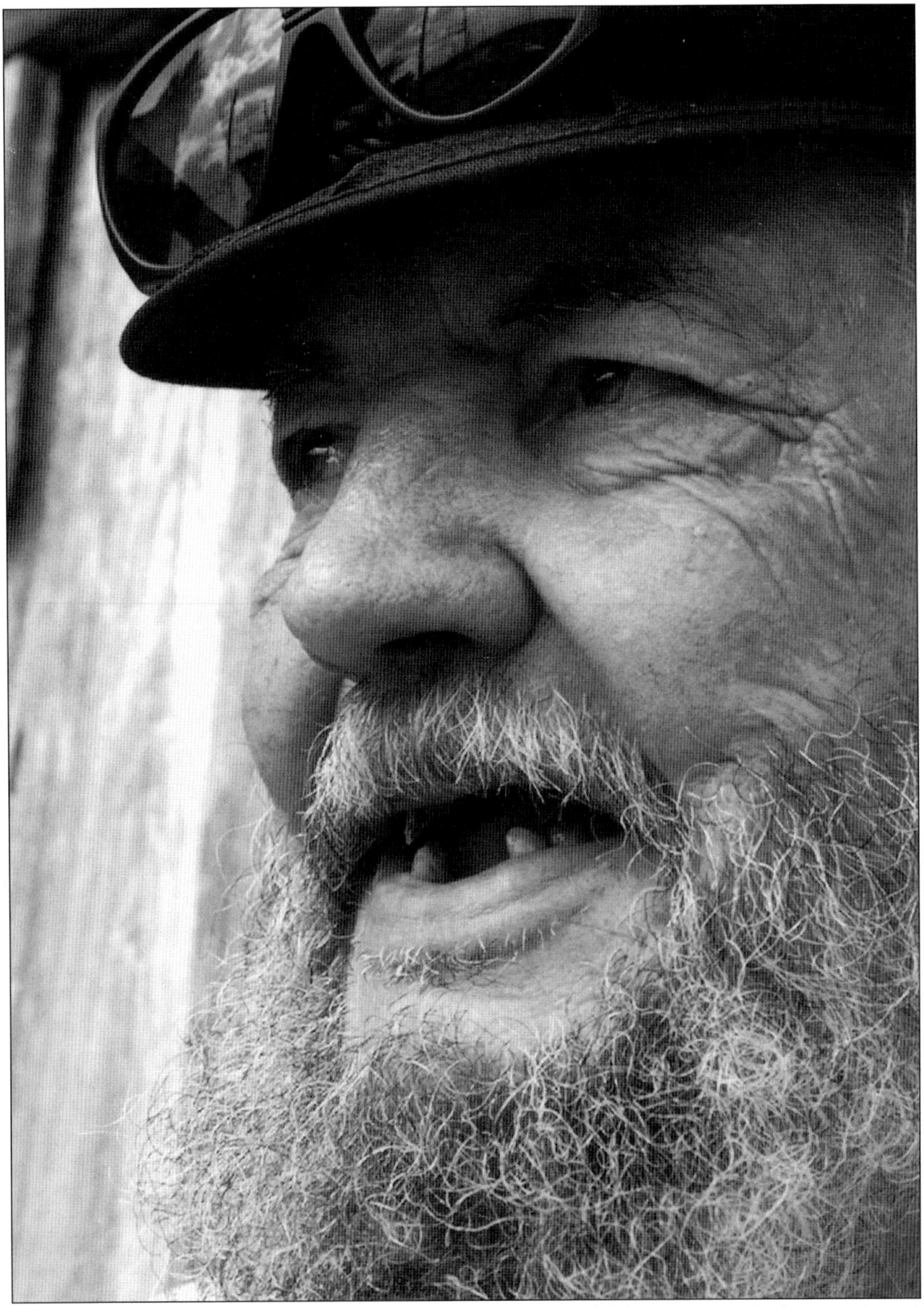

A true fisherman can read the signs of nature. A commercial fisherman can look at a tide and a sliver of moon and tell if the fish are biting in any given location within their fishing domain. This image of Bill May, a St. James City fisherman, taken by Mark Foley in 2000, reflects the rugged and robust nature of a Pine Island fisherman. (Florida State Archives.)

Five

World's Best Fishing

A Mr. Wood of New York took last week a tarpon measuring 5 feet, 8 inches, and weighing 68 pounds; tackle and reel.

—*Forest and Stream*, April 9, 1885

Under expert guide Capt. John Smith of St. James City, W. H. Wood's tarpon catch made on a rod and reel ignited a fishing frenzy still popular today. Not only did word of the catch spread through the fishing communities on Pine Island and Fort Myers, but eventually, the sports-fishing news traveled worldwide. Captain Smith put his boatbuilding skills to work by building wooden boats for visiting fishermen to rent. Other entrepreneurs followed Smith's lead by joining his family at the small fishing settlement. Two of the town's young boys, Elmo Pierce and Earle Hord, made a business of catching fiddler crabs, which they sold to the fishermen. Boom times had arrived in St. James City.

So began one of fishing's most popular sports: tarpon fishing. Not only was St. James City a destination for tarpon enthusiasts, Pine Island also provided the expert guides needed by the visitors. Most guides fished commercially in addition to the guide fishing, setting out from a 600-foot pier built across the shallow water off the town. Kay (Caputo) DellaBitta, the daughter of one such guide, Joe Caputo, remembers her father telling of how author Zane Grey considered him to be the best tarpon guide. Kay smiles as she remembers her father bringing home Grey's Western novels as gifts following the fishing outings. DellaBitta tells of a family routine centered around the books: "Mama would read us a chapter from Zane Grey every evening after we had gathered up all the dead mosquitoes on the floor from daddy lighting the Bee Powder."

Fishing also became a favorite of those stationed at Buckingham Air Force Base during World War II. News of catching fish with just the sinker—no bait needed—spread across the air base and all of Southwest Florida. Soon people stood shoulder to shoulder on both sides of the wooden bridge. Fishermen line the bridge to this day.

Fishing in Pine Island Sound and its environs guarantees the avid fisherman a variety of fishing challenges. From large game fish such as shark and tarpon, to elusive snook and redfish, the waters surrounding Pine Island area are home to the fisherman's dream catch.

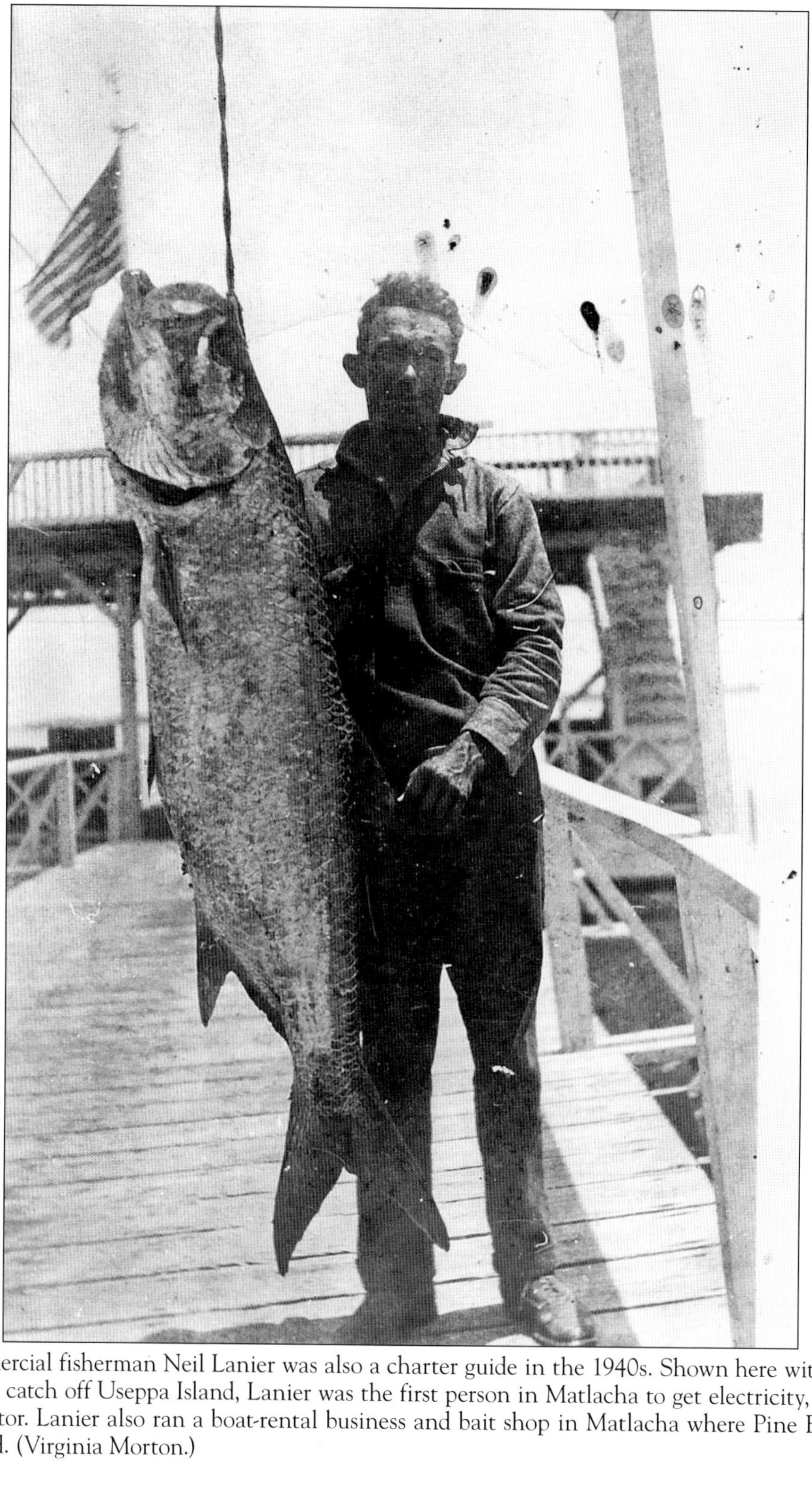

Commercial fisherman Neil Lanier was also a charter guide in the 1940s. Shown here with his tarpon catch off Useppa Island, Lanier was the first person in Matlacha to get electricity, via a generator. Lanier also ran a boat-rental business and bait shop in Matlacha where Pine Bay is located. (Virginia Morton.)

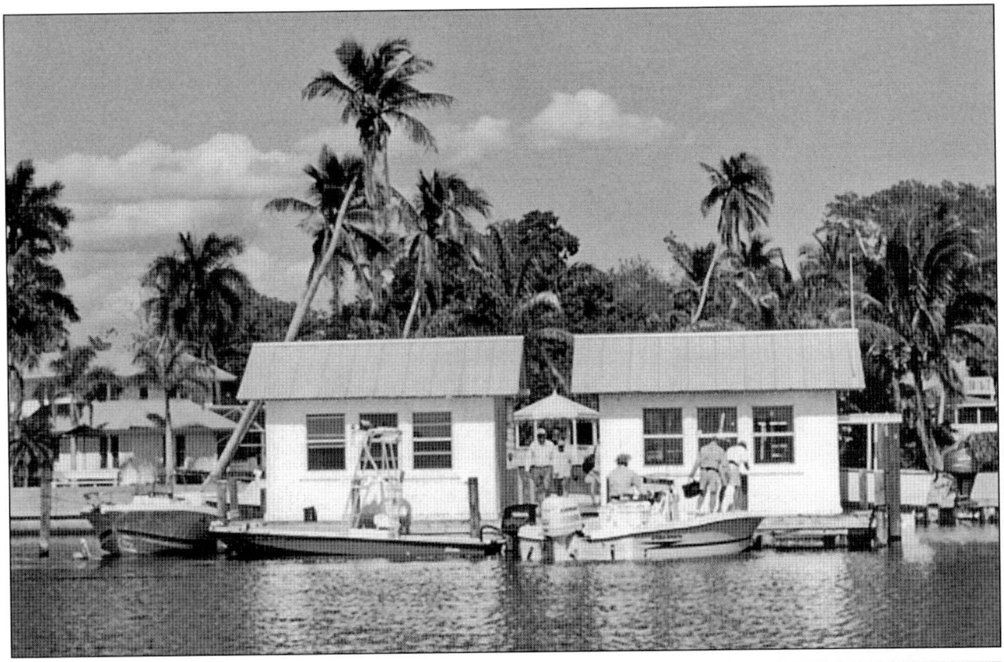

Built during the early days of tarpon fishing popularity in the latter 1880s, these "his" and "her" boat/bath houses were typical Victorian architecture. Allowing separate changing areas for men and women before and after fishing expeditions, patrons were never seen in public in attire unbefitting to the accepted protocol. These original Victorian boat houses (above), located on the dock behind the Tarpon Lodge at Pineland, were destroyed in Hurricane Charley in 2004. (Robert Wells.)

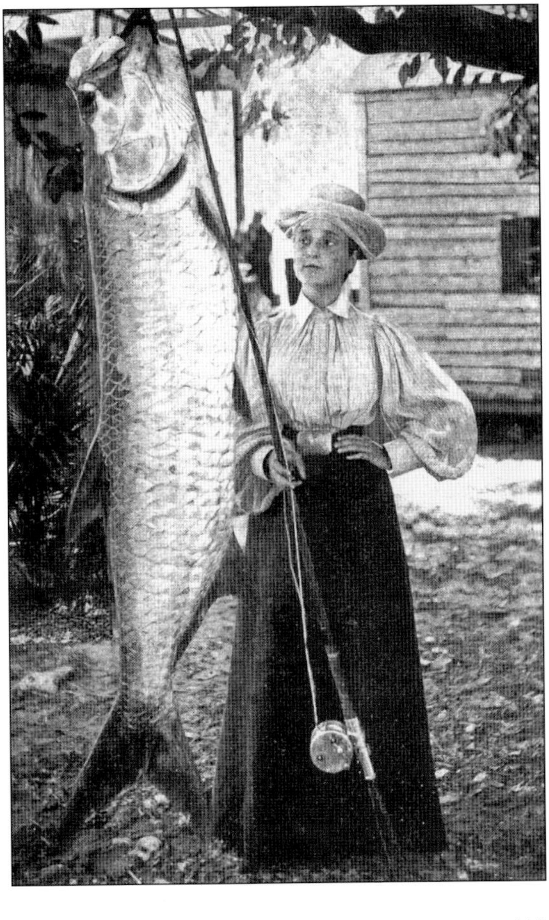

The idea of women anglers doing battle with a huge, powerful fish like this tarpon may well have been limited to freethinking individuals during the Victorian era. Taken in the early 1900s this postcard image is of one determined Victorian woman and her 185-pound tarpon caught on a spinning rod and reel. Enjoying the tropical setting, many women joined their husbands on fishing expeditions in the area. (Florida State Archives.)

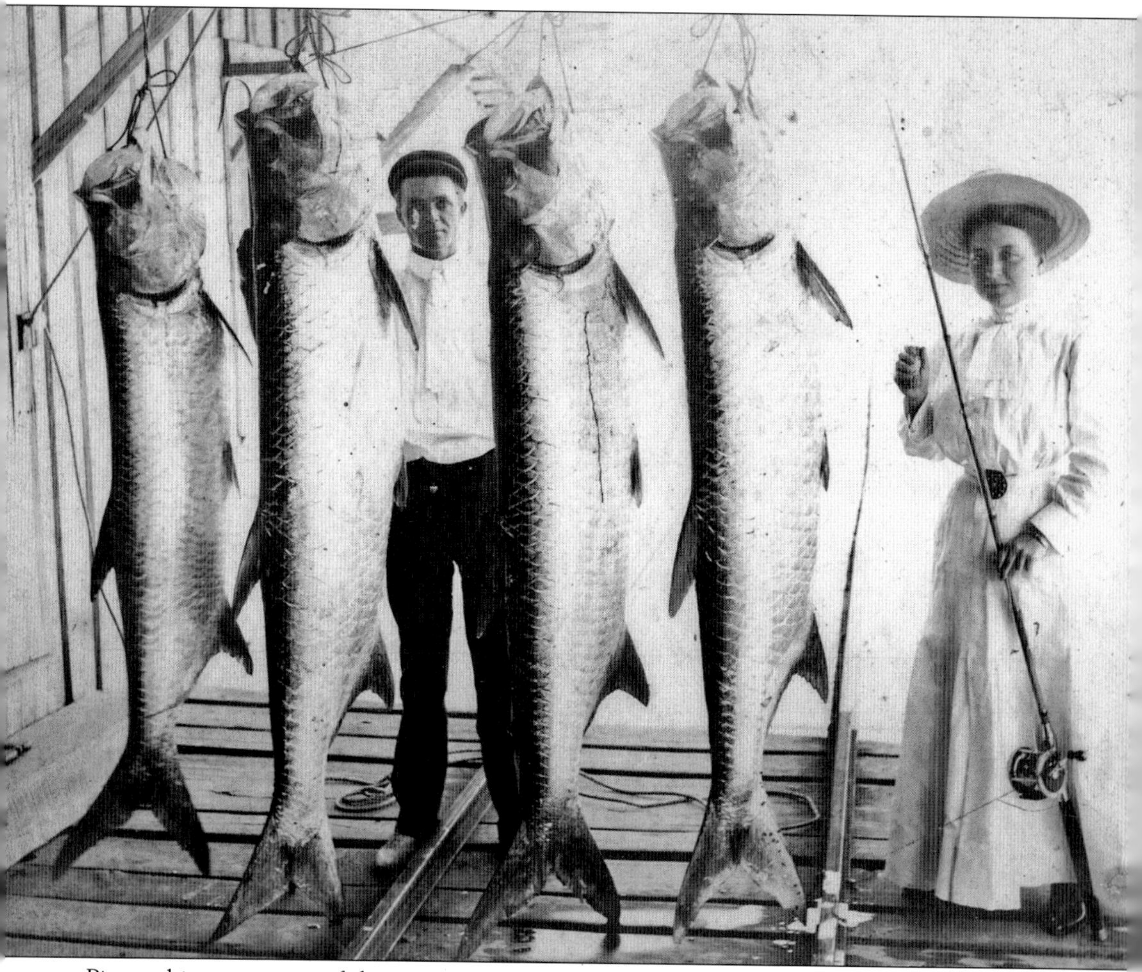

Pictured in appropriate fishing attire, this Victorian woman stands with her catch of tarpon. Perhaps she caught them off St. James City. In an article written in 1889, Robert Grant said, "At St. James City's there is a comfortable hotel [the San Carlos Hotel] maintained by Northern proprietors. A delightful spot [where] . . . ladies can accompany their husbands and brothers without risk of being otherwise than very comfortable." (Robert Wells.)

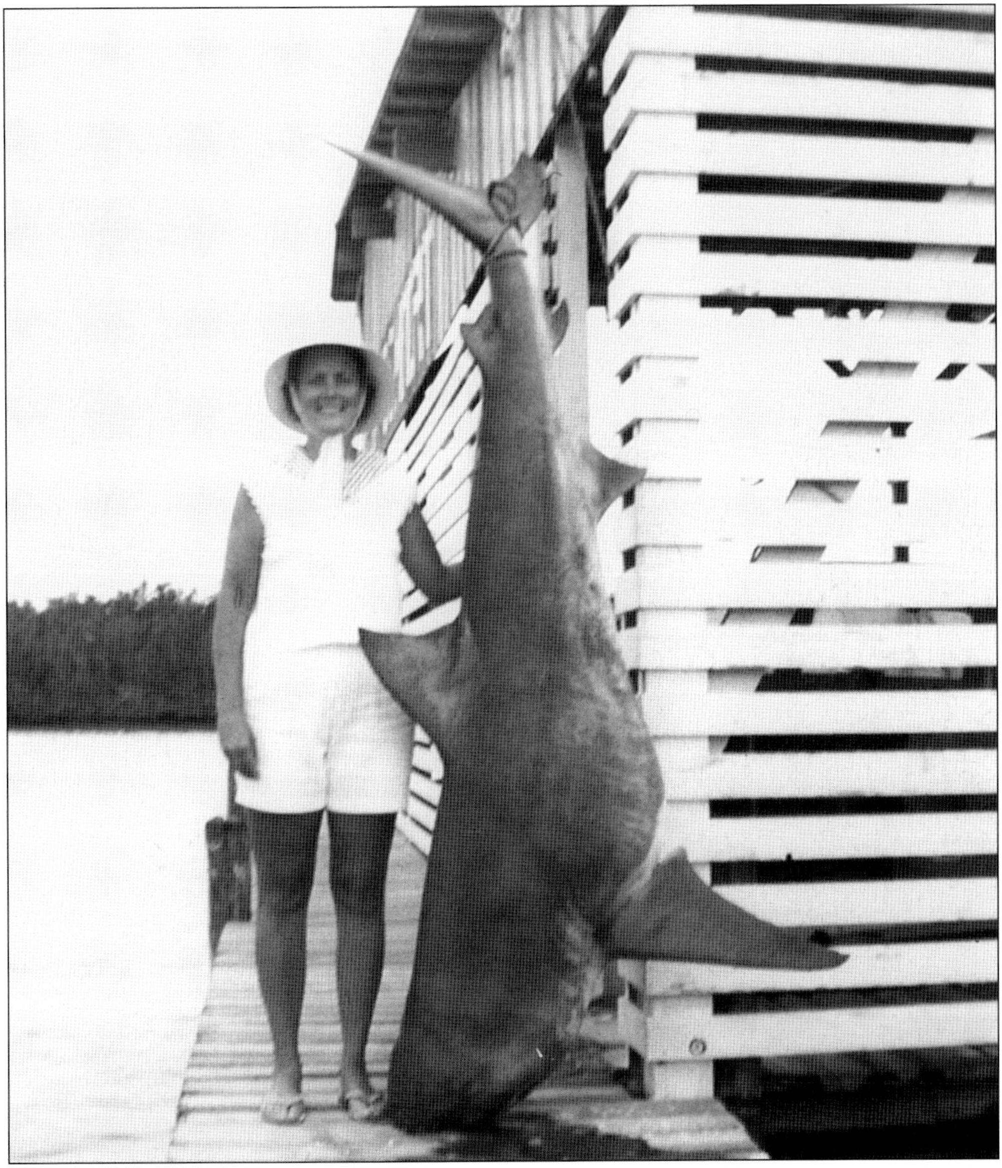

Using quarter-inch rope and chain with a 2-pound mullet as bait, Doris Stevens caught this 350-pound shark off St. James City at the mouth of the Caloosahatchee River in 1960. At one point during the reeling in, the shark charged the boat, jarring both the boat and fishermen. The guide yelled, "Cut the rope, Cut the rope!" But Doris kept reeling, landing the 8-foot-long shark. (Maurice Stevens.)

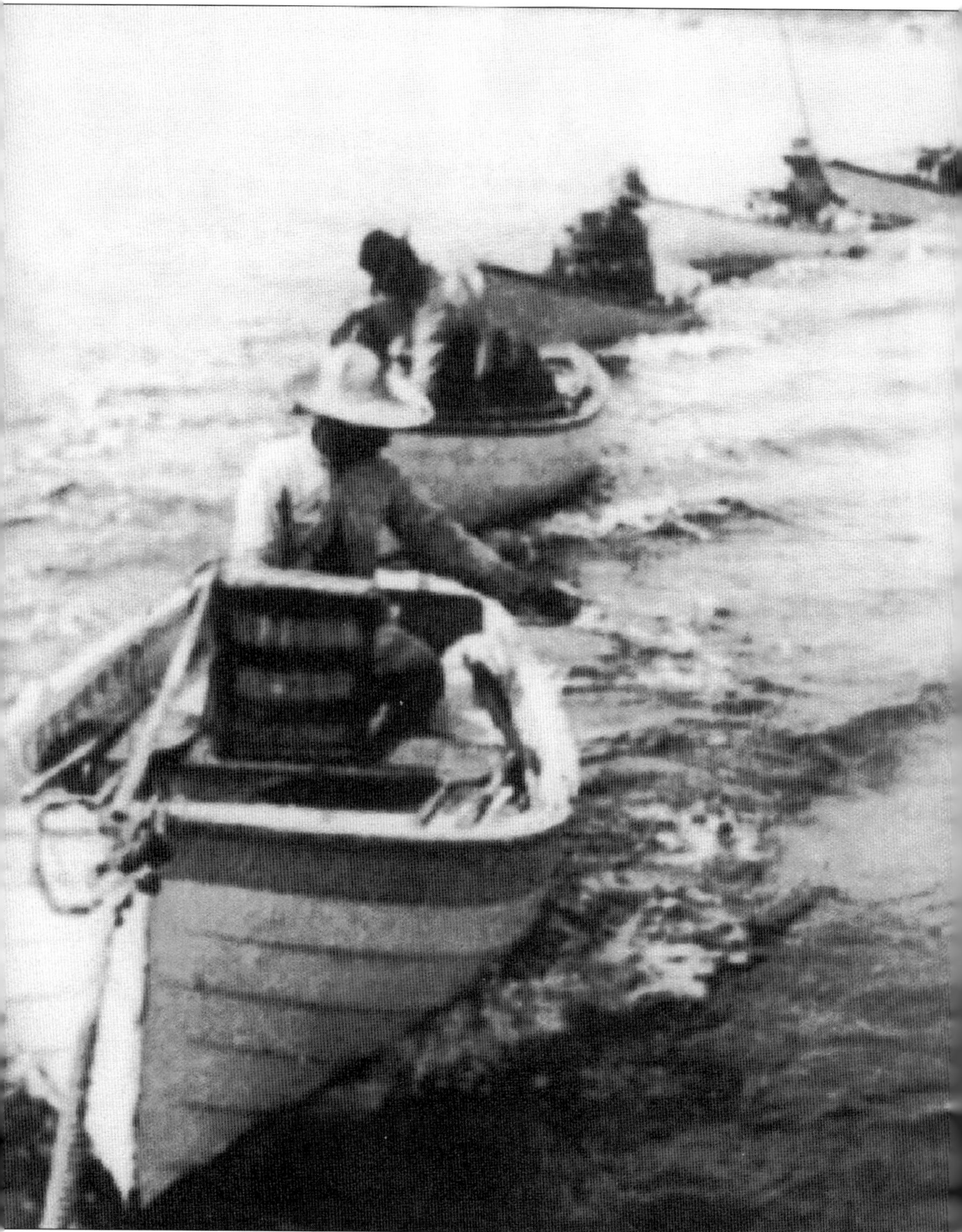

Motorboats did not arrive in the area until 1910, according to Richard Coleman, who is part of the Padilla family of the Pine Island area. In this early-1900s photograph, the lead boat, driven

by guide Jesse Padilla, has a motor, while the other 11 or more are pulled along from behind, thus giving the sports fishermen a trolling experience while fishing for tarpon. (Padilla Family.)

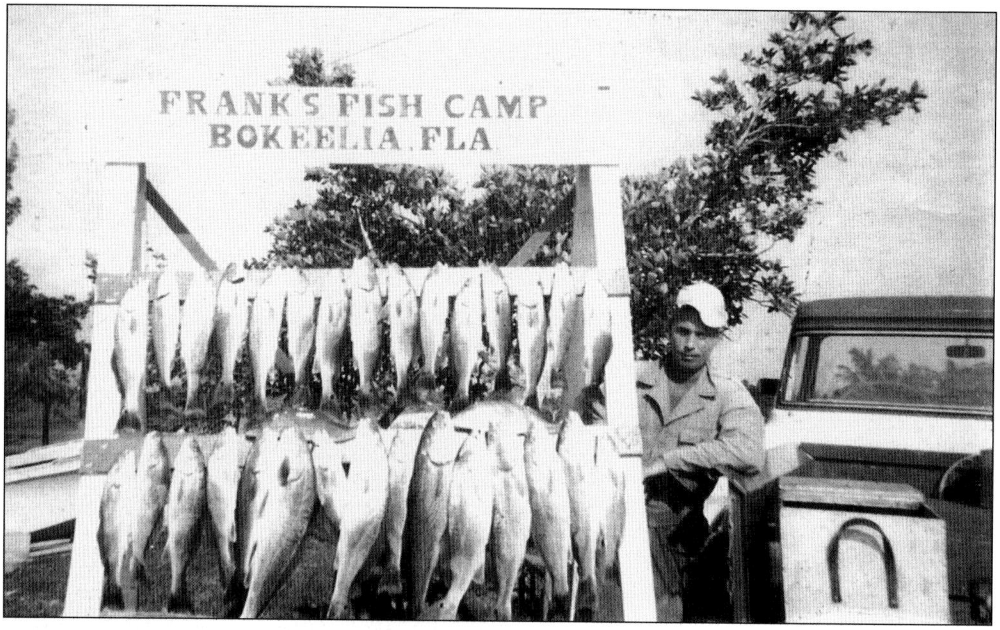

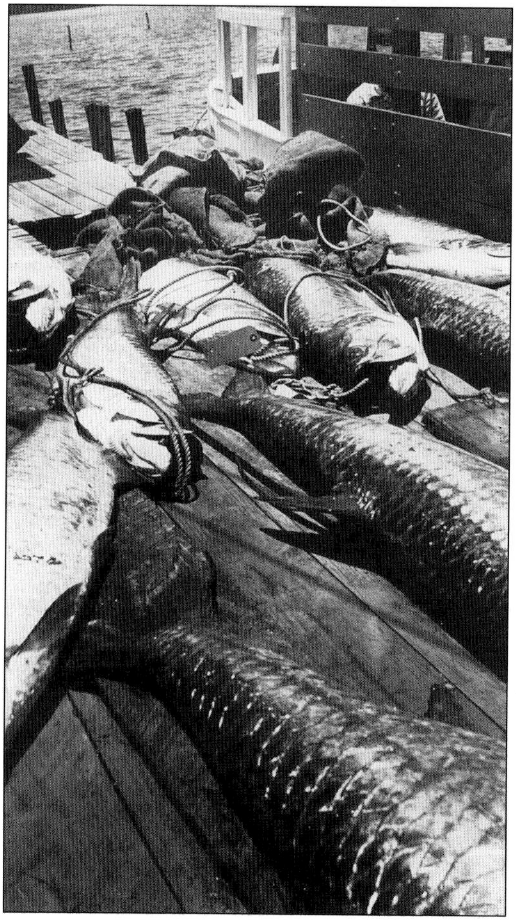

Frank DellaBitta stands with a large catch at his marina, Frank's Fish Camp (above), in the 1950s. Now known as Four Winds Marina, Frank and Kay DellaBitta purchased the property from Henry and Minta Martin of Bokeelia. (Kay DellaBitta.)

By the 1950s, tarpon fishing had reached a fevered level of excitement. Part of the fun was having the tarpon mounted and displayed back home. Here tarpon are piled on the dock at Frank and Kay's Fish Camp in Bokeelia, awaiting transport. Each weighing more than 150 pounds, the fish were shipped to taxidermists for mounting. (Kay DellaBitta.)

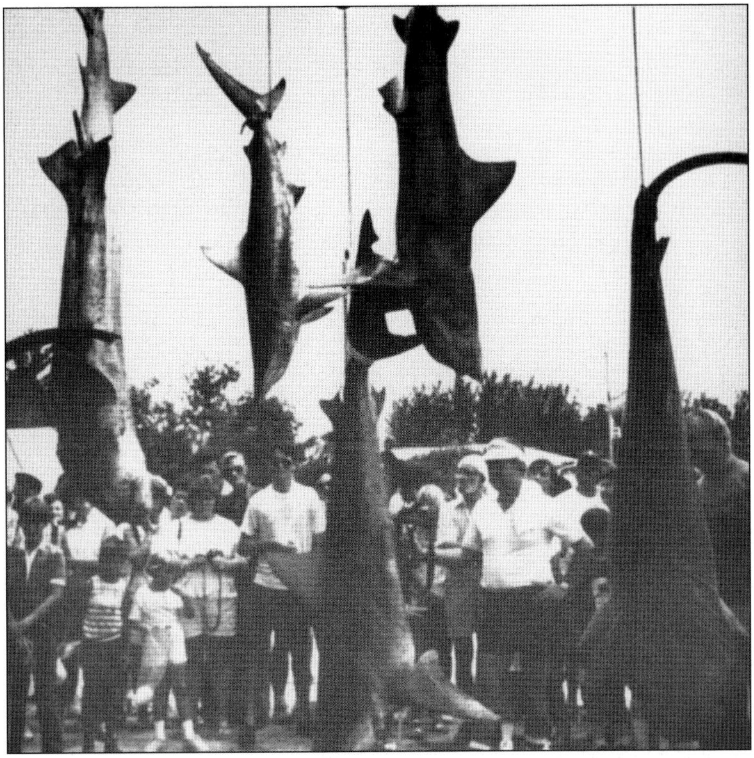

Popular in the 1980s, the Annual Shark Fishing Tournament was held at Pineland. The two-day event drew crowds of fishing enthusiasts to the weigh-ins, as pictured here in this weathered photograph. At the conclusion of the tournament, the participants enjoyed fresh Pine Island seafood. Once plentiful, the shark population has significantly dwindled, and the event no longer takes place. (Museum of the Islands.)

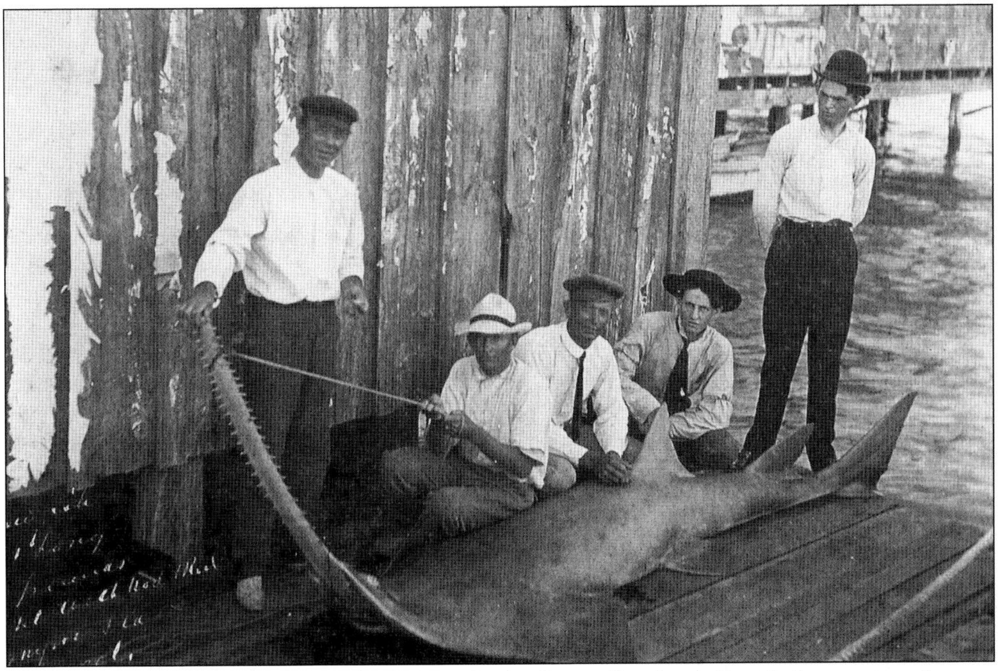

This photograph is on display in the Tarpon Lodge Bar at Pineland. Caught by a group of sports fishermen off Pineland, this was considered to be an extra-large sawfish. Sawfish are a group of extremely large shark-like rays that haunted the shallow water around Pine Island. Although they appear fearsome, sawfishes are docile. (Robert Wells.)

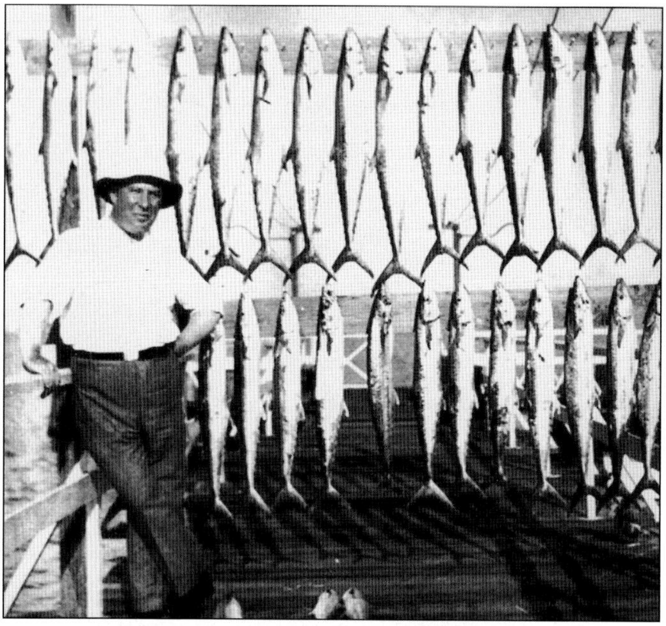

A Pine Island sports fisherman in the 1950s is pleased with his catch of king mackerel. For a fisherman with access to either a small boat or a long pier, the migrating king mackerel are often the target of choice from April to November. Using a bait of six chicken feathers bound together with a hook, then with two or three light jerks of the rod, the fisherman yells, "Fish on!," to warn fellow anglers of an impending fight with one of these high-speed beasts. (Robert Wells.)

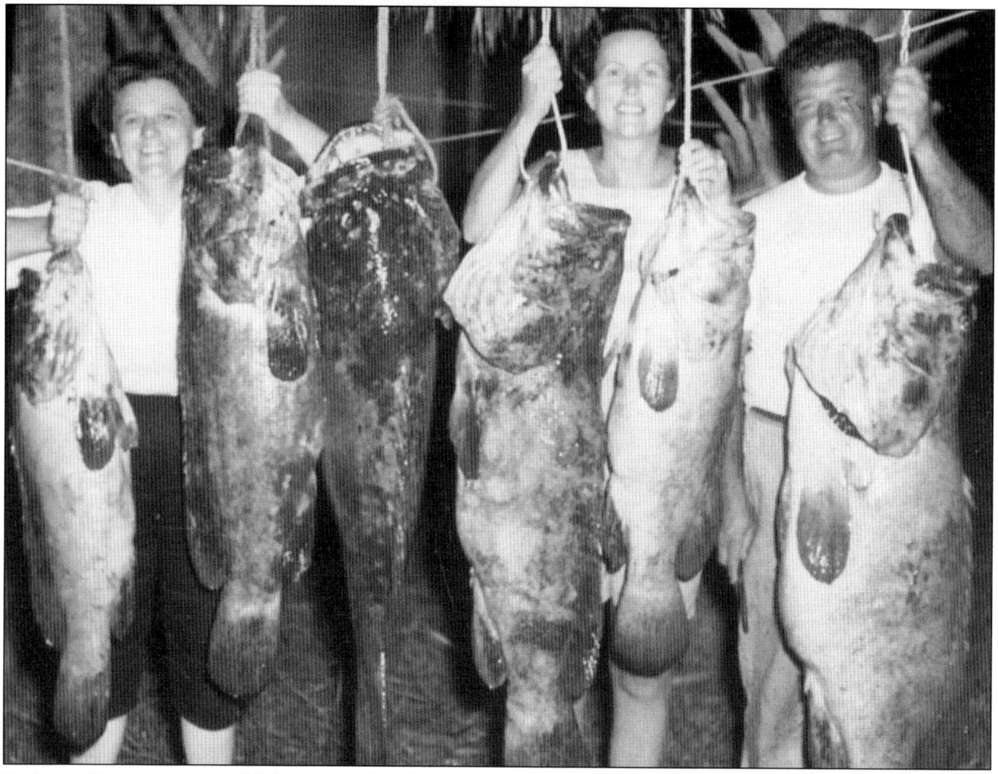

Robert Grant wrote of fishing in the St. James City area in 1889: "Fishing was excellent for Jew-fish and other monsters only too ready to carry off all one's line and disappear without showing themselves above water." Here (from left to right) friend Arelene Hawley along with Doris and Maurice Stevens, display their jewfish (now called Goliath grouper) catch in 1960. (Maurice Stevens)

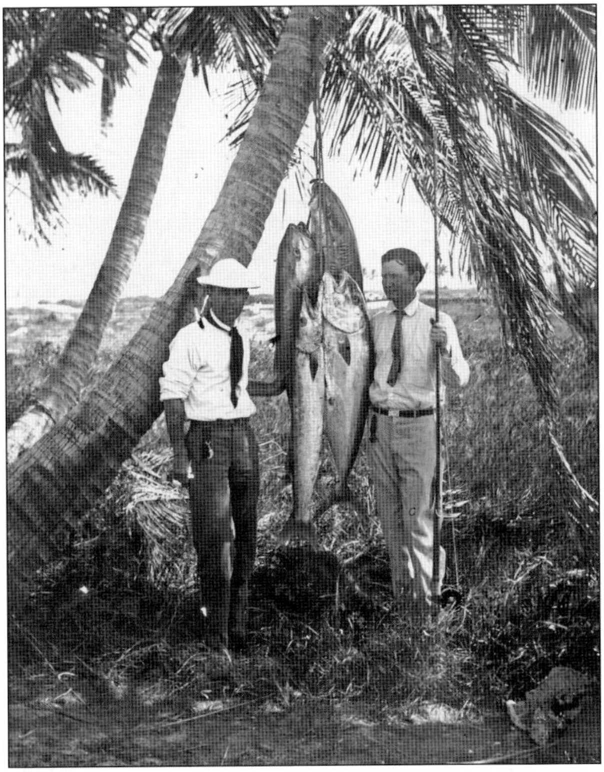

By the time of his death in 1939, author Zane Grey had managed to fish more remote regions of the globe than any other angler of his time, according to Bob Dunn and Peter Goadby in *Saltwater Game Fishes of the World*. Among his favorite fishing locales was Pine Island Sound. Pictured at right with his brother, R. C., in about 1917, Grey fishes for dolphin in waters south of Pine Island. (www.AntiqueFishingReels.com.)

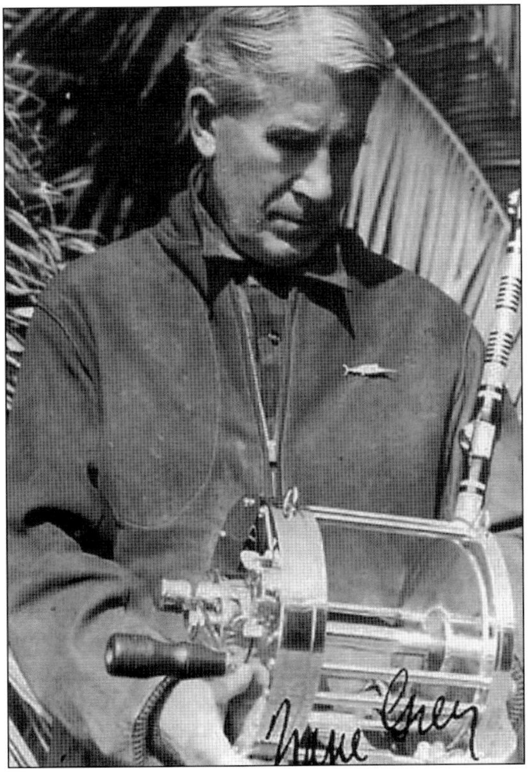

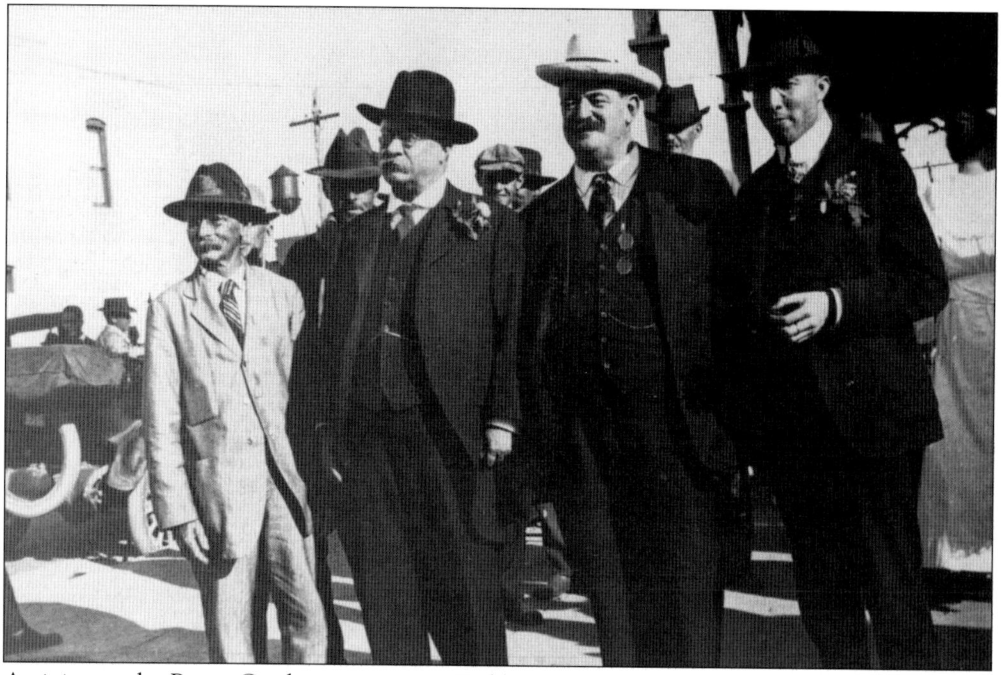

Arriving at the Punta Gorda train station, Teddy Roosevelt and his entourage awaited further transportation to Pine Island Sound, where they boarded Roosevelt's private "lightern" houseboat. An avid outdoorsman, Roosevelt not only fished for southwest Florida's prized game fish, he also conducted research on the shark and sting rays he caught. His interest was in determining the potential for marketing their preserved skins, much like how leather goods were promoted. (Fort Myers Museum of History.)

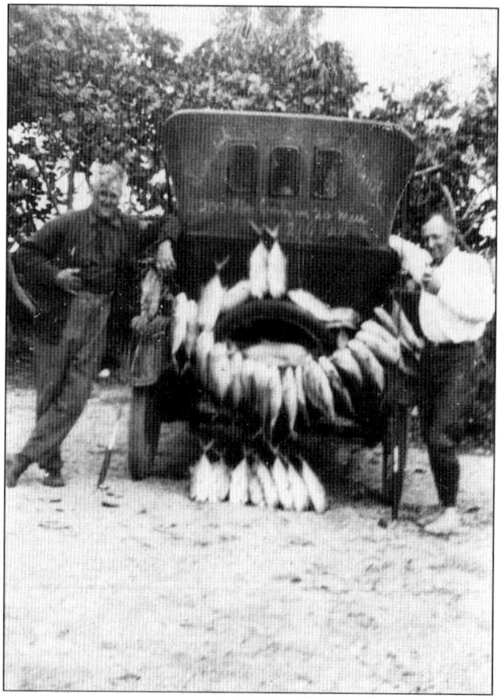

Sharing the waters with Pine Island fishermen in 1924 are Sanibel Island fishermen James Ross and Roy Rider. Sanibel Island was accessible to the mainland by a bridge and causeway built in 1962. However, there is no bridge access between Sanibel and Pine Island. The drive between the two islands takes at least an hour, while by boat it takes about 10 minutes. (Florida State Archives.)

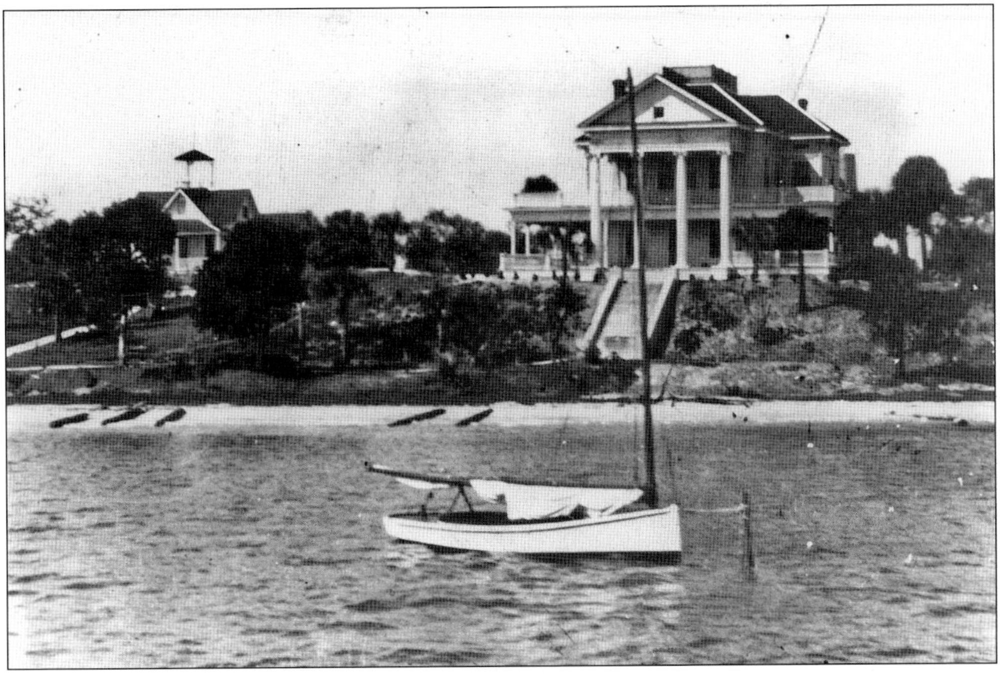

Built high on Calusa Indian mounds on Useppa Island, located outside Pine Island, the Collier Inn (above) was once the home of Barron G. Collier (right). Collier founded the famous Izaak Walton Club, after the author of *The Complete Angler.* The club was recognized as the leading fishing club in America, with its buttons sought after. Buttons were awarded as follows: silver for the first tarpon caught, gold for a 100-pound tarpon, and diamond for a 150-plus-pound tarpon. Under the direction of Collier, the club was responsible for beginning the catch-and-release practice of tarpon fishing. Tarpon that did not earn a button for the angler were released, while those of button-earning quality were kept for mounting. Taking the place of St. James City as the tarpon headquarters of the world after the San Carlos Hotel burned, the Collier Inn reigns as a prestigious fishing lodge today. (Florida State Archives.)

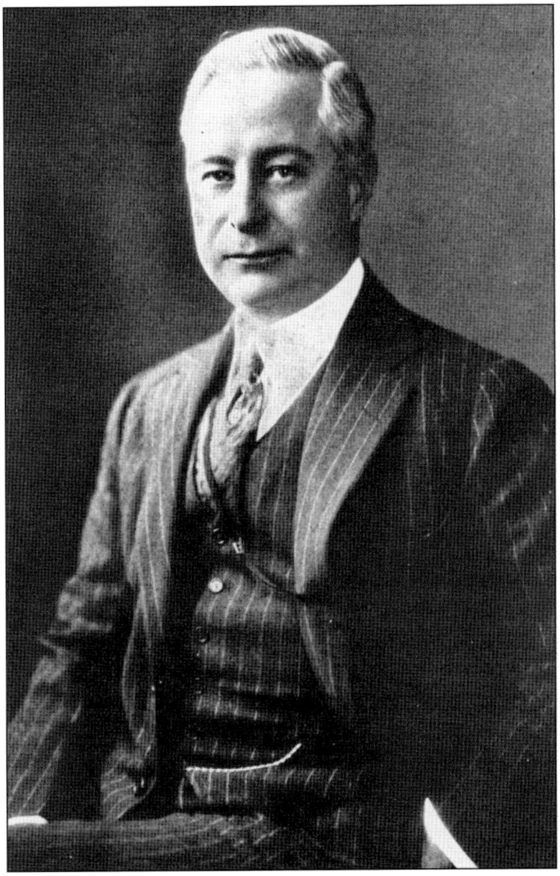

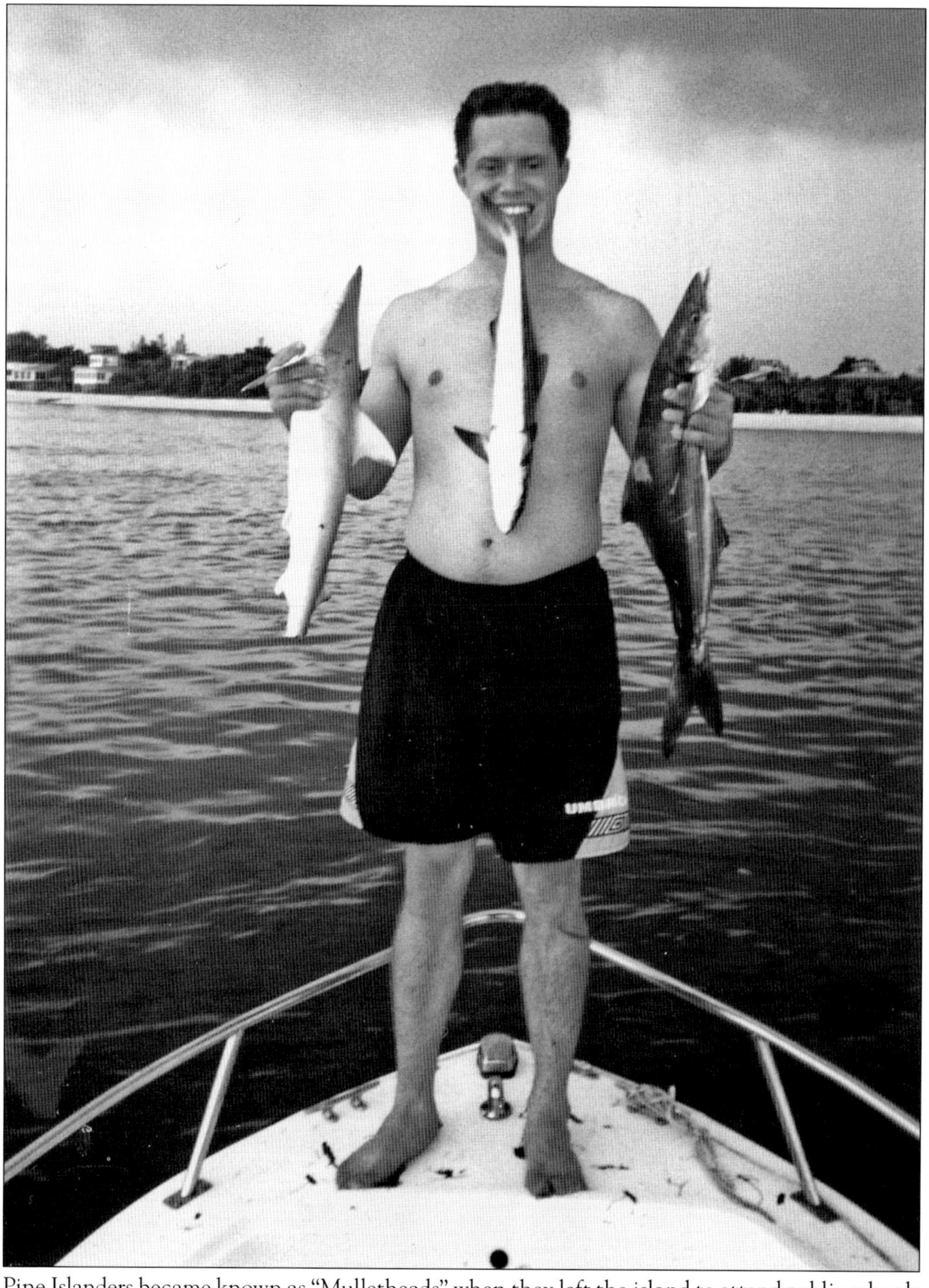

Pine Islanders became known as "Mulletheads" when they left the island to attend public schools in Cape Coral in the 1970s through the 1990s. So named for the island's predominant fishing catch of mullet rather than a haircut, the island's youth first rejected the seemingly derogatory term. Later they proudly adopted the label as their own. Here islander teen George Williamson poses with his catch in the early 1990s. (Craig Stevens.)

BIBLIOGRAPHY

Board, Prudy Taylor and Patricia Pope Bartlett. *Lee County: A Pictorial History.* Norfolk, VA: The Donning Company, 1985.

Dunn, Bob and Peter Goadby. *Salt Water Game Fishes of the World.* Portland, OR: Frank Amato Publications, 2000.

Edic, Robert F. *Fisherfolk of Charlotte Harbor, Florida.* Gainesville, FL: Institute of Archaeology and Paleoenvironmental Studies, Florida Museum of Natural History, 1996.

Jordan, Elaine Blohm. *Pine Island, the Forgotten Island.* Chelsea, MI: BookCrafters, Inc., 1982.

MacMahon, Darcie A. and William H. Marquaradt. *The Calusa and Their Legacy.* Gainesville, FL: University Press, 2004.

Oppel, Frank and Tony Meisel. *Tales of Old Florida.* Secaucus, NJ: Castle Book Sales, Inc. 1987.

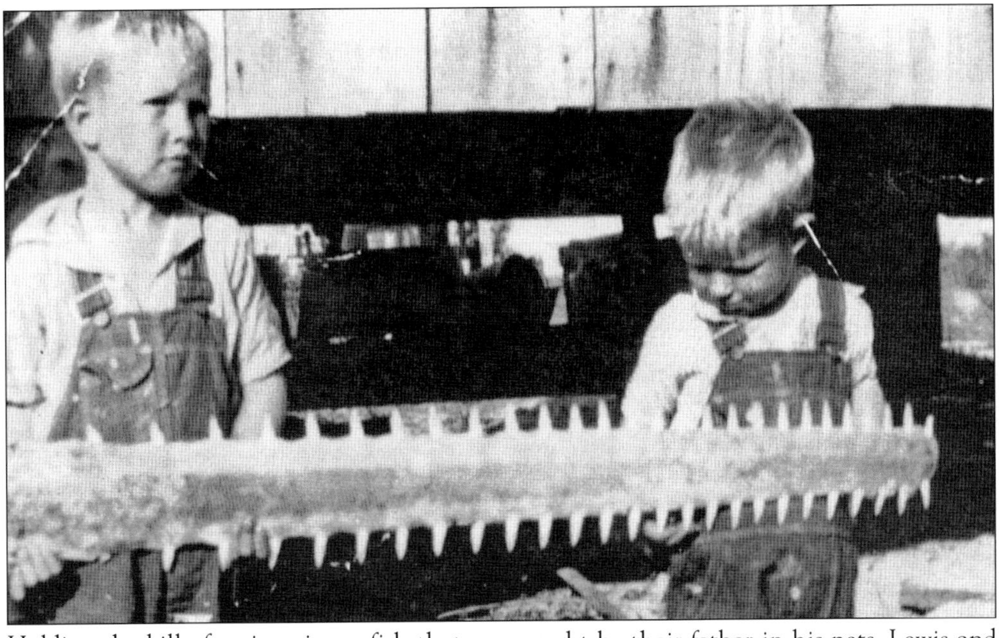

Holding the bill of a gigantic sawfish that was caught by their father in his nets, Lewis and Timmy Wade are shown in a 1930s photograph. Weighed in at over 1,000 pounds, it was of record-breaking size. A resident of Matlacha, their father was known for his unique generosity of providing the community with outdoor movies in the family's front yard along Pine Island Road. (Museum of the Islands.)

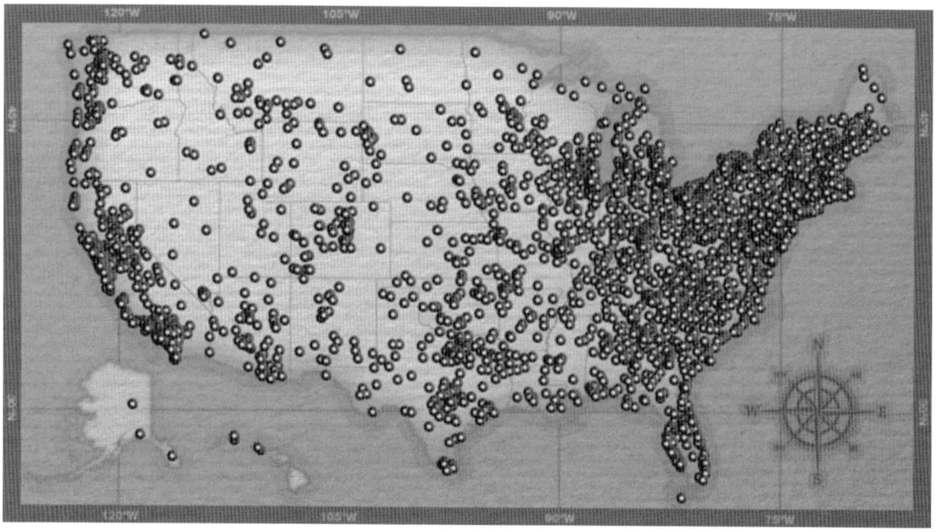